T0320422

NYU's Stern School of Business

Abraham L. Gitlow

NEW YORK

Stern School

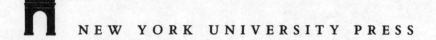

NEW YORK UNIVERSITY PRESS

# of Business

A Centennial Retrospective

■ NEW YORK AND LONDON

NEW YORK UNIVERSITY PRESS
New York and London

Copyright © 1995 by New York University

Library of Congress Cataloging-in-Publication Data

Gitlow, Abraham L. (Abraham Leo), 1918–
   New York University's Stern School of Business : a cen-
tennial
retrospective / Abraham L. Gitlow.
   p.   cm.
   Half title: NYU's Stern School of Business.
   Includes bibliographical references and index.
   ISBN 0-8147-3077-9
1. Leonard N. Stern School of Business.   2. Business schools—New
York (N.Y.)—History.   I. Title.   II Title: NYU's Stern School of
Business.   III. Title: Stern School of Business.
HF1134.S79G58   1995
650'. 071' 17471—dc20   94-49200
                               CIP

New York University Press books are printed on acid-free paper, and their binding materials are chosen for strength and
durability.

Manufactured in the United States of America

10 9 8 7 6 5 4 3 2 1

A tribute to the Leonard N. Stern School of Business, whose faculty educated thousands of entrepreneurs and professionals, and prepared them to make real the American dream.

Contents

Illustrations

Foreword

What we now know as the Stern School of Business at New York University began in 1900 as the School of Commerce, Finance, and Accounts. Its avowed purpose was the provision of practical training for young people hoping to make their way in the then burgeoning financial marketplaces of New York City. One hundred years later, from these humble origins has risen an institution which has become one of this nation's foremost institutions of management education, a School that has educated leaders of business enterprises across America and the world.

Such an extraordinary transformation is a worthy subject for thoughtful examination as we approach the School's centennial year of 2000. It is a story not only of our School, but of the nation and world of which it is a part, of the profound political and economic changes that have taken place over the last century. In many ways the School has been a mirror held up to the world at large, heavily influenced by the broad currents that have shaped that larger society—wars, depression, immigration, automation. The School's history is as well a history of academic life in America and of the changing role of professional education within the academy.

Capturing these events and placing them in their historical and cultural context are tasks of considerable complexity and difficulty. The Stern School is fortunate to have as its biographer and historian a person uniquely qualified for this role by virtue of his remarkable knowledge of the business world, higher education, and the Stern School, Dean Emeritus Abraham Gitlow. His special qualifications arise, in part, from the fact that he was one of the key players in the transformation he describes. In addition to his great institutional knowledge, Dean Gitlow displays remarkable perspective, gentle wit, and abundant humanity.

It is an important story told well. May you enjoy it as much as I have. And may the next century at the Stern School be as interesting and productive as the last.

—Dean George Daly
NYU Stern School of Business

Preface

It was a fine day in the summer of 1992. I had left the Violet, a New York University bistro located at the southeast corner of Washington Square in Manhattan's Greenwich Village. I was satisfied with the state of my immediate piece of the world. I had just enjoyed my favorite lunch, a bowl of chicken soup. It is even possible that a certain sense of smugness permeated my being.

Immediately after my exiting the Violet, Dan Diamond, a longtime friend and colleague who succeeded me as dean of N Y U's undergraduate business school, came along. We chatted for several minutes, and then he reminded me that the School would soon celebrate its centennial, in the same year as the arrival of the millennium. Dan added the thought that a centennial history of the School would be appropriate, especially since the School of Commerce, Accounts, and Finance, as it was known at its birth, was among the first six collegiate schools of business established in America. Further, its history, along with that of the Graduate School of Business Administration, which was established in 1921, was a microcosm of twentieth-century collegiate education for business in the United States. Its record was, in addition, representative of the transformation of collegiate education for business from a vocational, trade school character to one of rigorous intellectual standards. Moreover, New York University itself had been transformed during the century, so the story of the Stern School encompasses the spectrum of educational and philosophical issues and tensions that have marked higher education in America during the past hundred years.

I agreed with Dan, but demurred when he asked if I would undertake the task. He argued that my then 45 years as a faculty member, 20 of them as dean, placed me in a unique position for the job. My demurral reflected my reluctance to embark on a task that I guessed would consume a couple of years, especially after having undergone three major surgeries several years before. Although I had well recovered, the value of time had become much greater than it had been in younger years. Also, I had just completed a book, and was still concentrating on its publication and marketing. We parted, with Dan asking me not to reject the suggestion then and there.

As fall came and winter approached, Dan's suggestion kept popping into my thoughts. It would not go away, and I began to toy with a possible outline of what the history might be like, if I were to do it. I realized quickly that a compilation of dates, events, and uniformly laudatory comments did not interest me, although there was certainly much to praise, and a chronological presentation was a simple way to approach the matter of organization. What did excite me was the idea of an analysis of the educational and philosophical issues and tensions that marked the history of the School, and of American higher education in general in the twentieth century. I was given pause, however, by the further realization that such an approach had to be the work of an individual, not a committee. At least that is how it seemed to me. No matter how many others would be invited to examine the manuscript, to criticize, suggest, or otherwise comment on it, to be a coherent product of perceptions, values, and points of view shaped by four and a half decades of experience it could not be subject to the final judgment and dictates of a committee. But that meant, in my mind, that the history could not be official. It would have to be mine, and I did not know if that was what Dan had in mind.

Having sorted out those thoughts, I spoke again with Dan, explaining the conditions that I believed would warrant my undertaking the history. He replied that he had tentatively raised the idea of an official history with others, but, while everyone reacted to the idea favorably, no one seemed prepared to put resources into it. Under the circumstances, I told him that I, being beholden to no one, and free to follow wherever my research and analysis might lead me, would take on the task.

Now, some two years later, the task is done as best I can. Along the way, I have enjoyed the unstinting assistance of many people, none of whom, however, is responsible for the judgments and opinions expressed. I would be unconscionably remiss if I failed to mention the help of these people: Professors Emeriti Ernest Kurnow, Michael Schiff, Darrell Lucas, and Jacob Janis, who collectively represent some 200 years of memories of the Stern School, stretching back in Professor Lucas's case to the early thirties; former President James M. Hester, whose 13-year tenure from 1962 to 1975 was of critical importance in the transformation of NYU and its business schools; former Deans William Dill (later President of Babson College), William May, and Richard West of the Graduate School of Business Administration (covering the period 1970–1993); my successor dean at the undergraduate school, Daniel Diamond, and our longtime colleagues Associate Deans Harry Kelly and John Guilfoil; Professor Emeritus and former associate Dean of GBA, Gerald Glasser; Boris Kostelanetz, distinguished attorney, alumnus, and long-standing trustee of NYU; Professor Howard Gitlow, of the School of Business, University of Miami; Dolores Briante, executive secretary to GBA deans for more than four decades; Nancy Cricco, NYU's archivist; and Maureen George, whose contributions are more substantive than conveyed by the word secretary. Sylvia Viola must be mentioned too. Active in the undergraduate dean's office for 30 years, she searched the old files and discovered historical data of great value. There were also Richard Wines and Eunice Lang of the American Assembly of Collegiate Schools of Business, who were most generous in providing information about AACSB. Finally, many members of the administration and staff of the Stern School were helpful in providing information. Apart from all these academic people there was my dear friend Samuel Shapiro, former president of the American Society of Association Executives, a master editor and expert on organizational dynamics and development who provided invaluable insights and suggestions.

The Stern School history is clearly the beneficiary of the input of many minds, but the responsibility for the final product is individual and the author's alone. As always, my partner of 53 years provided patient and tolerant company from gestation to delivery. After all, it is Beatrice who gets me through the times when a project is stuck, and its outcome seems in doubt. May I continue to have projects and may she never run out of patience.

—Abraham L. Gitlow
Miami Beach, Florida

The Undergraduate School: Shaping the Culture

The Beginnings

The Stern School was born in 1900 as the School of Commerce, Accounts, and Finance, a two-year undergraduate entity in New York University. Located along with the Law School and the School of Pedagogy in a recently built and imposing multistoried structure at the corner of Manhattan's Waverly Place and Washington Square East, it offered a two-year program of studies between the hours of 8 and 10 every evening, Monday through Friday. The timing of class schedules reflected the founders' perception of the student body to be served.

The purposes of the founders were twofold. The first was to offer training in the "higher accountancy," to prepare students to meet the standards and requirements of the newly passed New York State Certified Public Accountants Act of 1896. That law provided for the issuance of a Certified Public Accountant (CPA) certificate, to persons who could pass an examination in the Theory of Accounts, Practical Accounting, Auditing, and Commercial Law.[1] The other major purpose was to offer training in subjects that would prepare students for careers in commerce: in business and the administration or management of business organizations.

Among the principal founders of the School were Charles Waldo Haskins, co-founder with Elijah Sells of the famous accounting firm of Haskins and Sells, Colonel Charles Ezra Sprague, president of the Union Dime Savings Bank, and Leon Brummer, an outstanding public accountant. Haskins was the founding dean. Sprague, Haskins, and some dozen other pioneers served as faculty (all part-time), and generally without any compensation.

The enthusiasm felt for the establishment of the School by the founders was not shared generally by the higher educational establishment. Higher education was centered in colleges and graduate schools of Arts and Sciences, and of theology. Classical learning, emphasizing Latin and Greek as well as philosophy and law, was still entrenched, although studies in the sciences were increasingly popular along with the study of such modern languages as French and German. Professional education continued to consist mainly of medicine and law, but engineering and pedagogy were increasingly strong. And the study of business administration at the collegiate level, introduced first in 1881 at the University of Pennsylvania's Wharton School, had been followed by schools of business at the University of California and the University of Chicago in 1898. In 1900, along with NYU's School of Commerce, Accounts, and Finance, schools of business were established at Dartmouth and the University of Wisconsin. Indeed, at the time of NYU's establishment of the business school, it was not even certain whether a degree or a certificate would be awarded upon completion of the program of studies. It was only a year later that NYU decided to follow the University of Wisconsin decision and issue the degree of Bachelor of Commercial Science (BCS).

The educational context in America's universities at the dawn of the twentieth century is captured clearly in these words, written in the fiftieth anniversary history of the American Association of Collegiate Schools of Business:

> The schools of business were not the outgrowth of pressures within the universities but developed primarily from the demands of business for collegiate instruction in business. At that time there were few faculty members qualified to teach in the fields of business. Little graduate work had been applicable to any field closer to business than economics. The behavioral sciences were not developed. And no one had firm conclusions concerning the nature of a curriculum which would prepare students for careers in business. Indeed, save for medicine, law, and theology, collegiate education was not expected to be of a professional nature.[2]

The uncertainty about curricular design was articulated clearly also by Dean Joseph French Johnson. In his 1912 annual report he wrote:

> The courses offered in the School are the result of evolution and *do not present a coherent curriculum designed to fit students for specific callings*. There

are exceptions, of course, notably in the Accounting and Journalism Departments. Plans are now under way to reorganize the curriculum so as to present more coherent and comprehensive courses aimed to fit the students for specific occupations. (Italics added)[3]

Commerce was not established to be an institution focused on graduate research. Its principal purpose was *teaching,* and teaching was done in the beginning by part-time faculty who were important practitioners. While they sought to extract from their experience general principles that they could teach to their students, they did not engage in the kind of research and publication that has become so dominant a consideration in faculty procurement and promotion in the closing years of the century. And the founders were explicit in emphasizing that the School would be *practical* in nature. The School's original *Announcement for 1900–1901* (i.e., bulletin) emphasized that:

> This school differs from the several Schools of Finance or Commerce recently established by prominent universities in America in that its entire instruction is intended to be professional in character. It is in no way to be confounded with or substituted for the course of liberal culture in a College of Arts and Science, but it may be advantageously connected therewith.[4]

How were Henry M. MacCracken, Chancellor of New York University, and his colleagues convinced that it was appropriate to establish the School of Commerce, Accounts, and Finance at N Y U? Perhaps the story is best told in the centennial history of New York University:

> In 1900, . . . the idea of professional training for business was generally looked upon with skepticism, if not with actual derision, not only in academic but in business circles. Fortunately, the men who approached Chancellor MacCracken were men of high character and deep sincerity, whose business success was proof that they were not visionaries. Notable among them were Charles Waldo Haskins, senior member of the accounting firm of Haskins and Sells, Charles Ezra Sprague, President of the Union Dime Savings Bank, and Leon Brummer.
> Mr. Haskins became the first dean of the new institution, but lived only long enough to see the School well established and on the road to success. Colonel Sprague was a member of the original faculty and remained active as a teacher until his death in 1912, at the age of seventy. Possibly more than any other one man, he was responsible for Chancellor MacCracken's final decision to accept the project of the founders. For when it seemed likely that the decision might be adverse, he rented the

house of one of the University professors during the summer vacation, came into close contact with the Chancellor, and, during frequent walks on the campus, was able to discuss the plan with him; and Colonel Sprague, a linguist and scholar as well as a man of remarkable personal charm, was able to impress Chancellor MacCracken as few others could have done.

What was equally important, Colonel Sprague was the type of man who could make the new venture a success. One who taught for the love of teaching—literally, since he accepted no compensation—he was able to inspire in his students genuine enthusiasm. His patience in explaining difficult points was seemingly inexhaustible; and he had a deep, personal interest in each of his students. Much the same might be said of Leon Brummer, who, like Colonel Sprague, served as a member of the faculty (though not continuously) for more than a dozen years. These two men, and others like them, formed the nucleus of the present faculty. All the courses were taught by business men, with the exception of the courses in Commercial Law, a subject in which the lecturers were drawn from the Law School.[5]

The persuasiveness needed by Colonel Sprague to convince Chancellor MacCracken is revealed in a recently discovered unpublished autobiographical manuscript. It contains the reminiscences of Professor George Burton Hotchkiss, who came to Commerce to teach Business English in Fall 1908. Hotchkiss, a pioneer in advertising and marketing, who later became a longtime chairman of the School's Marketing Department, retired in 1950. In 1908 he was an instructor in the English department of the University College of Arts and Sciences, located at the new University Heights campus in the Bronx. In Spring of 1909 Dean Johnson invited Hotchkiss to join the Commerce faculty full-time, eventually transferring his primary academic appointment from University College. Hotchkiss knew Chancellor MacCracken and sought his advice on this important career decision. Two aspects of the conversation between Hotchkiss and MacCracken are pregnant with meaning. Hotchkiss tells the story:

> I was to give up my work in the College, and devote myself entirely to the School of Commerce. Since it was purely an evening school, my days would be free for other work. *But instead of continuing my graduate study for a Ph.D., he (Dean Johnson) advised me to get a job on a newspaper. He thought it would be more valuable than the Ph.D. Moreover, it would help to prepare me better to teach courses in journalism which he had planned.*
>
> The decision required thought, for I sensed that it was a turning point in my career. I had been looking forward to the eventual teaching of

English Literature, and believed myself capable of interpreting such masters as Shakespeare, Browning, the lesser poets. . . .

The College at University Heights was at that time almost in the country, though the northward growth of the city threatened to engulf it, as it actually did a few years later. Life was pleasant there. I had a fine suite of rooms, more comfortable than any I had occupied at Yale, Harvard, or elsewhere. With few exceptions my colleagues were congenial. . . . Before answering Dean Johnson, I decided to consult the Chancellor, Dr. Henry MacCracken, a grand old gentleman. *He advised strongly against it. The future of New York University, he declared, lay at University Heights. Commerce would never amount to much. Perhaps if he had been at Washington Square at night and seen the line of students waiting for the two elevators, his view might have been different. At any rate, I decided to accept Johnson's offer.* (Italics added)[6]

The concept of collegiate education for business and the "higher accountancy" was one that met the needs and wants of the time. There was a huge hunger for the educational service that was now made available. Enrollments, hesitant at first, burgeoned. Indeed, they exploded.

The factors underlying the hunger for business education were explained in the Commerce bulletin for 1910–1911. The words were prescient, even prophetic, for they describe conditions in the present day too:

The methods of organization of the typical business concern of to-day are far different from those of the typical concern of twenty-five years ago. Three factors that have been prominent in the industrial world for one hundred and fifty years have operated with a higher velocity than ever before in the last twenty-five years, and are now rapidly altering the conditions under which business is conducted. First of these factors is the increasing use and the decreasing cost of transportation. Merchants and manufacturers in every section of the United States—and for that matter in every quarter of the globe—are liable to meet the competition of far distant merchants and manufacturers and in their turn, if they have sufficient knowledge and enterprise, may extend the sale of their goods indefinitely. The second factor is the proved economy of large scale production and distribution in most lines of business, thus bringing to the front larger concerns than have ever before existed. The third factor is the extension of facilities for securing credit through bank discounts, through the sale of securities and through mercantile accounts, thereby enabling men of ability, but without capital, to secure the use of capital more easily and on better terms than have previously been possible.

That as a result of these three factors competition to-day is keener, the margin of profits is closer, and the organization of business is more complex and more accurately determined, are statements not open to question. *It is also self-evident that changes in business conditions are more frequent and more sweeping than in the past.* Tradition, custom, local experience, rules of thumb, are not safe guides to action under such conditions. The successful business man of to-day must be shrewd, alert, far-seeing, honorable and tireless as good business men in all periods have always been, and in addition must have breadth of knowledge and scientific habits of thought beyond what has ever before been required. (Italics added)[7]

Evening Program

These programs of study were designed to serve students who were originally thought of as males, engaged in full-time work and taking classes only in the evening. Collegiate-level courses offered in the evening represented a radical idea. Many educators did not believe they could possibly be as rigorous intellectually as day offerings, because both students and teachers would be fatigued by the activities which consumed the normal working hours of the day. The Commerce bulletin of 1910–1911 recognized the issue and, quoting Dean Joseph French Johnson, argued contrariwise. The magic ingredient that Dean Johnson and his colleagues saw as carrying their argument was motivation:

Those who think that evening students who are employed in business during the day have not the time or energy to study and master a subject thoroughly probably fail to take into account the fact that our evening Schools of Commerce, Accounts, and Finance, do not burden their students with a large number of subjects at the same time. At the most a student is able to hear lectures for only ten hours a week, and experience in these schools has shown it to be wise to give the students only one topic for study on each evening. A two-hour lecture before ordinary college students would prove a very trying task, for it would be very difficult to hold their attention for such a long period. But in the university evening schools of accounts and finance, *so eager is the spirit of the students and so keen is their questioning spirit, that the two-hour period seems too short rather than too long both to the instructor and to the student.* During the day the student need have but one topic on his mind and need review but one of his note-books. Most of them find time for this usually between the close of business and the beginning of the lecture at 8 o'clock. (Italics added)[8]

Enrollment

The early enrollment figures are startling. Beginning with 60 students in 1900–1901, they grew rapidly to 441 in 1905–1906, reached 1,198 in 1910–1911, and by the 1913–1914 academic year amounted to 2,190.[9] And that was only the beginning. By 1936, the Commerce publication, *Glimpses of the Faculty,* boasted of an enrollment of about 8,000 students,[10] and a later publication spoke pridefully of 10,000 in 1941–1942.[11] There was great pleasure in these numbers, and in the fact that the School of Commerce had become the *biggest* business school in America, and hence in the world. But Commerce's *pride in size* reflected the larger culture at N Y U in those times, because the university as a whole took great pride in having become the largest private university in the land, in terms of student enrollments.

A fascinating aspect of Commerce enrollments is the appearance of significant numbers of foreign students. We discover them almost immediately after the establishment of the school. What is perhaps most surprising, however, is the degree to which the foreign student body was dominated by Japanese. Only nine years after the school's beginning the Commerce bulletin for 1908–1909 noted that the student body included 26 Japanese (20 in the degree program and 6 unclassified) and one Chinese student.[12] One year later the bulletin showed about 10 percent of the full-time student body (a minority of the total enrollment) consisted of foreigners; with 37 from Japan, 5 from Canada, 3 from China, 2 each from Argentina, Brazil, and England, and one each from Norway, Germany, Venezuela, Cuba, Greece, Egypt, Ireland, New Zealand, Sweden, Turkey, and Chile.[13] The foreign student presence persisted, for in 1942 the *Commerce Handbook* observed that "last year 129 students came from 35 foreign countries."[14] But we must not overlook the fact that these 129 students were part of a huge enrollment exceeding 10,000.

Commuters

While Commerce's enrollments contained an international element, the essential character of the student body was that it was composed of *commuters*. Washington Square was easily accessible by subway, bus, and elevated railways (now gone). Very few students were in residence at the Square, and the overwhelming majority of the student body came from New York City itself and its surrounding area in New York, New Jersey, and Connecticut. It was no mystery why N Y U became known to many, and not as a compliment, as "Subway University." For students who did seek residential status at the Square, the early bulletins (up to 1907–1908) pointed out that room and board were available in the area for $6 per week. In 1908 that rate moved up to $7 per week, which one year later was expressed as $7 per week "and upwards." By 1913 the rate had increased further to $8 per week and upwards, remaining at that level until America's entry into World War I in 1917.

School of Opportunity

A major Commerce characteristic from its beginning was its nature as a school of opportunity, one into which entry was easy. Candidates for the degree of Bachelor of Commercial Science (BCS) had to meet specified academic standards, for example, an acceptable high school diploma, successful completion of a year's work at a college of "good standing," or the New York State Regents Pass Card for 48 academic counts. But special students, that is, those lacking such credentials, could be admitted and pursue the same program of study. However, on successful completion of the program they received a Certificate of Proficiency, not the BCS degree.[15] Although entry was easy, successful completion was more difficult. From the beginning and as the School of Commerce exploded in its enrollments mass admission was accompanied by mass attrition. For the thousands who graduated, other thousands, far greater in number, dropped by the way. The survivors were a hardy lot, generally stubborn in their drive to succeed. And their nature was reflected in the remarkable record of success they achieved in their post-college careers.

Along with academic ease of access, there was another entry requirement; one which undoubtedly acted as a barrier to many who would otherwise have sought admission. Of course reference is made to the need to pay tuition and certain fees. Degree or certificate track students pursuing a three-year program in the evening had to pay $100 per year. Full-time students pursuing a degree or certificate program which could be earned in two years paid $150 per year. Viewed differently, the price of the BCS or certificate was $300. An additional $20 was required for a final exam and a $5 matriculation fee. These numbers seem paltry against the magnitude of contemporary tuition and fee structures. Perhaps the real impact is more easily seen when we compare the $325 total to the $6–$8 weekly cost for room and board in pre World War I years. At the $6 per week rate, the tuition fee level represented 54 weeks of room and board. At the $8 per week level it represented 41 weeks. Plainly, Commerce's tuition and fees were consequential. Special tuition rates were set for students taking fewer than the number of courses prescribed for the degree and certificate programs. One further point relative to tuition and fees; they remained remarkably stable for a long time, that is, from 1900 to 1917. However, the tuition structure shifted in 1916–1917 to a basis of $12 per 2-point course and $24 per 4-point course; or $6 per point. Yet, maximums of $100 and $150 for the three-year and two-year programs of study were retained. No doubt, changes like these reflected the large numbers of students enrolled in special short programs of study, for example, a one-year special course of study introduced in 1905, as well as those taking individual courses in what we would today regard as a form of continuing education.

The powerful upsurge in Commerce enrollments, coupled with severe space limitations at the Washington Square Center (the structure now known as the Main Building), led the School of Commerce to establish satellite operations. The first was set up in Brooklyn in the Eagle building, second floor, at Johnson and Washington Streets.[16] The year was 1912, and all first-year students from Brooklyn and Long Island were required to take their course work at this location. The second was set up in 1914, first in rented quarters, then in the old Trinity Church School building at 90 Trinity Place in February 1920. Known as the Wall Street division, it served students in the downtown Manhattan financial center. The Trinity Church School building also provided the quarters for the Graduate School of Business Administration after its founding in 1921.

Enrollment pressure had another effect. It stimulated the scheduling of courses in the late afternoon, and then also in the morning hours. By 1912, the Commerce bulletin spoke of four scheduling divisions; morning, afternoon, evening, and night. Every division scheduled classes Monday-Friday inclusive, with the time slots 10:30 a.m.-12:30 p.m., 4:45–6:30 p.m., 6:00–7:45 p.m., and 7:45–9:45 p.m.[17] Daylight course availability encouraged the enrollment of students freshly graduated from high school and pursuing their education on a full-time basis. What emerged in time was an academic dichotomy, with younger full-time students during the day and older part-time students in the evening and nighttime slots. But Professor Emeritus Darrell Lucas recalls that a number of day students took evening classes to get the benefit of the greater maturity and experience of the evening students.

Co-education

Before we depart from our discussion of student enrollments, we should note that the School was co-educational, that is, no barriers prevented the entry of women students. Despite no formally stated barriers, the language of the bulletins spoke only of men. One must conclude that the founders did not foresee a substantial attendance of women. Yet, women students appeared early.

What is remarkable is the numbers in which they appeared. Gladys H. Reutiman, adviser to women in the day division, reported an enrollment of women in the division exceeding 600 in the 1936–1937 academic year.[18] Since day enrollment ran about 4,000 in those years, women represented some 15 percent of the total (see Table 1.1). In addition, a substantial number of women enrolled in the evening, especially in a noncertificate status, that is, taking individual courses. Reutiman reported that the matriculated women students were distributed among the following major subject areas:

Commenting on the career choices reflected in Table 1.1, Reutiman emphasized a "desire for security." The time was part of the Great Depression of the thirties. A desire for security is easily understood, especially by this writer, who was in college at that terrible time. But one is still struck, given the strength of today's feminist movement and its emphasis on breaking "glass ceilings," by the picture of the Commerce women students drawn by Reutiman almost six decades ago. She said:

> On the average, our students are *cautious, subdued, unadventurous,* to be sure not as bitterly pessimistic about the future as those of 1932, but only mildly optimistic about their chances in the outside world. They have no idea of storming this outside world with college-bred confidence; instead they *simply want a haven in a job that is guaranteed to be safe and permanent.* Secretarial, teaching, and civil-service jobs look encouraging to them and seem to promise relief from economic uncertainty. The college girl of today realizes especially the benefit of secretarial courses. She knows that to break into the business world she must have something more concrete

TABLE I.I
Day Division Women Students, 1936–1937

Major	Program			
	BS	Certificate	Undecided	Total
Secretaryship	138	58	4	200
Commerce-Education	91			91
Accounting	70	4		74
Journalism	63	14		77
Marketing	60	5		65
Business Administration	40	2		42
Retailing	38	2		40
Management	34	11		45
Commerce-Law	7			7
Economics	5			5
Total	546	96	4	646

SOURCE: NYU, *Report of Officers to the Chancellor of the University, for the Academic Year 1936–1937*, 172.

to offer than a college degree and that typing and shorthand have the most value as that definite something. (Italics added)[19]

Reutiman went on, adding these words suggestive of potential problems for women at work, plainly not envisaged by her but obvious to contemporary eyes sharpened by current charges of sexual harassment:

Economic uncertainty has toned down that college-superiority attitude. Because the college girl has thousands of competitors for the business positions she wants, she has set her mind to being tractable and agreeable and will do everything possible to "fit in." This changed attitude should be reassuring to the business man who is always "leery" that the college graduate will be unwilling to do things that she is instructed to do without quibblings.[20]

Not directly relevant to the co-educational character of Commerce, but worthy of note, is the existence of the Commerce-Education and Commerce-Law programs among the majors listed in Table 1.1.[21] These were programs offered jointly by the several separate schools at Washington Square. The institutional openness that they represented is remarkable compared to the barriers to cross-school registrations erected later. Thus, the Commerce-Law program involved three years at Commerce and three years at the Law School, with the first year at the Law School serving as the fourth undergraduate year. The Commerce-Education program involved joint planning and implementation by the School of Commerce, the School of Education, the School of Retailing, and Washington Square College. That program prepared the student for a city teaching license in (1) accounting and business practice; (2) stenography and typewriting; or (3) merchandising and salesmanship. The underlying implication of the cross-school programs is that there was comparability of admissions and academic standards, although a screen undoubtedly existed at the point of acceptance into the major.

Diversity

We observed earlier that the student body, while overwhelmingly comprised of nonresidential commuters, had an intriguing touch of diversity in its foreign component. But there was another, far more significant, kind of diversity, and it involved the nature of Commerce as a school of opportunity. We must speak now of the profoundly important societal service rendered by the school to the thousands of Central, Eastern, and Southern European immigrants and their children pouring into New York City to seek a better life. Passing through the portals of Ellis Island, past the Torch of the Statue of Liberty, whose symbolism was so wonderfully well described by the immortal words of Emma Lazarus engraved on its base, they came to America, the Golden Land of rumor, to turn their dreams into reality. Eastern Orthodox, Catholic, and Jew, Polish, Russian, Rumanian, Greek, and Italian, they came in the gorgeous richness of their many cultural colors, and through the miracle that is America became Americans. And in that transformation, for thousands, the School of Commerce was the instrument, the catalyst of change.

The role of the School of Commerce in serving the educational needs and aspirations of newly arrived immigrants and their children was an integral part of the reemergence of the Washington Square area as the major center of New York University. The original University College of Arts and Sciences and the School of Applied Science (Engineering) had been moved from Washington Square to the bucolic, rural atmosphere of University Heights in the Bronx in 1894–1895. It was Chancellor MacCracken's dream to establish there a "residential college in the country." When the move was made, the Schools of Law and Pedagogy remained at Washington Square, to be joined by Commerce in 1900. For work in the Arts and Sciences, these units were served by a Collegiate Division of University College. But enrollments in that Division quickly mushroomed, as they did in Pedagogy and Commerce. However, unlike its parent, the Collegiate Division was co-educational. Perhaps more important, it assumed the character of its close academic colleagues at the Square by attracting and serving the same nonresidential, commuting stream of new arrivals to America.

A kind of cultural schizophrenia came into being at N Y U, for the student body at University Heights was of older, native stock. The institutional tension which resulted was described delicately in the university's centennial history. It spoke of the situation shortly before World War I in these words:

> There was, unfortunately, another aspect of the situation which was the most uncomfortable of all. Until the arrival of the Medical Preparatory freshmen there had been among the students of the University College less conflict between the older and the new strata of New York society than might have been expected in a college situated in New York City. Now, however, with the arrival of the premedical students, came a sudden and overwhelming influx of young men who seemed, rightly or wrongly, to the students of older American stock to be distinctly alien to their own manners and habits of thought. The social conflict that ensued may easily be exaggerated; but the University College of 1917 was a very different place from that of 1910.[22]

World War I did not ease the tension. In fact, at University College it became more intense. The centennial history continued:

> The chief problem, accentuated by the social and economic changes produced by the World War, continued to be the personnel of the students. More than ever, in 1919, the new social strata in New York City were pressing for admission to the professional schools, and to the colleges which prepared for them. The University College would, in the post war period, have no difficulty in securing students to almost any number it desired. The difficulty seemed to lie in the quality of the students; and the faculty in the spring and summer of 1919 devoted many an anxious hour to thoughts for the future of the College, into which, we may hope, went their reason as well as their emotion.

> Upon these men fell the responsibility of facing the questions which seemed in 1919 to threaten the future of the University College which they and their predecessors had known. The word "Americanism" was often, perhaps too often, upon the lips of the majority of our compatriots in 1919; and the majority of our faculty agreed, wisely or unwisely, with the majority of Americans, that "Americanism" was a quality that the student body of the University College had once possessed, was in danger

of losing, and must recover. In 1932 we are perhaps less sure of what "Americanism" is; but we can probably admit that the University College was being swamped in 1919 by an invasion of students of what, to the older American student and teacher, seemed wholly alien habits and manners. What should the College have tried to do? A conceivable answer is that it should have accepted the perhaps inevitable consequence of its location in New York City, and undertaken the duty of teaching "Americanism" to these "alien" young men. The sad facts of the case, however, appeared to be that for every "alien" student who entered, an "American" student disappeared, and that the College would soon be wholly "alien." If that occurred, how could "Americanism" be taught with no "American" students to serve as examples to the "aliens"? On the other hand, did not the University College have a duty to serve the community, and, if it were necessary to limit the enrollment, what fairer tests for entrance could be employed than those of a purely intellectual character? Such were the questions which agitated, not only the faculty of the University College, but those of many similar colleges after 1919.[23]

Further comment on this point is warranted. Although Commerce served as a marvelous school of opportunity for the newly arrived immigrants streaming into the New York City area, the attitudes that stirred the cultural waters at the University Heights were not altogether absent at Washington Square. Dean Joseph French Johnson, that most remarkable man who engineered the growth of Commerce, wrote these suggestive and disturbing words in his 1919–1920 annual report to the Chancellor:

> Another significant feature in connection with the development of the day division which is becoming more and more apparent, is the fact that we are drawing an increasing number of students from beyond the confines of New York City. The calibre of these out-of-town students is distinctly superior to that of the student body drawn from within the limits of New York City. In this group lies a powerful medium for spreading the good name of the School of Commerce, Accounts, and Finance and of New York University in general. Undoubtedly, the New York University Alumni Clubs which are springing up all over the country will increase the flow of this highly desirable element in our enrollments.[24]

One is intrigued. In what respects were the out-of-town students "distinctly superior"? What made them a "highly desirable element"? Academic records upon entrance? Some perception of unusual intellectual power and potential? It seems unlikely that these were the characteristics the good dean had in mind. It seems rather more likely that they appeared less alien and hence more attractive in a cultural sense, that is, more "American."

Once again, Professor George Burton Hotchkiss fills in the picture. In his autobiographical reminiscences he writes about the effect of the post World War II GI Bill of Rights, and its effects on the numbers and nature of Commerce students.

> One regrettable (and I hope, only temporary) effect of this congestion, was that the student body of the undergraduate School of Commerce became more strongly local in character. We had to take care of all of our former students, and did. But in admitting new freshmen, we felt obligated to give precedence to graduates of local high schools, and although the Government asked us to stretch facilities to the limit, we had little room for transfer students or new students from distant localities. Since most other institutions, especially the State Universities, followed the same policy, the result was to make all of them more provincial. *It was particularly bad for us, because New York notoriously has an unduly large proportion of foreign-born and second-generation Americans, including some well-defined "blocks."*
>
> In the United States as a whole, no racial or religious group has ever been able to secure dominance, and few have attempted it. In the affairs of an institution or municipality, such a group has sometimes seized the reins of power, and has used the power ruthlessly. The attitude of such a minority group, if it has formerly been oppressed, seems to be, "now it's our turn." Because of the lack of dormitories and other reasonably priced residential quarters at Washington Square, our percentage of out-of-town students had always been small, but it had been sufficient to keep the balance of races and religions somewhere near that of the nation as a whole. Now in the day school, at least, conditions were unbalanced. The evening school and the Graduate division at Wall Street were less affected.
>
> The students who have come to us from distant states have probably been no brighter than those from the Metropolitan area, and certainly have been no better prepared. If they have accomplished more, as I think they have, it has been due either to a greater degree of the individualistic pioneering spirit, or to greater concentration upon university affairs. . . . And unfortunately, too many of the students of this latter period expected more of the teacher than any teacher could deliver. (Italics added)[25]

Faculty: Teaching, Research, and Consulting

The faculty, in the beginning, were all men of affairs, involved deeply in the practical realities of daily business life. Spoken of already and most prominent among them were Charles Waldo Haskins, Charles Ezra Sprague, and Leon Brummer. They were part-time teachers, bringing to Commerce classrooms lessons learned from vast experience. It was not too many years, however, before full-time faculty made their appearance, the first being Joseph French Johnson in 1901–1902. Certainly the enormous growth of the School and its extension of instruction into the daytime hours made this development inescapable. But, while a full-time faculty and administration became fairly quickly the academic base and core of the School, significant use of part-time teachers continued for decades to mark the character of Commerce. And always the justification was the practical nature of the program, and the importance of practitioners in achieving this purpose. That other purposes, less worthy, came to be served will be spoken about later.

Numerically, the Commerce faculty began with 18 authorized slots, of which 4 were vacant. By 1910 the size of the faculty had grown to 36, and by the 1916–1917 academic year it had expanded further to 97.[26] The 97 consisted of 12 professors, 2 associate professors, 11 assistant professors, 34 lecturers, 29 instructors, and 9 assistants. While the lecturers were probably part-time, the other categories were not committed exclusively to academic activities. It was part of the Commerce culture to expect full-time faculty to be engaged actively in business consulting. Professor George Burton Hotchkiss pointed out, in this connection, that practical experience was only one aspect of outside consulting by faculty. Another aspect was its importance as a source of additional income. He states that "for all except the War period my total annual earnings were usually double my salary."[27] Parenthetically, we note the appearance of the first woman faculty member in 1913–1914, Jeannette Hamill, JD and MA, an assistant in economics. And two years later Eva Vom Baur, AB, appears as a lecturer on Women in Industry. Describing the Commerce faculty in 1936, Dean John T. Madden wrote:

> Dean Johnson was able to bring to the faculty outstanding business executives and financial experts . . . who served as lecturers for varying periods. In choosing his full-time instructors, Dean Johnson sought men of proved ability in business affairs. *He encouraged them to maintain some business connections* so that they could enrich their lectures with the fruit of their practical experience. *In judging candidates, he gave more weight to teaching ability than to academic attainments.*
>
> To this day, in the courses of professional character, there has been no deviation from the principal that business education should represent the

effective combination of sound theory with sound practice. (Italics added)[28]

A look at the 1920–1921 Commerce bulletin for the Wall Street Division reveals how completely Dean Johnson had established the character of the faculty. Of 30 faculty listed as teaching in that division, 17 were part-time, drawn from business firms, government, and the High School of Commerce. Thirteen held full-time faculty rank, of whom 5 had only the BCS degree. Two others were CPAs, and the other 6 held BS or BA degrees. Six of them held also the law degree (LLB). *Not one faculty member teaching at Wall Street possessed the doctorate.*[29] Professor Archibald Wellington Taylor, head of the Department of Trade and Transportation, director of the Wall Street Division, and later dean of the Graduate School of Business Administration (GBA), held an AM degree. And Professor Arthur Henry Rosenkampff, affectionately known as "Rosie" by generations of Accounting students and longtime head of the Accounting department, had only the BCS degree. He later earned the CPA. But in the following year, 1921–1922, when Archibald Wellington Taylor became dean of GBA and the faculty almost doubled in size to 58, we find 6 doctorates among the faculty (4 PhDs and 2 ScDs). Fifteen held law degrees. Ten possessed no college or university degrees.[30] The sharp increase in faculty size undoubtedly reflected the increase in course and section offerings associated with the full launching of the new Graduate School of Business Administration.

Almost ten years later, as the terrible decade of the Great Depression began in 1930–1931, the Commerce Wall Street Division listed 146 faculty.[31] Sixty-eight held professorial rank (i.e., full, associate, or assistant), 72 were instructors, and 6 were lecturers. Of the professors, 14 had the PhD degree and 6 held other doctorates, 6 had law degrees, 5 were CPAs, 31 possessed master's degrees, 10 had baccalaureates only, and 4 had no college or university degree. Some were double counted because they had double credentials, for example, CPA and law. Of the 72 instructors, 3 had PhDs, 1 had the DCS (Doctorate of Commercial Science), 17 were lawyers (3 with JD degree and 14 LLB), 7 had the CPA, 17 held master's degrees, 17 held only bachelor's degrees, and 11 possessed no degrees. Again, there were some with double credentials. And of the 6 lecturers, 2 were PhDs, 1 was a CPA, 2 had only baccalaureates, and 1 had no degree. The presence of 16 faculty who possessed no college or university degree reflects the value placed on practical experience and knowledge. It must be noted with equal force that the presence of possessors of doctoral degrees was becoming increasingly evident.

Cash Cow

The School of Commerce, a big, bustling, brash educational beehive, had become a power center in New York University. But in the eyes of the more traditional segments of the institution (essentially, the Arts and Sciences), this did not happen because of its intellectual or academic quality. It happened because of its financial might. Commerce had become an enormous "cash cow," generating large surpluses of funds over and above its operating costs. Its operational costs were moderate, especially when compared with university units needing expensive laboratory facilities. And its large-scale employment of part-time faculty provided relatively low salaried instructors. Although feelings were mixed, the School's administration took some pride in its record of financial success, probably seeing in that success a valid justification for its emphasis on practicality as an educational virtue.

Professor George Burton Hotchkiss made some pointed comments about the extensive use of part-time faculty.

> Education for advertising has benefited by the fact that many advertising men have been willing to teach for small compensation, or none at all. At the start, and for many years afterward we paid an instructor $400 for a sixty-hour course. This was the usual rate in other departments. However, we increased the standard rate to $500 and then $600. Sometimes we paid more, and even went as high as $1,000 for a man we particularly wanted. Even at $600, we had no difficulty in getting men whose business salaries were at the $15,000 level or above. This state of affairs was not an unmixed blessing, for a full-time teacher usually had the equivalent of six courses, which if taught by part-time men would cost only $3,600. Even at $1,000 per course they would cost only $6,000, which is too small a salary for a first-rate full professor. Thus the willingness of advertising practitioners to become teachers in their spare time operated as a depressing influence upon the salaries of those who made teaching their profession.
>
> Much the same condition prevails in other fields of business and partly explains why the founders of the School of Commerce in 1900 were able to assure Chancellor Henry MacCracken that the School would never be

a drain upon the resources of the University. And it has not been. On the contrary, it has almost every year turned over a surplus of income over expense, to offset deficits incurred in other schools.

By no means all of us in the School of Commerce were in sympathy with the policy of earning a surplus to be devoted to the Schools that were not self-supporting. Dean Johnson and Dean Madden, however, had inherited it, and found it difficult to break away from it. While I was Chairman of the Marketing Department I did not allow it to interfere with the plan of building up a full-time faculty. In some years we may have operated at a loss, for our subject used more man-power and had more expenses than some others, but over the entire period, we managed to break even. I believe we continued to do so under Professor Agnew, although I cannot be positive, since I no longer was responsible for our budget.[32]

An apocryphal story about Dean John T. Madden circulated among the faculty when I came to the School of Commerce in 1947. The story captured and revealed a significant segment of the range of attitudes about undergraduate professional education for business which characterized the Faculty of Arts and Sciences and the Faculty of Commerce at the time.

It was said that at a meeting of deans, Dean Madden was chided by his Arts and Sciences colleague for presiding over a school that prostituted higher education. To which Dean Madden was reported to reply that there was one thing worse than being a prostitute, and that was to be the pimp living off her earnings. While the rejoinder was clever, note that it chose to attack the morals of the accuser rather than reject the substance of the accusation. Indeed, it is probably true that a substantial part of the Arts and Sciences shared the sentiment that undergraduate professional education for business was inferior and tolerated only because it generated large tuition revenues for the university. At a later time this tolerance diminished, and most markedly during the decade of the sixties when Commerce enrollments plummeted and the "cash cow" suffered a period of financial adversity.

After World War II

But in 1947 Commerce seemed impervious to adversity. Its enrollments continued to be huge, buttressed by the great wave of World War II veterans taking advantage of the GI Bill and inundating America's colleges and universities. Students were registered in large sections, assigned to a classroom, and instructors rotated to each section. The original class scheduling module of the School still prevailed, that is, a course involved two hours of meeting per week and yielded two points of academic credit. However, the old BCS degree program of 96 points had been abandoned in 1926 and replaced by a 128-credit BS degree program. For full-time day students this meant a four-year program of 32 credits per year (16 credits per semester, in eight courses). The load of eight courses per semester could be alleviated to a degree by mixing in some double courses yielding 4 credits each.

Faculty were accommodated in large, open "bull pen" department offices, with senior professors enjoying the privilege of a desk along the outer window wall of the Commerce building. Junior instructors and part-time faculty shared desks. It was an educational factory, a fully matured creation which was true to the intent and purposes of its founders. It was practical, focused on teaching rather than research, successful in producing graduates who were employable across a wide spectrum of business and vocations. It met the needs of prospective employers. It was also the biggest of its kind in the country, and essentially nonresidential (a commuter school). It was an easy, mass admission school, but not nearly so easy to gain graduation, and so a mass attrition school. It was split roughly evenly between full-time day students and part-time evening students, richly diverse in its student body, co-educational, and an enormous financial success (a "cash cow").

The School was a marvel and not to be scorned, although some looked upon and magnified its weaknesses. But its strengths were great and richly fulfilled the hopes of the founders. It was above all else a magnificent school of opportunity, a place where the ambitious, energetic, eager, even driven children of immigrants found their way to the fulfillment of the American dream. It was an educational beehive, in a sense a bustling factory, but with many brilliant teachers who inspired as they taught. While many of them lacked advanced academic credentials, those who had them gradually increased in number and relative importance, portending future changes in the character of the School. It is these changes to which we now turn our attention.

The Undergraduate School: Transforming Trends in the First Half-Century

Dean Charles Waldo Haskins, along with Charles Ezra Sprague and a few others, set the School's direction. But its nature was truly determined by the two deans who followed, and who between them accounted for 45 years of its history. They are Joseph French Johnson, 1903–1925, and John T. Madden, 1925–1948. The culture described in Chapter 1 emerged under their leadership.

Evident pride was taken in the School's size. Perhaps the best illustration of that pride was the Fiftieth Anniversary Dinner of the School, which was celebrated by a lavish dinner in 1950 in the great art deco ballroom of New York City's Waldorf-Astoria hotel. The highlight of the affair was the award of 50 honorary DCS degrees to that number of America's major chief executives. The dais was spectacular, peopled by multiple tiers of honorees, School and University administrators, and other leading citizens. It was big, like the school itself, and it manifested a certain naive faith in size. That faith would be tested severely in the coming decades, and finally displaced by a new set of values that gradually came into greater conformance with stricter, more rigid standards of academic quality. Remarkably, in the process the School did not lose its soul as the open door to expanded opportunity for a widely diverse student body.

The internal trends which underlay the School's transformation are more easily perceived retrospectively than they were prospectively. These five trends are probably the most significant: (1) the gradual growth of a full-time faculty of "professional" academics, whose professorial status became tied initially to the degree of Doctor of Philosophy and later to output of research; (2) the gradual tightening of admission standards, first in terms of increasingly rigorous specifications of courses required to be completed in high school, second, in terms of minimum high school grade point averages and third, but much later, in terms of the College Entrance Examination Board (CEEB) examinations; (3) expansion of number of credits required for the baccalaureate degree to 128 points (1926), and the broadening of the subject scope of the degree with the introduction of the Bachelor of Science (BS) degree that eventually displaced the old BCS degree; (4) the establishment of the Graduate School of Business Administration, which gradually intensified pressure on the faculty to have the PhD and to be actively engaged in research; and (5) much later, changes in the educational levels of businessmen and, consequently, in the sense of what constituted an adequate education for business (in itself, probably a reflection of the vastly more complex technology which developed in twentieth-century America).

Faculty

The transformation of the faculty eventually led to research being valued more highly than teaching, with faculty becoming more self-focused and less concerned with the classroom and its students. Teaching suffers as a consequence. And students come to feel that they are not a primary interest of the School and university, except as a source of tuition revenue with which to sustain the faculty in pursuit of its separate interests. Alienation of students from faculty is a serious matter that is now attracting more attention from the academic establishment. Of course, a faculty significantly involved in business, either full-time or part-time, may be less attentive than desirable to student needs and interests. Where does the best balance lie? The question is important.

What made the doctorate so important in American universities? It was the gradual triumph of the German university model of the late nineteenth century, which emphasized research and possession of the doctorate as evidence of one's ability to do research. Research was important because it was seen as extending man's horizon, thereby enlarging knowledge, improving society, and advancing civilization. These are all most worthy objectives, and in the German model the university was the place where it happened. Herein lay the mystique of the doctor of philosophy degree, and the role of its possessor as a knight girded to push back the forces of ignorance. It follows that as PhDs became dominant figures in the American academies, emphasis shifted from undergraduate to graduate education, and from teaching to research. It also follows that weakening occurred in the voice raised in behalf of teaching and of "professional" education at the undergraduate level.

The very same issue, seen through different eyes, was discussed by the Syndic[1] of New York University in his 1912 annual report. The title, long since abandoned, would today be recognized by hardly any American academic. But the issue, stubborn and persistent, will not die. In the Syndic's words:

> It is coming to be generally recognized that if the present tendency is permitted to continue un-checked, the Ph.D. degree will come to be merely a professional degree for teachers, to be acquired in the ordinary routine, very much as it is in Germany and as the M.D. degree is acquired in this country; that its commercial aspect will be increasingly emphasized, and that it will cease to mark the pursuit of science for science's sake, for which purpose it was originally designed. This fact was recognized some time since by the University when it created the degree of Doctor of Pedagogy, and it was the hope of the University that that degree might serve the purpose of a professional degree for those who pursued advanced studies only in order that they might fit themselves for teaching. Other universities, however, do not seem to have felt the necessity of preserving the Ph.D. in this way, and it is now probably too late to save it from becoming distinctively a professional degree. Unfortunately, the ideals for which the Ph.D. stand are not necessarily the ideals which develop the best teachers for all grades of schools.[2]

Table 2.1 emphasizes the point, as it emerges from the half-century experience at the School of Commerce between 1910 and 1960. Several major observations may be deduced from the data; namely, (1) the doctorate was associated overwhelmingly with the professorial ranks and was uncommon among instructors and lecturers; (2) the huge reliance upon the latter ranks for staffing implies dependence on a relatively inexpensive "labor" pool for financial rather than academic reasons; (3) yet, the relative decline of lecturers and instructors indicates the gradual professionalization of the faculty; and (4) the "sea change" in this connection between 1950 and 1960 foretells later trends which practically mandated possession of the PhD and the almost complete disappearance of the lecturer ranks. We shall return to these observations in Chapter 4,

TABLE 2.1

Commerce Faculty Having PhD or Other Earned Doctorates, by Rank, 1910–1911, 1920–1921, 1930–1931, 1940–1941, 1950–1951, 1960–1961

	All Professorial Ranks			Instructors/Lecturers		
Year	Total No.	Total No. Earned Doctorates	% Earned Doctorates	Total No.	Total Earned Doctorates	% Earned Doctorates
1910–1911	7	2	28.6	7	1	14.3
1920–1921	35	13	37.1	106	3	2.8
1930–1931	76	18	23.7	148	8	5.4
1940–1941	95	34	35.8	127	11	8.7
1950–1951	106	46	43.4	138	7	5.1
1960–1961	133	74	55.6	92	6	6.5

SOURCES: New York University Bulletins, School of Commerce, Accounting, and Finance, Academic Years Noted at Head of Table, Faculty Listings.

when we discuss the resurgence of the School in the seventies and eighties.

Admissions Standards

We observed earlier that the School of Commerce, in addition to admitting high school graduates and people who had successfully completed the first year of study at an acceptable college, admitted holders of the BS degree or its equivalent. Also, the School of Commerce admitted *special students,* that is, those who did not possess these credentials. But special students could not receive the BCS degree, unless they satisfied the admission requirements specified for degree track students. Instead, upon successful completion of the identical program of study, they received a certificate of proficiency. Eventually, the certificate of proficiency was abandoned, and along with it the admission of special students who lacked the high school diploma.

A second major step to raise admission standards involved specifying the composition of courses required to be completed in high school. Effective September 1924, all regular (i.e., degree track) students had to have 15 required units in high school. Those units had to include 3 or 4 units of English and 1 unit of Elementary Algebra, an early recognition of the importance of mathematical ability to a business school graduate. But, of the 10–11 elective units, 5 had to come from these subject group areas (3 from any one area and 2 from any other area): (1) a classical language other than English; (2) a modern language other than English;

(3) Mathematics other than Elementary Algebra; (4) History, Civics, and/or Elementary Economics; and (5) Sciences.[3] The remaining 5–6 "elective" units could be offered from *any subject* accepted by secondary schools for graduation, for example, commercial subjects like Stenography and Typing. In September 1927, a unit of Plane Geometry was specified as required, in addition to Elementary Algebra, making a minimum 2–unit Math requirement. A further tightening occurred in 1928 when the choice of 5–6 elective units was reduced to 5, and they could no longer include subjects such as Physical Training, Hygiene, Music, and so on.[4] And in the next year's bulletin (1929–1930), footnote 2 on page 17 noted that "No entrance credit (is) allowed for less than two units of a classical or modern foreign language."

The direction of change apparently altered somewhat in the years that followed. By 1947, when I arrived at Commerce, the math standard had been relaxed, that is, the specific math requirement (elementary algebra and plane geometry) had been dropped. Instead, in addition to 4 units of English, 6 units were required in other academic subjects (i.e., mathematics, classical language, modern foreign language, science, history— including civics, economics, problems of American democracy), and 6 more units in academic and/or commercial subjects. The total required units were 16,[5] one more than the 15 in 1924.

A minimum high school grade point average was required for the 16 units. It had to exceed "the passing grade of the secondary school by at least 20 percent of the difference between the passing grade and 100 percent." While the usual high school passing grade was 65 percent, the required minimum in the minds of the Commerce faculty was probably 60 percent (the minimum percentage equivalent of a D grade). Hence $100 - 60 = 40 \times 0.2 = 8 + 60 = 68$. This writer wonders whether the GPA requirement was followed in practice. He has a strong memory of the first faculty meeting he attended in the Fall of 1947 when one of the major topics of faculty debate was raising the minimum required GPA for admission to Commerce. Many faculty expressed deep concern over the impact of such a change on enrollments. Unhappily for the accuracy of memory, the faculty minutes for the October 1947 meeting make no reference to such a discussion.

Finally, but not of major importance until a later period, the high school graduate had to take the Scholastic Aptitude Test (SAT) of the College Entrance Examination Board, an association of college and secondary schools formed to conduct uniform college entrance examinations. What is significant is that the College Entrance Examination Board (CEEB) issued a certificate to those who passed its college entrance examinations. And in 1924 the School of Commerce accepted this certificate for entry into its regular degree programs of study.[6] But no requirement existed that applicants to Commerce degree programs had to take the SAT as a condition of entry, or that they had to achieve some minimum score. Those conditions would come in the yet distant years ahead and would be associated with the academic transformation of the School. However, the first move in that direction was made in 1924, not long after the establishment of the CEEB. By 1947 there had been no further change.

Curriculum

Curricular developments also manifested a tendency to *become more stringent academically*. Concurrently, they broadened the programs of study leading to the degree. Perhaps the major move in this direction was the introduction of the four year (full-time day) Bachelor of Science (BS) degree program in 1926, which did not change in its essential nature until the traumatic latter part of the fifties and in the sixties.

Seen in the light of present-day academic standards, the harsh reality seems to be that the original BCS degree program of the School of Commerce was substantively thin. It consisted of 10 contact hours of instruction per week, Monday–Friday, scheduled in the late evening hours from 8 to 10 p.m., and it extended over two semesters per year for two years. If one contact hour equals one credit hour, then we see a 40–credit hour degree program with its course offerings concentrated entirely in the professional (practical) subject areas of Accounting, Finance, Commerce, and Law.[7] In the following year, 1902–1903, the program of study was divided, one requiring greater concentration in Accounting, while the other continued with the more general pattern shown above and now identified as the course in Commerce and Finance.[8]

A major enlargement in the program occurred in the 1904–1905 academic year.[9] For evening students it was expanded by 50 percent, from 10 full courses to 15, so that this program now required a minimum of three years to complete. A "full" course ran for two hours per week for two 15-week semesters, making a total of 60 class contact hours, or 60 credit hours. Students who could attend school full-time could earn the degree in two years. But they had to take 16 full courses, that is, an extra course making a total of 64 credit hours. The 16 courses had to include at least two in Accounting, two in Commerce, two in Finance, two in Law, and one in either Modern Languages or Science. Of particular interest, especially in light of difficulties in cross-school registration in later decades, the 1904–1905 bulletin pointed out that "lectures on the less technical subjects, such as Political Economy, Economic History, Theory and History of Banking, they will hear during the day either in the University College or in the Washington Square Collegiate Division. The lectures on law will be taken in the Law School." [10]

A further major expansion took place three years later, in 1907–1908.[11] For evening students, in addition to the completion of 15 full courses, at least two years' successful experience in business to the satisfaction of the faculty was required. For day students the program was extended to require the completion of 20 full courses, that is, 20 hours per week for two academic years of 30 weeks each. The 1908–1909 bulletin added that the faculty may require at least 60 hours of instruction in English or other subjects.[12] Class scheduling was extended to the earlier hours of 4:45–6:45 p.m. in 1909–1910. The English requirement (Business English) was made mandatory in 1912–1913, the same year in which classes were first scheduled in four time slots (10:30 a.m.-12:30 p.m.; 4:45 p.m.-6:30 p.m.; 6:00—7:45 p.m.; and 7:45 p.m.-9:45 p.m.).[13] And in the following year the "day" program became full-blown, so that full-time day students could schedule *all* their courses during the daylight hours.[14]

Within a brief span of 13 years Commerce, which had begun as a School for older students who worked full-time, had become also one serving younger people directly after graduating from high school. It was inherent in this development that the presence of a full-time cadre of professional academics would emerge and gradually grow with the expansion of the day program. Eventually, as suggested earlier, the professional academics in the faculty would take their cue as to the key elements of academic quality from colleagues in the Arts and Sciences and in the graduate professional schools who emphasized the doctorate degree and research. But not yet, and not for many more years.

The tendency toward increasing strictness showed itself also in ways that now seem amusing. The 1914–1915 bulletin spelled out penalties for unexcused class absences, and for late arrival or early departure from class.[15] Excused absences were limited to three per subject. Late arrival or early departure (more than 10 minutes) resulted in an absence. And absences had to be explained by an excuse signed by an employer, physician, or relative and left in the appropriate School office immediately following the absence. Late excuses would be disregarded.

By 1920, further major changes in the BCS curriculum had become effective. Evening students seeking the degree had to complete 72 points of course work, representing 18 points per year over four years of 30 weeks each. A minimum grade point average of 70 percent had to be achieved. A further 24 points of credit was granted for at least three years of successful experience in business while in school, or a total of 96. Day students seeking the BCS degree had to complete 96 points over three years of 30 weeks each, and with a minimum grade point average of 70 percent.[16] The curricular screws were tightened again in the next year. Twenty-four of 50 points of elective courses had to be taken in advanced courses, that is, courses with prerequisites of at least four points of specified prior work. The remaining 26 remained elective. Further, the minimum required grade point average for the degree was raised to 75 percent.[17] In 1923–1924 the required core in the evening BCS degree program was expanded to include Management 1 and 2.[18]

The requirement that 24 points be taken in advanced courses implies that a significant number of students were pursuing too many introductory, basic courses and avoiding more difficult advanced courses. A further curricular change in 1924–1925 implied that a significant number of students were excessively concentrating their advanced course work in a particular department, and hence harmfully narrowing their academic exposure. In any case such a tendency would explain the faculty's decision to limit students to no more than 50 percent of their total degree credits to any one department (i.e., 48 credits for day students and 36 credits for evening students).[19]

The method of computing grade point averages was converted from percentages to credit hours in the 1925–1926 academic year.[20] Letter grades were to be given on the basis of the following:

A   Highest excellence
B   Superior Work
C   Satisfactory Work

D   Inferior Work, but passing

E   Failure with privilege of reexamination

F   Bad failure, with no reexamination privilege

An overall average of C was now required for graduation, with the average computed on the basis of credit hours. Given the 2-point contact hour course module, the letter grades for such a 2-point course yielded the following equivalents:

A   6 credit hours

B   4 credit hours

C   2 credit hours

D   0 credit hours

Consequently, in addition to 96 points (contact hour credits) required for the BCS degree, 96 credit hours also had to be earned. Grades of D, yielding 0 credit hours had to be offset by countable credit hours in additional courses; or by Bs or As in other courses. But students could not make up the deficiency by repeating the course in which the D was received. Also, students receiving an E and passing a reexamination could not receive a grade higher than D. And a student receiving a grade of F had to repeat the course to remove the deficiency.

The 1925–1926 bulletin cautioned students about cheating, an early indication that the School of Commerce, so extraordinary an educational enterprise in many ways, was not an academic Garden of Eden. The bulletin set down specific rules for examinations, for example, no books or papers could be brought into the exam room. Those students who were apprehended and found to be cheating were subject to expulsion. As a onetime member and later chairman of the School's discipline committee several decades later, I can testify at first hand that the warning was not idle. Indeed, it was taken very seriously, and some students were dismissed in academic disgrace.

A more profound transformation of the Commerce Curriculum came in 1926–1927. In that year a new Bachelor of Science degree, requiring 128 credits of course work, was introduced.[21] John T. Madden had become dean the year before, and this change had his active support. The change reflected also a new set of standards adopted by the American Association of Collegiate Schools of Business (AACSB). The essential feature of the new BS degree program was its requirement that substantial course work had to be taken in the Liberal Arts and Sciences.

A new BCS degree program of 128 credits was concurrently introduced, but it was not as demanding in that respect. As examples, the new BS degree program required 12 points of work in modern foreign languages, but the BCS degree program did not. Also, where the BS degree required courses in science, the BCS degree refers to Outlines of Science, Chemistry in Industry, and Physics in Industry. Note that science is taught in the framework of its practical application to business and industry. Students following the old BCS and certificate programs of study, that is, those who entered Commerce before June 1926, had to complete their course work by June 1932. After June 1932, the old programs of study disappeared. The 1926–1927 bulletin noted also that at least 32 points of work toward the degree had to be taken "in residence" at Commerce. In effect, this limited the amount of transfer credit that a student could apply toward a Commerce Degree.[22]

The difference between the new BS and BCS degrees was stated explicitly in the 1929–1930 bulletin:[23]

> The BS program is made up of 64 points in arts courses and 64 points in business courses; in other words, the program leading to (that degree) is composed of two years of arts work and two years of business courses. The arts courses are taken concurrently with the business courses. One of the chief differences between the program for the bachelor of science degree and that for the bachelor of commercial science degree is that the first has two full years of business courses, whereas the latter has three full years of such courses. Students who desire to continue their study of foreign languages and who wish to have a larger percentage of arts work in their program should register for the (BS) degree. Students who desire to take as much work as possible in business courses should register for the (BCS) degree.

The new BCS degree program curtailed sharply the credits that could be granted for business experience and research. Evening students working full-time in business and entering Commerce after September 1926 (that is, new program), could earn no more than 10 points toward the degree based on their business experience. But to get those credits they had to do an annual thesis "representing original research in the business" in which the students worked, and such research had to be satisfactory to the faculty (the Committee on Supervised Research and Business Experiences). Further, a limit of four credits per year could be earned in this way.[24] Day students could earn credit also for actual business experience, as an "equivalent of advanced laboratory courses in the student's field of specialization," but only to a maximum of 8 points. The "new" 128–credit BCS degree program was discontinued in September 1936, after which only the BS degree was offered by the School.[25]

Although the 1929–1930 bulletin stated that the BS degree required that one-half the courses (64 credits) be taken in the arts, the program of study outlined in the 1926–1927 bulletin indicated an Arts minor of 12 points and Arts electives of another 24 points. If we add to the total of 36 points another 4 points in Math, Science, or History, two years of required modern foreign language (8 points), and 4 points of English composition, we have a grand total of 52 points out of the 128 required for the degree. This excludes Economics 1 and 2, which could count also as social science and which would bring us close to the one-half mark. Yet, there was confusion because the 1936 publication *Glimpses of the Faculty*, speaking about Basic Cultural Courses, said:

> Both the alumni and faculty of the School have long recognized that a sound training for success in business consisted of two main elements: (1) a training in the fundamentals of such professional subjects as accounting, advertising, finance, etc.; and (2) a study of such nonprofessional subjects as history, literature, psychology, etc. The kind of business man the School attempts to produce possesses both skill in his chosen field of specialization and a knowledge of the civilization in which he lives, and an acquaintance with the arts and science that have produced that civilization. *To this end, approximately thirty per cent of the bachelor of science curriculum is composed of cultural subjects. The School seeks to train its students not only to make a living but also to live a well-rounded life.* (Italics added)[26]

A look at the School's *Programs of Study for the Academic Year 1948– 1949* confirms the statement in *Glimpses of the Faculty* indicating "approximately thirty percent of the bachelor of science curriculum is composed of cultural subjects." Perhaps the most liberal major was the one in General Economics[27] which allowed 44 credits of general cultural or nonprofessional course work, 24 credits in the School's basic professional core (Banking and Finance, Management, Marketing, Accounting, Business English, Economics), 24 credits in the professional major, 12 credits in a professional minor, and 24 credits for professional electives. Forty-four credits amount to 34 percent of the 128 credits required for the degree. The Accounting major, much more prescriptive, allowed 40 credits of cultural (Arts and Sciences) courses, with zero credits for a professional minor or for professional electives. That program mandated

44 credits in the professional core, plus another 44 credits in the professional major. The basic majors in Banking and Finance, Management, and Marketing, as examples, paralleled generally the General Economics structure in the proportions of the program allowed to cultural courses, and to professional minors and professional electives. But each department offered also narrower, more specific majors targeted toward particular industries and occupations. Thus, Management offered a program in Production Management. In that program, only 32 credits of work were offered in cultural courses and no work was permitted in professional electives. Instead, the professional major required 52 credits. The leaning toward specialization could be seen also in the 24 certificate programs of 64 credits each offered to evening students over a three-year period. These programs were for students unprepared to undertake the BS degree program, yet desiring preparation for a specific occupation. In the language of the Programs of Study, the certificate programs were designed "to provide . . . a certain amount of preparation for (a) particular field of business . . ."

One other feature of the Commerce curriculum demands explicit recognition. Commerce students did not take their nonprofessional course work in the Washington Square College, with the Arts and Sciences students. Instead, this work was taught by the General Course department of the School of Commerce, a mini Arts and Sciences faculty under the jurisdiction and control of the School of Commerce.

The General Course department was established in Commerce in 1926–1927, under the direction of Professor Edward J. Kilduff.[28] It was concurrent with the introduction of the new BCS and BS degrees, and retained the Liberal Arts and Sciences course work under the control of Commerce. The new department offered these courses in 1926–1927: Outlines of Literature, Outlines of History, Outlines of Science, General Mathematics, General Sociology, General Psychology, Introduction to Art, and Ethics. In 1927–1928 the department added Logic, Physics in Industry, and Chemistry in Industry. This was not a completely new direction for Commerce. The School had been offering courses in Sociology since 1913–1914. And it had also taught foreign language courses since the earliest years of its existence, principally, German, Spanish, French, and Italian.

Given the cross-school arrangements at Washington Square in the earlier decades of the century, one wonders how and why this separation occurred. Did the College distance itself from the Commerce students? Did Commerce deliberately erect this structure, perhaps for budgetary reasons (i.e., to retain the course enrollments and associated tuition revenues)? Did Commerce create the separation based on dissatisfaction with the orientation of the course work and the faculty in the College, that is, that the courses were somehow irrelevant to the "real" world, or that some of them were antibusiness in tone? Whatever the reasons, one consequence was surely to strengthen any bias in the College that inclined its faculty and students to regard Commerce as inferior intellectually and academically. After all, they had a convenient query to support such bias; namely, if Commerce students were of equal quality, then why did they not take the cultural course work in the College? The fact that they did not seemed a damning proof of inferiority.

In spite of grand statements of purpose, the aspiration of real balance between professional and nonprofessional courses would not be fully achieved until much later. Clearly, less than half of the course work in the BS degree was typically in the arts. Also, the 1948–1949 Program of Study showed that the School listed 29 major fields.[29] In addition to such broad functional fields of business as accounting, finance, economics, management, and marketing, the Program of Study listed narrower vocational and industry-specific areas such as brokerage, real estate and insurance, investments, production management, public utilities, retailing, and so on. Twenty-four certificate programs were listed.

A couple of additional comments are appropriate. First, the curricular structure which had emerged in the School of Commerce by 1936 was essentially unchanged by 1948, a year after I arrived. The curriculum, as shown above, continued to require 128 credit hours for the BS degree, consisting essentially of 2-credit courses. Full-time day students typically took eight courses per semester to complete the program in four years, while evening students could do the program in six years. Of course, work taken in the summer would make possible earlier completion. The program of studies continued also to be characterized by a multitude of courses, since the 2-credit module, coupled with an enrollment of many thousands, encouraged massive proliferation of course offerings. This tendency, in turn, may have encouraged faculty to propose large numbers of narrowly focused and highly specialized courses. Also the departments usually liked to satisfy the desires of the faculty. Apart from an inducement to attract students into narrowly focused courses, no financial problem for the School or the university was involved, as long as enrollments continued to be large. But that would change when enrollments fell significantly.

Second, negative perceptions about the nature and quality of the curriculum miss a fundamental point. The Commerce curriculum of the first half of the twentieth century developed in response to the needs and demands of business and society. From that standpoint we see programs of study that developed enormously over the half-century, from exclusively "professional" and "practical" in the beginning to significantly broadened and substantively enhanced by 1950. Important steps had been taken to produce a graduate knowledgeable about the history of society and with an interest in the larger world beyond business. That more substantial steps would be needed and would be taken later is no ground for condemning the progress that was already achieved, and remarkable in itself.

Introduction of Graduate Degrees and Establishment of the Graduate School of Business Administration

Later chapters will limn the story of the Graduate School of Business Administration. That segment of the Stern School story comes into the picture now only because: first, it was an outgrowth of the development of the School of Commerce; second, the two components of today's Stern School continued to be intimately involved with each other throughout their existence; and third, their interrelationship was attended by various tensions which emphasized some fundamental issues of professional education for business in the university, and of university and school governance.

Although Commerce was established as an undergraduate school and originally offered only the BCS degree, it admitted students to its program who already had baccalaureates, and even more advanced degrees. These students included lawyers and others who desired some business education exposure to complement and enhance their existing education. But there must have been an educational problem in the wide degree of heterogeneity in so broad a spectrum of educational backgrounds as existed in the early student body. In any event, in the 1908–1909 academic year Commerce introduced a Master of Commercial Science (MCS) degree program.[30] The MCS program was for holders of the

BCS or other equivalent college degrees. It required completion of 180 hours of advanced work, plus a thesis in commerce, accounts, or finance which showed evidence of original research and thought and which was approved by the faculty. A possible oral examination was also mentioned, but not indicated as necessary.

With the opening of Commerce's Wall Street Division in 1914 and its acquisition of the Old Trinity Church School building at 90 Trinity Place in 1920, the MCS degree migrated downtown along with the BCS and certificate programs. In 1916 a Graduate Division of Business Administration was formally created within Commerce. It became the Graduate School of Business Administration in 1921, remaining at the Trinity Place location for the following three-quarters of a century. In 1921–1922 Archibald Wellington Taylor, who was concurrently director of Commerce's Wall Street Division, was listed in the bulletin as dean of GBA.[31] In the same year the bulletin introduced the Master of Business Administration (MBA) degree.[32] The MBA program was designed for holders of the Bachelor of Arts (BA) or Bachelor of Science (BS) degree, or an equivalent degree. The three-year (96 credit) scope of the BCS degree and its narrow curricular content made it necessary to distinguish between holders of that degree, and those holding the BA or BS degree.

No doubt, the educational needs of both classes of students differed. Since both Commerce and GBA were authorized to award graduate degrees at that time, it is difficult to comprehend how work was divided between them. It is plain that at that juncture Commerce was dominant in enrollments, faculty numbers, physical plant, and finances. It is equally plain that the relative weight of the two divisions continued that way for many years. Eventually, however, the issuance of graduate degrees became the exclusive province of GBA. The Doctor of Commercial Science (DCS) degree was first granted in June 1928 and the Doctor of Philosophy (PhD) degree in June 1938. The last DCS degree was granted in June 1948.[33] Thus, the MCS and DCS degrees were dropped in favor of the MBA, the PhD, and certain (MS) degrees.

As long as Commerce enrollments and financial strength continued great, some fundamental issues were kept under the surface and relatively obscure. But, when enrollments and "cash cow" power began to slip in the 1950s, and then collapsed in the sixties, those underlying issues and tensions burst out and threatened the continued life of the undergraduate school. Prominent among those issues were the philosophical and educational justifications for an undergraduate professional business program. Was not the ideal intellectual preparation for a business career an undergraduate liberal arts or sciences degree (BA or BS), coupled with an MBA? Would not such a course of study truly produce a person with a broadly based educational background, with a grasp of the development of Western civilization and the forward march of science, and having as well a sound substantive professional preparation? The questions will be addressed later, but it is necessary to raise them here because the growing strength of GBA ultimately led to a significant split among the faculty on this issue.

Consider also the academic pecking order. Graduate is mightier than undergraduate in terms of academic status and reputation. As a consequence, the creation of GBA inspired a desire in many Commerce faculty to be assigned graduate courses as a sign of peer recognition of academic merit. To be denied such assignment was easily construed as a symbol of deficiency. Faculty oriented to the graduate programs came to look down, in greater or lesser degree, on the quality of the undergraduate programs and faculty. And many of them eventually became proponents of cutting out Commerce. Similar developments occurred at other universities, and in some they did result in the discontinuance of the undergraduate programs (e.g., Northwestern, Tulane, Pittsburgh). But not at N Y U, and that is an important part of the Stern School story.

Finally, consider the relative emphasis given to teaching and to research, as well as to the "practical" character of the curriculum and the involvement of the faculty in outside consulting (i.e., in maintaining ongoing involvement with practical business affairs). Once again, developments at N Y U paralleled those in other American B-schools, as business schools are commonly called, and universities. Emphasis on research grew while that on teaching weakened, and was reflected in decisions on tenure, promotion, and salary increments. Research itself tended to become more esoteric. And those doing such research came to view themselves with increasing boldness as the purest and noblest at the academic round table. Faculty doing research of an immediately practical kind, for example, consulting with industry, came to be viewed by their academically chaste colleagues as money-grubbing pursuers of personal material gain, who compromised their intellectual integrity in the process.

These issues were and are consequential. We will revisit them.

The Changing Attitudes of Business Leaders

Our discussion of the huge increase in Commerce enrollments that occurred in the first half of the century, from the small beginning in 1900 to the 10,000 of 1941–1942, observed that it was a reflection of the needs and demands of our society. Transportation, communication, and information were exploding technologically. A more sophisticated and better educated labor force was needed. Our educational establishment responded to that need.

By 1950 the horse-drawn wagon was largely gone, replaced by truck and auto. Commercial aircraft were already displacing oceanliners and freighters, except for heavy, large bulk cargo. And tractor-trailer trucks competed with railroads. The computer age dawned and nuclear energy was at hand, although about to be beset by fear of potential disaster. The educational level of American society at the turn of the century could not accommodate such revolutionary changes. For example, in 1900 only 6.3 percent of the population 17 years old were high school graduates. In 1970 the figure had risen to 75.6 percent.[34] And in 1991 it had increased to 78.4 percent.[35] The percentage of the population having completed four years of college or more rose from 10.7 in 1970 to 21.4 in 1991.[36] In 1900 the percentage of college graduates was minuscule.

Not only technology fed the demand and need for advanced education. So did a corresponding psychological and social factor. As larger proportions of the population became high school and college graduates, no less a level of competence was perceived as mandatory for their children. The role of the famed GI Bill of Rights, which financed advanced education for legions of World War II and Korean War veterans, was highly significant in this societal transformation.

Of more immediate importance to America's B-schools, and to both Commerce and GBA at NYU, was a profound shift in the attitude of American business leaders toward the educational credentials required of their employees, and particularly of those employees aspiring to managerial and top executive positions.

Being the Boss, a book about leadership and power in American business, spoke to this point, citing the results of a *Fortune* 1985 survey of the chief executives of the 500 largest industrial and 500 largest service companies:

Five hundred twelve CEOs responded to the survey anonymously, and *Fortune* compared its information with data on U.S. CEOs provided by earlier studies for 1900, 1925, and 1950, and reported in Mabel New-comer's *The Big Business Executive* in 1955. Using the Newcomer findings as a model, *Fortune* had also done a survey of CEOs in 1976, so that its 1986 report provided data for 1900, 1925, 1950, 1976, and 1986.

The most striking trend over the eight and one-half decades is the powerful push to higher education and advanced degrees by chief execu-tives. Thus, in 1900, fully 60 percent of the CEOs were only grade school or high school graduates, while some 10 percent attended college, about 20 percent were college graduates, and under 10 percent indicated just graduate study. In 1986, in sharp contrast, the picture was more than simply reversed. Then, fully 60 percent indicated post-graduate study, 30 percent were college graduates, about 7 percent attended college, and a minuscule 3 percent had no more than a grade school or high school diploma. It is no overstatement to say that a college education, coupled with post-graduate study, is a major element today in preparing oneself for the chief executive's position. [37]

But nowhere is it set down that the manager's need for advanced education could be satisfied only, or even best, by a B-school degree. Indeed, as we shall see, a considerable body of opinion developed among business leaders that a broad educational exposure in the Arts and Sci-ences was superior and hence preferable to the programs of study offered by undergraduate business schools. They thought a professional educa-tion for business was best achieved at the graduate level with the MBA degree. Of course, they had not yet experienced the comparative perfor-mance capabilities of the graduates of the best undergraduate B-schools with those of the best Arts and Sciences colleges. They would be con-fronted with that experience in the seventies and after, and it would be in many ways a chastening and eye-opening experience. Of equal and perhaps greater significance, they had not yet dealt on a large scale with the promotion and compensation expectations of newly minted MBA graduates of our top B-schools, nor had they yet compared these MBA holders on any cost-benefit basis with people holding baccalaureates from schools like Stern or Wharton. In any case the stage is set for the next scene.

The Undergraduate School: The Traumatic Fifties and Sixties

Enrollments

Decline, decay, demoralization, and despair came to characterize Commerce in the ten years from 1955 to 1965. The surface manifestation of this trauma was a devastating drop in enrollments. The peak enrollment of 1941–1942 was quickly recovered after World War II, as the veterans financed by the GI Bill flooded into the School. A temporary drop around 1949–1951 was overcome by the arrival of the Korean veterans. But as the mid-fifties arrived, a precipitous enrollment decline began.

By the Fall semester of 1960–1961 the huge enrollments of 8,000–9,000 had fallen to 4,813, of which number 2,779 were day students. Ten years later, in the Fall semester of 1970–1971 the total enrollment stood at a puny 1,422, of whom 1,051 were day and 371 evening students. As bad as the implosion of day student enrollments was, the relative contraction of the evening student enrollments was worse, from 42.3 percent of total enrollment to 26.1 percent.[1]

What could explain so cataclysmic a collapse of the School of Commerce? An extraordinary number of forces came together to produce the collapse, some external to the university and School, some external to the School but internal to the university, and some internal to the school itself.

Forces external to the School and the university. Among these forces were: (1) the end of the wave of World War II and Korean war veterans who came to the school under the GI Bill; (2) the enormous expansion of tuition-free and low-tuition city and state universities; (3) popularity of the liberal arts and sciences in the mid- and late sixties, and the concurrent rise in unpopularity of study for business; (4) the impact of the Gordon-Howell (Ford Foundation), the Pierson (Carnegie Foundation), and CED (Committee for Economic Development) reports, which were highly critical of collegiate education for business; and (5) the large-scale population movement to the suburbs, and the growth there of two-year community colleges offering relatively inexpensive and locationally more convenient alternatives to Commerce.

Forces external to the School but internal to the university. Among these forces were: (1) the major and lasting impact of the NYU Self-Study report (1956), which was produced during the presidency of Henry Heald (1952–1956), and which called for massive changes in the character of Commerce; (2) NYU's 1963 application to the Ford Foundation for a $25 million development grant, which repeated in essence the demand for the transformation in Commerce that appeared originally in the NYU Self-Study report; (3) the resulting and real threat by the university's central administration to discontinue the School of Commerce, which reached a peak in 1963–1965; (4) the public announcement by Washington Square College in the early sixties that it was going to discontinue its evening studies program, which created a public perception that all NYU divisions at Washington Square were withdrawing from evening studies; (5) perhaps of greatest immediate significance, university pressure on Commerce to raise greatly its standards for admission to the School; (6) the adoption by the university of a flat fee tuition arrangement which charged students registering for 12 or more points as full-time students, thereby presenting evening students with a quandary; (7) the almost concurrent adoption of the so-called four-course plan, which forced the undergraduate schools at Washington Square to move from 3-credit to 4-credit courses. As a consequence, evening students taking three courses, that is, 12 credits, fell into a full-time status and were charged the same tuition as full-time day students. Although this problem was later corrected for Commerce students, it had an immediate negative impact. To avoid the full tuition charge, when it was in effect, an evening student had to limit his courses to two per semester, which meant eight years to obtain the degree (excluding summer work) instead of six.

Forces Internal to the School. Among these forces were: (1) the report of the faculty "Think" committee in 1964; (2) a year later, the report of the

Faculty Committee to Study the Schools of Business; and (3) attitudes adverse to continuance of the School of Commerce held by a significant segment of the faculty of the Graduate School of Business Administration.

While all the foregoing forces had a negative effect on Commerce, some of them contained the seeds of regeneration and renewal. These resulted in a profound transformation of the School, concentrated in the decade and a half from 1960 to 1975 and resulting in a remarkable resurgence, which catapulted Commerce into the position of one of America's leading undergraduate schools of business (in qualitative rather than quantitative terms, although enrollments also greatly recovered).

We will not deal with all of the above-mentioned forces impacting the school, but confine ourselves instead to those which were most important in bringing about its transformation.

The N Y U Self-Study Report

Henry T. Heald became president of N Y U in 1952, leaving in 1956 to assume the leadership of the Ford Foundation. In that brief span of four years he set in motion profoundly powerful forces which would in the following three decades completely change the character of the university, and most particularly the School of Commerce. President Heald moved quickly to set those forces in motion. In the Fall of 1952, immediately following his arrival at Washington Square, he spoke with Charles Dollard, president of the Carnegie Foundation, and requested a grant of $250,000 to underwrite an evaluation of the university's educational program.[2] The project went forward under the aegis of an Office of Institutional Research and Educational Planning established on June 14, 1953.

Early in the report these comments were made, having particular relevance to the School of Commerce as a "cash cow".

> For some decades there was no other financial resource that could be counted upon. A large number of fee-paying (i.e. tuition) students in low-cost instructional areas produced a transferable "surplus" however ephemeral. The unfortunate by-product was that these academic units in the "black" were able to keep up this appearance only because they failed to plow back into the programs the money that would have produced superior results. The price was paid—and is still paid to some extent—in

large classes, overload in research supervision, crowded offices, laboratory, library, and campus deficiencies, and more subtly in a shortage of "risk" capital.[3]

How aptly the Self-Study's words applied to Commerce, and for how long it had been true, can be perceived in this poignant appeal to the university Chancellor, penned by Dean John T. Madden and submitted on October 1, 1930.

> This school closed its thirtieth year with the largest enrollment in its history and produced a surplus from operations, *over and above overhead,* approximating $300,000, which was contributed to the general deficit of the University. It was another year in the series of years of sacrifice made necessary by the lack of adequate free endowment for the university. It is fitting that public attention be called to the sacrifices of faculty and students in the hope that generous donors may supply the means so sadly needed. Our instructors are carrying a heavier teaching and administrative load than their confreres in other institutions. Many of our classes are too large for effective teaching, necessitating the use of the lecture method exclusively in these sections. We are dangerously undermanned and our salary scale is not in line with that which prevails in other schools of our class. This, together with our greater teaching load, does not present an inviting picture to those whom we would like to add to our faculty. Our scholarly production and scientific research necessarily suffer. But these handicaps and others were overcome in great measure by the loyalty and devotion of the staff to the University and students. I shall mention only one example which is characteristic of the spirit which prevails. The organization of the day section of the Graduate School of Business Administration placed an additional burden on the budget of the School of Commerce. Our professors voluntarily offered to carry an additional graduate course without compensation, if necessary, in order that this important step be undertaken. Of course, *the time will ultimately arrive when emergency measures required under present conditions will no longer avail.* The physical strain on the staff must soon begin to tell. (Italics added)[4]

Yet, 26 years later the same conditions prevailed and were described in the Self-Study. It went on to express these convictions about the substance of B-school education:

> 1. . . . there has been no adequate test of whether business education is "better" training . . . than . . . liberal arts, or other types of training. Such testing is extremely difficult because of the variety of business courses offered, *the lower intellectual rating of business students in most institutions (until recently), and the disposition to offer descriptive courses in business.* . . .

3. The extreme specialization in business of some years ago is now under fire, and most schools are taking wholesome steps to develop more balanced curriculum, with reasonable provision for liberal arts, especially at the undergraduate level.

4. An extremely able student who intends to enter business, and who can afford to spend the necessary time and money, is perhaps better prepared if he takes his undergraduate training in liberal arts, engineering, or science and then spends two years at a good graduate school of business, than if he pursues business studies as an undergraduate.

5. On the other hand, there is ample justification for the undergraduate program in business. . . .

6. Schools of business should experiment with less specialized, more integrated, and *more rigorous* undergraduate programs for qualified students.

7. The graduate school of business should seek to develop a professional attitude toward business. . . . Thus far very few schools have graduate instruction that differs significantly from the undergraduate offerings. (Italics added)[5]

Finding substantial interrelationships of programs and faculty among the School of Commerce, the Graduate School of Business Administration, and the School of Retailing, the Self-Study report made this major structural recommendation: that is, that all three administrative units be consolidated to form a single School of Business, to be headed by an executive dean; that Commerce be renamed the College of Commerce and be the undergraduate unit with a dean; that GBA should be the graduate unit of the School of Business with a dean; and that the School of Retailing should become the Division of Retailing within GBA. Administrative control over the staff and major activities of the College, the Graduate School, and ancillary units would be placed in the hands of the executive dean.[6]

The Self-Study report was much more than shadows on a wall. It was prophetic in its convictions and its recommendations. It foreshadowed the essential points made in the Gordon-Howell (Ford Foundation) and Pierson (Carnegie Foundation) studies of B-school education in 1959, as it did those made in the reports of the Commerce "Think" Committee report in 1964 and the 1965 report of the Faculty Committee to Study the Schools of Business. However, it fell into limbo between Heald's departure and Hester's assumption of the presidency. In fact the "Think" Committee did not have it before them during their deliberations and arrived at their conclusions minus any conscious awareness of the concurrence between their own conclusions and those of the 1956 NYU Self-Study. But President Hester had read it carefully, and accepted its conclusions.

The Gordon-Howell and Pierson Reports

Thomas L. Norton, who had been dean of the Baruch School of Business at the City University of New York and also president of the American Association of Collegiate Schools of Business (AACSB), became dean of the School of Commerce in 1955. He was a leader among America's business school deans, and his acceptance of the Commerce deanship was important for the School. It was, at that moment, facing reaccreditation issues with AACSB, because some departments had too few course sections taught by PhDs. AACSB, as well as NYU's Self-Study report, had already perceived the directions that would have to be taken by America's B-schools to win the respect of their academic colleagues, and regain the confidence of America's business leaders. But Tom Norton could not have perceived in 1955 that he was accepting the captaincy of a vessel that could have easily turned out to be an academic *Titanic*.

In 1959 two foundation-supported reports appeared on collegiate education for business. They were *Higher Education of American Businessmen* by Robert A. Gordon and James E. Howell, financed by the Ford Foundation, and *The Education of American Businessmen* by Frank C. Pierson, financed by the Carnegie Foundation.[7] Dean Norton, in a review paper, observed that "together, they assume formidable proportions and present many major recommendations, which may appear new or even revolutionary."[8] No doubt their impact, which was enormous, benefited from their sponsorship by two of America's leading foundations, by the voluminous and careful research they reflected, and by the recognized scholarship of their authors. Yet, as observed earlier, their essential recommendations had already been foreshadowed by the NYU Self-Study report, even though awareness of that report's conclusions was minimal among the Commerce faculty. The reports were preceded also by an AACSB research report entitled *Faculty Requirements and Standards in Collegiate Schools of Business* (1955).[9]

The AACSB findings relative to undergraduate business education were:

> 1. Definition of specific goals by each school and formulation of educational and research programs consistent with these aims.

2. Strong emphasis on general education.

3. A large and broad professional core of business subjects.

4. Avoidance of over specialization.

5. Courses on a high intellectual level, organized to present an intellectual challenge to students.

6. Discouragement of highly specialized and narrow technical courses.

7. Reexamination, with emphasis on experimentation, of methods of instruction

8. Higher levels of standard of performance.

9. Emphasis on improvement of the caliber and effectiveness of the faculties of schools of business.

10. Full recognition of the importance of imaginative and farreaching programs of research as a part of the activities of schools of business.[10]

Dean Norton commented that "none of the recommendations in the Ford and Carnegie reports is at variance with these conclusions arrived at by the association's conference in 1955."[11] He added: "The Curricula recommendations in the two reports, reduced to the broadest generalizations, are that the General Education base should be expanded; the Business base should be expanded; and the amount of time devoted to a field of specialization should be reduced."[12]

Why then did the two reports have the huge impact on America's B-schools that they did? More was involved than the prestige of the foundation sponsors and the academic repute of the authors. Important also was the publicity which attended their publication. The internal reexaminations and soul-searching which were going on in NYU and some other universities, as well as in AACSB, did not command a high level of public awareness. But the Gordon-Howell and Pierson reports did. Consequently, the pressure on the B-schools to make changes increased enormously. Also, the impact of the two reports was strengthened because of the extensiveness of their discussion, the number of specific special studies underlying that discussion, and, perhaps most significant, the specific and detailed suggestions that they made for curricular changes.

The NYU Ford Foundation Proposal and Grant

Dean Norton's ability to press forward at Commerce with the changes demanded by the foregoing internal and external reports and the pressures they unleashed was compromised by illness, which afflicted him during his last several years in office. Major opposition to the changes also came from the Commerce faculty and some administrators. But this opposition was overwhelmed by the foresight, determination, and energy of James M. Hester, who became N Y U's president in 1962. President Hester picked up the N Y U Self-Study report's recommendation of 1956, and moved decisively to implement much of its substance. In particular, it became clear that Commerce had to effect profound changes, or face the risk of being "terminated."

The essence of the story is told in J. Victor Baldridge's study of N Y U, entitled *Power and Conflict in the University*. Baldridge quotes Hester as saying:

> The University was confronted with critical conditions. We had to undertake action that was radical from the standpoint of many people in the university. Some of these changes had to be undertaken over strong opposition and were implemented by administrative directives. In two of the undergraduate schools a number of faculty members had accepted the "school of opportunity" philosophy as a primary purpose of their school. This had been justifiable at one time, but no longer. Many faculty members simply did not recognize that circumstances had changed and did not accept the fact that the service they were accustomed to performing was now being assumed by public institutions at far less cost to the students.
>
> At this point the administration had to be the agent for change. It was incumbent upon us to exercise the initiative that is the key to administrative leadership. In the process, we did interfere with the traditional autonomy of the schools, but we believed this was necessary if they and the university were to continue to function.

Among the Commerce faculty, one bitter professor told Baldridge:

> The School of Commerce was about to have its throat cut and we didn't even know about it until after the blood was flowing! Sure, Hester came over and gave us a little pep talk about how much this was going to improve things, but he didn't really ask our advice on the issue. He didn't exactly say it was going to be his way "or else," but we got the point.[13]

Of course, later events would prove President Hester completely correct, and the bitter professor utterly wrong. But it took years of painful effort and the dislodging of more than a few faculty before the desired end was achieved. A critically important move was N Y U's proposal to the Ford Foundation[14] requesting a $25 million development grant. That proposal, which was based on the N Y U Self-Study report,[15] was submitted in November 1963, and it was successful. The following excerpts from the proposal tell the story:

New York University is committed to a policy of attaining in all its divisions the academic superiority that characterizes its leading schools and colleges. . . .

Inherent in the University's plans is the intent to set new standards in the evolution of urban higher education. *To this end the university will maintain only those divisions that can achieve high standards of performance and leadership.* . . .

Vigorous steps are being taken to strengthen the composition of the student body. *A progressive raising of minimum admission standards to a common level is reducing the proportion of marginal students, while additional financial aid, from university funds as well as from outside sources, is increasing the number of outstanding students.* . . .

In the undergraduate colleges, emphasis is being placed on encouraging the fully-committed full-time students and reducing the number of part-time students. . . .

Through the decade ahead the University will concentrate a substantial part of its financial resources to effect a shift toward a more full-time, fully-committed faculty. . . .

The University recognizes the fundamental position of the Arts and Sciences in all higher education and the importance of a broad liberal arts foundation for graduate and professional study. *Strengthening this area will be achieved primarily through a new Commission on Coordinated Liberal Studies, whose first task is bringing all required liberal arts work in the undergraduate colleges in Washington Square into a unified program.* Through this plan, the first two years in the School of Education, School of Commerce, and Washington Square College will have a common core of courses taught by All-University Arts and Science departments. . . .

In order to improve the total effectiveness of the several schools teaching business administration, an *Executive Dean of the Schools of Business has been appointed, and proposals are under study for the establishment of a common faculty of the Schools of Business.* A Joint Committee on Curriculum will examine the various business curricula to identify those areas of instruction which can be given jointly. . . .

The former School of Retailing has been replaced by the Institute of Retail Management, which is oriented toward research and special non-degree programs and does not itself provide a degree program. . . .

The undergraduate School of Commerce will participate in the new Program of Coordinated Liberal Studies along with the other undergraduate colleges in the Washington Square Center. The School itself *will concentrate on the upper division of undergraduate work.* (Italics added) [16]

The governance changes gave a sharp point to the demand for substantive curricular change, as well as to a tightening of admissions standards and faculty standards for appointment and promotion. Nothing less than a profound transformation of the Commerce culture, which had been shaped over six decades, was being mandated. It seemed clear that a failure to effect that transformation might well bring about the end of the school. The message was inherent in the appointment of Joseph Taggart, already dean of GBA, also to be executive dean of the Schools of Business, with Dean John Prime of Commerce reporting to him. And the conversion of the School of Retailing into the Institute of Retail Management, as a division of the Schools of Business, was done by fiat of the central administration. No one could be blind to the implicit "or else."

The Commerce "Think" Committee Report

Reaction was not long delayed, for in the Fall of 1963 a subcommittee of the School of Commerce Curriculum Committee was appointed. Chaired by Professor Alfred Gross, it included Professors Abraham L. Gitlow (Economics), J. Harold Janis (Business English), Ernest Kurnow (Statistics), and Benjamin Newman (Accounting). It was known as the "Think" Committee, and it reported in September 1964.

According to the introduction to the Committee's report:

> Despite significant improvements in our own admission standards, curriculum, and mode of instruction, the School of Commerce remains subject to . . . criticism. Our specialized programs are still, to a significant degree, narrow in their aims and concepts, our courses are over-segmented and insufficient in their intellectual demands, and our faculty is not uniformly prepared to cope with the educational demands of the business revolution we are now experiencing. Thus, while our higher standards of admission are too high to attract the large numbers of students we used to have, we have not been able to acquire the reputation needed to attract students of the caliber now filling the better, liberal arts and science-oriented institutions.[17]

Confronted with the situation described, the Committee saw three alternatives: (1) abandon the undergraduate school; (2) lower admission standards to attract local students turned away from the City colleges; or (3) create a school that could survive and prosper in an academic community whose only criterion is excellence. It should occasion no surprise that the committee opted for the third alternative. Viewed retrospectively, it is somewhat surprising that the goal was not only achieved, but was achieved so completely. Not immediately however, but only after years of pain. Meantime, the outcome often seemed uncertain.

The "Think" Committee summarized its report by expressing the belief that the curriculum of an excellent undergraduate business school "must rest on a firm liberal arts base, that its programs must be interdisciplinary in character, and that its specific courses, limited in number rather than breadth must lean toward the conceptual and analytical and away from the purely descriptive. Withal, the graduate must be equipped with the substantive knowledge he needs for entrance into a particular profession or business area."

Specifically, the Committee recommended:

1. Convert the School of Commerce into an exclusively junior-senior college with high admission requirements and a broad business curriculum that, in rigor and substance, matches the standards of other professional curriculums and forms a natural extension of the discipline of the arts and sciences.

2. Reorganize the curriculum on an interdisciplinary basis, achieving desirable balance between the quantitative, behavioral, and environmental aspects of business, while reducing the number of specialized programs to five.

3. Remove control over the specialized programs of study from the functional departments and put it in the hands of interdisciplinary subcommittees of the Curriculum Committee.

4. Pare drastically the number of courses given and strengthen the courses retained or added so that they may be equated with their counterparts in the graduate school.

5. Draw on the resources of the liberal arts schools of the University in instances where they have the faculty and courses that can benefit our students in any particular program. Encourage reciprocal use of our programs and facilities.

6. Retain the School of Commerce and Graduate School of Business as separate institutions, but with a common faculty, administration, and departmental structure.[18]

The report was dynamite. At any earlier time it would have probably been greeted with demands that its authors be lynched from the highest tree in Washington Square Park. Some faculty, seeing their obsolescence so starkly outlined, may have had so black a thought. Others, more numerous, saw the power so decisively applied by President Hester in the appointment of Dean Taggart as executive dean and in the creation of the Coordinated Liberal Studies Program (which was associated with the dissolution of the large Commerce General Course department and the transfer of the Journalism department and its program of studies to Washington Square College). They had no stomach for a fight. Still others, like the members of the "Think" Committee and some sympathetic colleagues, applauded the report. Opponents were in disarray. Proponents were strengthened. Fence sitters were prepared to yield to the pressures forcing change.

The Faculty Committee to Study the Schools of Business

The "Think" Committee's call for governance changes that would merge the Commerce and GBA faculties, administration, and departmental structure was perceived with alarm by a significant and influential segment of the GBA faculty. They felt that GBA had vastly improved itself in recent years, and that a merger with Commerce would saddle them with inadequate but tenured faculty. They felt also that the reputation of the School of Commerce, whatever it may have been in its days as a pioneer among B-schools, was now so low that it would contaminate the emerging prestige of GBA. Other less lofty motives could have included fear that Commerce would be a financial burden and restrain improvements in salary, research support, and other areas.

Given this context, a joint faculty committee of the two schools was appointed to study the Schools of Business. It began holding meetings in the Spring of 1965 and concluded its work later that year.[19] The committee consisted of Professors Jules Backman, Robert Kavesh, Ernest Kurnow, and Benjamin Newman. Dean Taggart presided and Assistant Dean Raymond D. Buteux served as secretary. Backman and Newman were perceived as primarily Commerce, Kavesh as primarily GBA, and Kurnow as equally oriented between the two units. In the June 5, 1965 meeting, Professor Backman urged the committee to call for the complete integration of the faculties while Professor Kavesh pointed out the concerns of many GBA faculty that Commerce had not improved in quality as had GBA, that GBA would suffer in its ability to recruit able young faculty because of a surplus of tenured Commerce faculty, and that a significant number of GBA faculty would not like to teach undergraduate courses. Two decades later, when the prestige of Commerce had risen so that it was recognized as one of America's leading and finest undergraduate business programs, these concerns, except for a lingering distaste for teaching undergraduate courses, had disappeared. In any case the merger of the faculties did not actually occur until eight years later in September 1973, by which time the qualitative improvement of Commerce was unmistakable. But a merged graduate-undergraduate Statistics department, under the chairmanship of Professor Ernest Kurnow, was created in 1963.

Earlier, in the May 3 meeting of the Committee, consensus on these major points was reached:

1. An acting dean should be appointed for the School of Commerce.
2. The administrative arrangement of having a single chairman for both the undergraduate and graduate departments should be furthered.
3. The basic administrative structure of the Schools of Business should be an Executive Dean with a Dean for both Commerce and GBA.
4. The budget of the two schools should be handled jointly.
5. There should be joint hiring.
6. There should be a single curriculum committee.

The committee then agreed to recommend Professor Abraham L. Gitlow as acting dean of the School of Commerce. A merger of the Commerce and GBA faculties was not recommended at this time. With respect to curricular change, the Committee agreed with the main thrust of the "Think" Committee report.

The Outcome

What happened in the School of Commerce, sketched in broad outline, was set down by J. Victor Baldridge.[20] He recognized the completeness with which the Commerce culture had become inculcated with and dominated by the "school of opportunity" philosophy and the "practical" outlook that characterized the School's founders and their successors. He observed what that philosophy and outlook meant in terms of admission standards, type of full-time faculty preferred, use of part-time faculty, "vocational" orientation of curriculum and courses, proliferation of courses and consequent narrowness of many of them and, cumulatively, overall academic quality. And he understood the stubbornness with which so many of the Commerce faculty and administration re-

sisted change. In his words, "probably the majority of the Commerce
faculty was opposed to major changes in their basic philosophy or to
changes in admissions policies. Moreover, the administration's chief
representative on the scene, Dean John Prime, was not totally convinced
that the changes were desirable. Dean Prime resisted many of the
changes, and many faculty were strongly behind him. A real power
struggle developed, but in this battle the administration had most of the
weapons."[21] Baldridge goes on to observe that a breakthrough in the
contest came about with two major changes in the Commerce leadership. First, in April 1962, Dean Joseph Taggart was appointed executive
dean of the Schools of Business, continuing concurrently in his position
as dean of the Graduate School of Business Administration. Second, in
August 1965 Dean Prime resigned and was succeeded by Acting Dean
Abraham L. Gitlow. Baldridge makes the laconic comment that "To no
one's great surprise both Executive Dean Joseph Taggart and Dean
Gitlow favored the administration's plan for upgrading quality in the
School of Commerce."[22] He quoted one Commerce professor as saying,
"This would not have happened a few years ago when the whole univer-
sity lived off Commerce's surplus money."[23] Baldridge summarized the
transformation, saying:

> Without a doubt the changes hit Commerce very hard. A resisting faculty
> was cut to the bone; a resisting dean retired; the autonomous School of
> Commerce was placed under an executive dean who was also in charge of
> the Graduate School of Business; many courses were wrested away from
> Commerce and put in the coordinated Liberal Arts Studies program; the
> full-time student enrollment decreased from a high of 2800 to a low of
> 1000. On the other hand, the quality of the students, faculty, and program
> was vastly improved. Most people at NYU—even present members of the
> Commerce faculty—now feel that these changes were necessary. Never-
> theless, in the political struggle the old School of Commerce died and one
> of the most powerful organizational interest groups on campus was
> hobbled.[24]

Before we back up and flesh out the foregoing description of events,
to make matters more real, an aspect of the story should be noted. It is
my retrospective realization, although I was a significant participant and
player in the events, that I was not fully aware at the time they happened
of their *historical sweep*. In particular, I did not appreciate the prescient
quality of the NYU Self-Study report of 1956. Now a senior citizen, I
search my memory and conclude that the realization of the powerful

pressures which were building did not truly strike home until after the Gordon-Howell and Pierson studies appeared. Of course they did strike home in the early sixties, and for the next two decades I was up to my earlobes in the transformation and revival of the School.

The massive transformation described above inspired a visiting accreditation team in the 1968–1969 academic year to make these comments:

> The New York University programs in business at both undergraduate and graduate levels have standards of excellence manifestly exceeding minimum criteria of the Association. *The only doubt at all on this question might have arisen some four years ago* when the School of Commerce had very large enrollments taught to a considerable extent by part-time faculty and some nonterminal full-time faculty. . . .
>
> The most striking observation of the revisitation of New York University in 1969 is the spirit of change and innovation in an old and distinguished institution; . . . we find a major qualitative thrust of gargantuan proportions in the critical characteristics of the School of Commerce over the last few years. This new direction plus new resources and new spirit would be hard to match nationally and is still going on. (Italics added)[25]

Some Quantitative Support

Enrollments, which were still almost 5,000 in 1960–1961, dropped to almost 2,500 in 1964, and then plunged further to a bottom of just above 1,000 in 1972. But the high school grade point averages of entering freshmen rose from 2.2 (about 77 percent) in 1960 to 3.40 (a bit below 90 percent) in 1993. Concurrently, combined verbal-math SAT scores rose from 897 in the earlier year to 1,231 in 1993. And a previously mass admission-mass attrition school took on the academic characteristics of America's premier institutions of higher education, that is, selective admissions with very low attrition. It is a wonder that the School remained a "school of opportunity," in the best sense of the term, for it continues to serve new immigrant streams seeking to fulfill the promise that is America, in addition to the children of those already part of the mainstream.

From a governance standpoint and to avoid an immediate and crushing financial disaster, drastic cutbacks had to be achieved in the numbers of courses and sections scheduled, and in the number of faculty. Profound curricular changes were mandatory to make possible the reductions in number of courses, sections, and faculty. Let us look first at what was done in these three areas.

Using registration reports retained from my administration, we find a reduction in the number of courses scheduled, from 148 in Fall 1964 to 66 in Fall 1970. In the same period, the number of sections scheduled declined from 315 in Fall 1964 to 97 in Fall 1970. Of course the large relative decline in sections was achieved through a severe cutback in multiple sections of individual courses. Points of enrollment, a key to tuition generation, dropped from 24,169 in Fall 1964 to 10,612 in Fall 1970. But the 24,169 points in 1964 included 9,472 points of instruction in other university divisions (8,335 points in the Coordinated Liberal Studies Program), while 9,009 points in other divisions in Fall 1970 (6,106 in CLSP) were excluded from the 10,612. Thus, on an apples to apples comparison, the 24,169 points generated by Commerce students in Fall 1964 compared with a total of 19,621 points generated in Fall 1970. In the early years of the CLSP, Commerce received no budgetary credit in its revenues for the CLSP points taken by its students, although it was charged for all direct and overhead costs associated with their attendance at NYU (including scholarship support). This inequity was remedied by the end of the sixties. In the meantime, it distorted perceptions of the Commerce budgetary picture.

In view of these changes, what happened to the numbers of faculty, both full-time and part-time? Full-time faculty fell from 90 in 1964–1965 to 71 in 1970–1971, which understated the change. In the later year the number of faculty included people in the newly merged Department of Economics at Washington Square who had primary appointments in the Arts and Sciences faculty and who were not in the 1964–1965 figure. Part-time faculty dropped from 58 in 1964–1965 to 17 in 1970–1971.

Plainly, the presence of a substantial number of part-time faculty who lacked tenure status provided a *flexible* segment of the labor force, and, hard as it was in human terms, advantage was taken of that flexibility. Another source of flexibility was nontenured full-time faculty in the assistant professor and instructor ranks. In 1964–1965, 30 were in those categories, a third of all full-time faculty. By 1971–1972 that number had fallen to 20. More than 10 had been dropped, because new hires had been made. Standards for promotion and tenure became very strict, and were enforced. Also, the associate professor rank declined from 29 to 19, despite the promotion of a group of highly qualified assistant professors.

Associate professors and full professors possess tenure, so it is implicit that a significant number of them must have retired or resigned. How was that accomplished? The book *Being the Boss* provides the answer:

> Tenured full-time faculty were carefully reviewed. Those without the characteristics desired were divided into two groups; first, those who were near retirement age (68, under university rules, but 62–65 under social security eligibility rules) and had medical problems; and second, those who were younger.
>
> For older faculty, age 62 and over with medical problems, an early retirement buy-out plan was developed, based on several key elements:
>
> 1. While working, a faculty member faced deductions from base salary for social security and the university's TIAA-CREF pension plan.
>
> 2. When retired, that faculty member's disposable income would no longer be subject to those deductions.
>
> 3. The university's contributions for social security and TIAA-CREF would end when the faculty member retired, representing a saving.
>
> 4. Since enrollments were declining, replacement faculty would not have to be hired, so that a faculty member retired three to four years before age 68, as an example, would represent a saving to the university of that number of years of base salary, plus the additional contributions for social security, TIAA-CREF pension, unemployment compensation, and so on.
>
> 5. Given the prospective university savings associated with point four, the university could well afford to make a lump-sum contribution of one to two years base salary to the faculty member's TIAA-CREF pension, bringing his or her after-tax disposable income in retirement up to or about even with what it would be if he or she worked to age 68 (the lump-sum contribution was allowable at the time under existing tax rules).
>
> The arrangement was welcomed by several faculty suffering from medical problems. Word of mouth spread to others, including some older faculty whose health was fine. They came forward and requested similar deals, to which the university readily agreed. As a consequence, a number of tenured older faculty retired early. Younger tenured faculty who did not fit the academic profile of the future were interviewed and told candidly that, while they would be treated courteously in terms of teaching assignments, they should not expect to share in future salary increases. Also, leave arrangements were offered to make it easier for them to relocate, and a number accepted.[26]

The numbers provided and the changes they reflect fail to give complete insight into the cataclysm which engulfed Commerce between 1955 and 1970. A glance back to the post World War II years gives the perspective needed to grasp the full dimensions of the transformation of the School of Commerce. Thus, aggregate enrollment of students in 1947–1948 numbered 10,064, with 8,594 enrolled in Fall 1947 and 8,847 enrolled in Spring 1948. The difference between the Fall and Spring enrollment figures, on the one side, and the aggregate enrollment of individual students for the year indicates the turnover in the student body.[27] Those enrollments generated 252,244 points of instruction. And they produced 1,567 degrees and certificates at Commencement in June 1948 (1,537 BS and 30 certificate). I attended the Commencement ceremonies on Ohio Field at University Heights in the Bronx, and remember well the roar of the crowd when the huge mass of Commerce grads rose for the conferment of their degrees.

The huge enrollment of 1947–1948 was served by a full-time faculty of 227, of whom 98 were of professorial rank and 129 were instructors,[28] plus a very large corps of part-time faculty. My attendance at the first faculty meeting of the 1947–1948 academic year is fresh in my memory, and I can see again the mob of well over 300 people present in old Lassman hall of the Commerce building. With the all-time peak attendance of 1950–1951, the full-time faculty had swelled to 244, of whom 106 were of professorial rank and 138 were instructors (plus 16 lecturers). Significantly, the number of full-time faculty had contracted to 206 (123 professorial rank and 83 instructors) by 1954–1955 plus 5 lecturers. But by 1960–1961 it had grown a little to 225 (133 professorial rank and 92 instructors) plus 6 lecturers, despite the persistent decline in enrollments from the early fifties. Perhaps this reflects Dean Norton's illness at the time, coupled with inaction by Dean Prime in the face of the gathering storm.

We stated earlier that the administrators and many of the faculty of Commerce took pride in the huge numbers of those years, just as they were overwhelmed and dismayed by the collapse that ensued. A look at the dean's annual reports to the Chancellor of the university for the years 1946–1947, 1947–1948, and 1950–1951 is illuminating. In 1946–1947, Dean Madden wrote that "the surplus [of the school] after all charges allocated to the School, stood at approximately $1,000,000." He went on to say that "during the period from the academic year 1925–1926 and including the year just ended, the aggregate . . . surplus amounted to $9,263,157."[29] And those were years when a dollar was still a dollar! Put differently and perhaps more dramatically, those $9,263,157 dollars of 1947 purchasing power were equal to $60.0 million dollars of 1993 purchasing power.[30] 1926–1947 were also years which were coterminous with Dean Madden's stewardship of Commerce. He continued, with perhaps a touch of bitterness because he was already desperately ill with cancer, to which he succumbed a year later:

> This extraordinary surplus was devoted to sundry university purposes other than those directly affecting this School. The results were accomplished by sacrifices of students and faculty, by constant economy, sometimes almost to the point of penuriousness, and they could only be justified by the beneficial results which flowed to the University as a whole. It is to be hoped that a remedy may soon be found for a state of things which is grossly unfair and which no one who has in mind the interest of the University as a whole, wishes to see continued. *It must ultimately prove disastrous.* (Italics added)

But things did not change. The university continued to be addicted to Commerce surpluses, just as surely as a drug addict cannot shake off the curse of his affliction. And so we find Dean Collins complaining in his report for the 1950–1951 academic year that, while academic conditions at Commerce continued to be poor, the School produced a pure surplus of some $1.8 million in 1949–1950, and not much less in 1950–1951.

Why didn't the deans and their faculty revolt? The question is pregnant with implications for university governance. Have things changed since those days? Are deans and department chairpeople managers, in the sense that they are in private, profit-centered business, or are they representatives and spokespeople for faculty?

The quiescence of the deans and faculty to compensation and other conditions in Commerce demands examination. They were not ignorant of their situation, either in absolute or relative terms. Dean Madden made lengthy reports on the state of the School at faculty meetings, and his words are recorded in the official minutes. The following comments made by him at the faculty meeting of December 11, 1946, are suggestive of answers to our questions:

> I have been scrutinizing the recently published Report of the Treasurer of New York University for the year 1945–1946. And I should like to take a moment of your time to discuss with you some of the outstanding items in that report because you, with your expectancy of tenure, have an important stake in the future of the University and should keep yourselves informed regarding the financial health of the University. Moreover, if

you have a knowledge of the financial condition of the University you can better understand what can and cannot be done for you and our school.

In the year 1945–46, . . . the budget receipts hit the all-time high of 11 1/2 millions of dollars, yet the excess of income over expenses was only 23 1/2 thousands of dollars. I cannot see, therefore, how we can expect warranted and proper increases in salaries. . . .

With respect to an increase in tuition fees. I feel that the present tuition fee of $13.50 per point for the School of Commerce is too high in comparison with what the members of our faculty receive in salaries. And I made a strong protest at the time against raising the fees of the School of Commerce from $12 per point to $13.50 per point unless the Faculty received more money. The student gets his money's worth at $13.50 per point; but his money does not go to the professor to the degree it should. *Too much of the surplus earned by large sections and by the "sweat and tears" of our faculty goes to making up the operating deficits of other schools* and not enough to providing better facilities for students of the School of Commerce and better salaries.

I suppose I have been charged by the Central Administration with not taking "the University point of view." As an accountant, I know a little of their difficult financial problems. . . . But at the same time, I believe that unless better salaries are paid to our Faculty, we cannot attract and hold good men. The quality of teaching may deteriorate, we may fail to maintain our prestige, and *we may kill the goose that certainly lays golden eggs for the University*. (Italics added)

Shortly after Dean Madden made the foregoing remarks, at a special meeting of department chairmen on January 15, 1947, he spoke at great length and with strong emotion about the obligations of full-time faculty to the School and university. In his remarks he contrasted full-time faculty with part-timers, emphasizing that the latter owed their primary and overriding duty and responsibility to an outside employer rather than to the University. It is a fascinating note that Dean Madden observed in this connection that the point applied even to "part-time" faculty who carried the equivalent of full-time teaching loads, that is, 24 points per academic year (or, 12 points per semester). One must wonder what sort of service could be rendered to "primary" employers by people carrying such teaching loads, or, alternatively, what sort of service was given to the school.

But that facet of the matter must be set aside for the moment. What is important is that Dean Madden pressed powerfully his belief that full-time faculty were on call *at any time* to assume classroom duties, to attend student functions, to participate in public conferences, to be available for student advising and registration, to maintain definite and reasonable office hours, and to be available for committee assignments. These people, unlike part-timers, were eligible for promotion, tenure, participation in annuity plans, and so on. But full-time faculty could engage in compensated work outside the School. In fact, the dean thought such activity was desirable and beneficial, enhancing the teachers' understanding of the business world and thereby enriching the experience brought to the classroom. More, Dean Madden strongly opposed setting School rules which would specify and limit the individual faculty member's ability to exercise his own judgment of the extensiveness of such outside activity. He expressed the belief it should rest with the individual's sense of integrity and conscience, but "subject to supervision by the Dean and the Administration."[31]

Was the dean's attitude conditioned by an idea that faculty free to earn significant sums through outside work would be less likely to rebel against the poor compensation and other unpalatable conditions at Commerce? Perhaps. But one should not rush too rapidly to an adverse judgment, for, at the same meeting, Madden reflected on his own personal experience in this connection. He told his colleagues, the assembled chairmen, that in 1916 he and a colleague formed a private firm for the practice of accounting. He went on and told them that the new firm prospered beyond the dreams of the founders, and the income from fees mounted quickly and greatly. And this was his career plan, that is, to continue as a faculty member but with this highly remunerative outside work. In 1922 then Dean Joseph French Johnson became ill, and the University Chancellor asked Madden to become an assistant dean, backing up Dean Johnson who was not expected to survive very long. Madden felt deeply obligated to Johnson, and so he accepted. But Johnson survived for three years. As Madden perceived that his commitment was becoming long-term, he withdrew from his partnership and private practice. He said that two reasons compelled his decision: first, he felt that his academic position gave him an unfair competitive advantage over other private practitioners; and second, he felt he could not do justice to both jobs. And so, although no rule prohibited him from continuing with his dual arrangement, he says he made up "his own canon" and gave up private practice. He added "I refuse to think any more about the financial loss that that decision cost. I can only say that I would not have to work today if I had continued in public practice. I could have retired many years ago with all the capital I should ever want. However, I think that despite this, I made the wiser choice."

Remember that Dean Madden was fatally ill with terminal cancer when he spoke the words. And, what he never revealed to his colleagues, but what is known to me from old faculty salary records, is that Dean Madden received a salary of $10,000 per annum as dean of Commerce in 1929, *with no increase in that salary until his death in 1948.* This is the man who produced a pure surplus of over $9 million for N Y U between 1926 and 1946. More, the Commerce surplus was some $1 million when the total university budget was $11.5 million, and the net at the bottom line was only $23,500 in the black. Yet Madden spoke to his faculty of the need to understand the university's financial position, while arguing with the central administration that persistent reliance on Commerce surpluses, coupled with a failure to reinvest resources in the School, would lead to disaster.

Dean Madden was an extremely loyal man, to N Y U and to Commerce. It is easy to understand why he was loved, even revered, by so many fellow faculty and students. He must have felt a profound duty to support the University, though that required operating Commerce in a sacrificial, even exploitive way. He used the word "penurious" in one report to the Chancellor. He argued with the central administration that the road being followed was likely to lead to disaster, but, simultaneously, he explained to his faculty the need to sacrifice for the benefit of the entirety. And so he did not revolt. Nor did his associates, the chairmen. Put bluntly, they were managers and they performed their roles as they perceived them. Indeed, Professor Emeritus Darrell Lucas remarks: "As academics, we did not consider that our academic compensation was poor! We just accepted the fact that academic compensation was modest compared with commercial."[32] One must comment that the academic world, including N Y U, has changed markedly in this respect. No doubt, many people today would judge Madden a fool for both his self-sacrifice and his acceptance of the sacrifices required of his colleagues. I cannot embrace that judgment, feeling rather admiration and respect for his sense of integrity and honor. And I have those feelings even though I suspect I would have done differently.

The matter of faculty compensation and teaching loads should not be left without some comments about "overloads," that is, teaching loads above 12 hours per week by full-time faculty for extra compensation. Such arrangements were common in the hectic environment of the post

World War II years, and it was not unusual for faculty to teach 14 or even 16 hours per week. Of course, such an arrangement was not conducive to advancing research productivity or the intellectual quality of the enterprise. But it was financially profitable for the university. It must be noted that the practice did not end until the arrival of Henry Heald as university president. Thus, Professor Emeritus Michael Schiff recalls that Heald mandated an end to the practice of assigning over-loads, making it palatable for the faculty affected by allowing their "overload" compensation to become part of their future base salaries. This single and highly dramatic action signaled the direction that Henry Heald intended for the university, and foretold the institution's future path.[33]

Curriculum Changes

The curriculum of the School of Commerce had changed substantially over its first half-century, and the cumulative impact of the changes was great. From a thin, limited, altogether practical program of study for evening students in 1900, it had evolved to a four-year Bachelor of Science program in 1950. At mid-century it had a significant core of general education courses, intended to graduate people with a much broader intellectual exposure than envisaged by the founders. Admission requirements had become more stringent, as had the performance standards to be satisfied to graduate. But, as we have seen, the curriculum was still regarded by many outside and by some inside the business school as too narrow, too vocational, too descriptive, too lacking in intellectual rigor, and generally inadequate.

Major changes occurred in the fifties and sixties. The most important were probably: (1) the shift from 2-credit freshmen courses to 4-credit ones in 1956, and the almost concurrent shift to 3-credit courses in the upper class years; (2) the university's creation of the Coordinated Liberal Studies Program in 1963–1964, which removed Arts and Sciences offerings from the large Commerce General Course department, involved the termination of that department and the transfer of many of its faculty out of Commerce, and involved also the bodily transfer of the Journalism department, along with its faculty and students, to Arts and Sciences; (3) the associated reorganization of the remaining Commerce departments and the large reductions in number of majors offered by the School; and (4) the adoption of the so-called 4-course plan by Washington Square College, and its impact on Commerce. While these changes will be discussed at some length, we should note also that admission standards were significantly tightened in 1961. The depression decade slippage in high school academic unit requirements was reversed, so that 2 units of math were again required. Also, 2 units each in any two of these four academic subject areas were now required: classical language, modern foreign language, history and social science, and/or science. The SAT was also mandated. Between 1961 and 1966 the combined mean SAT scores of entering Commerce freshmen rose from 897 to 1,139.[34]

Four-Credit and Three-Credit Courses

We noted before that the Commerce curriculum from the earliest years of the School featured a 2-credit course module. Oddly, this scheduling module persisted through decades of vast growth and curriculum change. Even the shift to day classes and the later introduction of the bachelor of science 128-credit degree program in 1926 did not alter the module, so that students had to take eight courses per semester. Inherent in the arrangement was a fragmenting of student attention over too many offerings per semester, plus a compounding factor in the need to take eight separate examinations at the end of each semester. Given the unsatisfactory nature of the arrangement, its persistence is remarkable. It was changed for freshmen courses in 1956, when the first-year students were taking their basic core courses. The remedy was simple. Instead of taking each core course over two semesters, the courses were concentrated into single semester 4-credit entities. Half the courses were taken in one semester, and the other half in the second semester. The earlier fragmentation was removed, and the students could concentrate their attention on just four courses per semester.

While this arrangement did not carry over completely to advanced courses, they too shifted from the 2-credit module to a 3-credit one. Consequently, the educational disadvantages noted above were ameliorated for the upper class years of the Commerce curriculum. If the faculty saw sound educational reasons for changing the module for the freshman year, then why didn't they follow through and apply the arrangement for upper level classes? Unhappily, the real answer probably does not lie in pedagogical theory. It is more likely to be found in a desire to preserve as many course offerings as possible. It had been so easy to proliferate them in the years of huge enrollments. No doubt, each faculty member, enamored of his or her courses and convinced of their intellectual and educational merit, did not find it difficult to rationalize and justify maintaining a rich spectrum of course offerings. But, in the larger scheme of things, as enrollments plummeted, the huge superstructure of narrowly conceived, specialized courses could no longer be sustained. It had become a tight skin which constrained the curriculum and made it rigid. And it had to be torn apart to achieve freedom for change and flexibility.

In any event, a major reworking of the School's curriculum and courses occurred in 1956 and 1957. The 3-credit course module probably appeared to be a reasonable middle road to follow for the upper class courses. While it necessitated a significant change in curriculum and number of courses offered, it was not as wrenching a change as adoption of a uniform 4-credit module would have been. In general, the most consequential result of the curriculum and course revisions was a substantial increase in flexibility and a great broadening of the surviving programs of study. The required General Education core was increased to 60 credits, essentially half the 128 credits in the degree program. But these courses continued to be taught by the Commerce General Course department, maintaining an insidious basis for biases among Arts and Sciences faculty. While the change was significant, its impact was undoubtedly vitiated by the continued teaching of the Liberal Arts courses under the jurisdiction of Commerce (even though a bulletin footnote stated in fine print that Commerce students could take these courses in the Washington Square College).[35]

Concurrently, the professional core was expanded. In addition to Accounting, Banking and Finance, Economics, Management, and Marketing, courses were now required in Law, Statistics, and Business Policy. The 12-credit professional minor was dropped. But the professional major, that is, the department core, continued to be determined solely by the department and restricted as the department might determine. Departmental jurisdictional lines and, implicitly, job territories continued to rule. The changes made were important, but they failed to go far enough. That would become apparent in the years following. Yet they were clearly perceived as major by contemporaries.

The Coordinated Liberal Studies Program

Henry Heald served as president of New York University only a short time, from 1952 to 1956. Yet, he left the N Y U Self-Study report, which foretold the university's direction. But the "road map" was not followed by Heald's successor, Carroll Newsom. He was an agreeable man who served as president from 1956 to 1962. But his presidency was an interregnum that ended with the installation of James M. Hester in 1962. It was Hester who seized the initiative, and, using the power at his command, began to implement the recommendations of the Self-Study report. A major move was the creation of the Coordinated Liberal Studies Program and its implementation in 1963–1964. This move was a raw exercise of executive power by central administrative fiat. It was not submitted to votes of the faculty of the School of Commerce.

The General Course department of the School of Commerce was dismantled and its faculty were transferred to the relevant Washington Square College departments, for example, History, Sciences, and so forth. The several undergraduate schools at the Square designated representatives to sit as members of a Commission on the Coordinated Liberal Studies, to approve and supervise new general core course offerings for the College, Education, and Commerce students. The chairman of the Commission was the dean of Washington Square College, then William Buckler. The deans of Commerce and Education were members. Inter-school faculty committees, as appropriate, discussed the core course syllabi and content and made their recommendations.

The ship was launched, passengers and crew were aboard, but the sea was not smooth. Washington Square College faculty were initially worried about the effect on their hiring, promotion, and tenure decisions with the introduction of a number of tenured professors from Commerce. The former Commerce faculty were worried over their treatment by new colleagues who, in addition to the material concerns noted, did not always regard them as professional and academic equals. With time these worries were assuaged and eventually disappeared through the attrition of retirement and death, as well as by eventual acceptance. But it took time.

Another aspect of this change, and far from unimportant, was financial. With the dismantling of the General Course department and the shift of all general course work from Commerce to Washington Square College (the new courses were designated "A" courses), the tuition revenue generated in those courses was automatically credited to the College. Initially and for several years no revenue credit went to either the School of Commerce or the School of Education for the credits taken in the "A" courses. In the case of Commerce an immediate consequence was an enlarged budgetary deficit, further aggravated by the concurrent bodily transfer of the Journalism department from Commerce to Washington Square College. Perhaps this move was based on a perception that journalism, which involved written exposition, was more akin to the work of the English department than to business. In any case its impact on the Commerce budget was significant and compounded the financial effect of the Coordinated Liberal Studies Program. I believe the financial effect stimulated and strengthened the resolve of those who demanded additional reforms and restructuring in the School of Commerce, failing which the School should be discontinued.

Later Commerce Reforms

One is intrigued by the picture just painted. Major reforms in curriculum, course offerings, and structure were being made in Commerce. Yet the critics continued to cry out criticism and condemnation. What did they want? Reform or destruction? Did they see themselves as latter-day Christs driving the money handlers from the Temple? Whatever their convictions and the strength of their criticism, beyond doubt, Commerce had lost its most potent defense, its financial clout. Also doubtless, it is much worse to be poor and not command respect than to be rich without respect. Commerce used to be a tough target. Now it was an easy one. The challenge to the School, even more important than the immediate budgetary situation, was to get respect, both within and without New York University.

Further major reforms were made by 1964–1965, as an outcome of the "Think" Committee report. The number of departments and course offerings was reduced. Business English, Public Utilities, Real Estate, and Secretarial Studies disappeared, as did most, if not all, of their course offerings. A new Department of Business Administration was created to pick up the remnants of Business English and its faculty, and to administer a General Business major for students not wanting to major in a specific functional area, for example, Banking and Finance,

Management, and Marketing. The surviving departments, in addition to Business Administration, were Banking and Finance, Accounting, Economics, Management, Marketing, and Statistics (which had in 1963 been removed from the Economics Department and made a separate entity). Despite these efforts, respect was not yet won.

In 1965 Dean Prime retired and Professor Abraham L. Gitlow became Acting Dean.

A key year came in 1965–1966. Enrollments continued to drop and the budgetary situation remained serious. But, somehow, a resurgence of spirit and morale appeared, and with it there gradually came respect. The essential story was set down earlier. The Business Administration department was dismantled. Most of its faculty were retired early with individual buyouts, or transferred to the School of Education's Department of Business Education. A few remained with Commerce, reverting to surviving departments with which they had been affiliated earlier. Early retirement buyouts were arranged for still other tenured faculty. Nontenured faculty were reviewed carefully, and those without doctorates or with them but showing little progress in research were given notice of termination. Part-time faculty were cut out almost completely. Course offerings were slashed further, and multisection courses were reduced in numbers to achieve minimum enrollment targets.

Since the number of full-time faculty was not reduced as drastically as the number of courses and sections, it was possible to reduce teaching loads concurrently. That improvement in working conditions enabled the School to insist on stronger research performance and possession of the doctorate as conditions for promotion and tenure. These were essential elements in gaining academic respectability, from the faculty of the Graduate School of Business Administration as well as the faculty of the other university divisions. Along with all these moves, Dean Gitlow got President Hester's approval to renovate faculty offices so faculty got a sense of privacy, and to create the Dean Thomas L. Norton Faculty Lounge, an attractive and handsomely furnished room. As the perception grew that the School was on the move, Dean Gitlow's position was altered and "acting" was removed from his title. That change of status was, in itself, a heartening signal to the Commerce faculty.

A central element in the profound reform which marked 1965–1966 was the complete reworking of the Commerce curriculum. We have seen already that important reforms had been made earlier, but the integument of vocationalism that had for so long encapsulated and contained the School's courses and program of study, while significantly weakened, continued to be dominant. The aura of vocationalism still clung to Commerce. The enclosure finally burst apart completely in 1965–1966.

Consult Table 3.1. It shows a program with 60 credits in liberal studies and 60 credits in professional studies, leaving 8 credits of free electives which could be used in both groupings, or concentrated in one or the other. It is truly a program with equal exposure to liberal and professional courses. Further, it is essentially a layer cake curriculum, with the liberal studies concentrated in the first two years and the professional studies in the last two years. Of the professional courses, only Accounting and Statistics are taken in the sophomore year, an arrangement resting on the belief that those two courses are necessary tools which add significant substance to professional courses. The business base, or professional core, is reserved for the junior year, and the department core (a major limited to 12 credits, i.e. 4 courses), along with an integrating business policy course is placed in the senior year. Breadth of exposure is the hallmark of the program. Gone is the sense of narrowly conceived, highly specialized, largely descriptive professional courses. Gone also are the multitude of departments, majors, and minors that had so long marked Commerce. The surviving departments are seven in number, as noted earlier. The surviving majors equal the departments. The number of courses are drastically cut, from 140 in 1965–1966 to 90 in 1966–1967.[36]

Adoption of the Four Course Plan

On May 31, 1967, at a meeting of the Commission on Coordinated Liberal Studies, Dean Buckler of Washington Square College (WSC) submitted a memorandum suggesting that the undergraduate colleges at the Square consider adoption of a four-course plan. The essential idea was to reduce the 128-point undergraduate baccalaureate curriculum from some 42 3-point courses to 32 4-point courses. Given the participation of all three colleges, WSC, Commerce, and Education, in the Coordinated Liberal Studies ("A") plan, it was important that the 4-point proposal be jointly decided.[37] A major pragmatic reason for wanting a joint decision was the desire to keep the credit arrangement for

TABLE 3.1

Educational Program of the School of Commerce, 1966–1967

Liberal Studies	Freshman	Pts	Sophomore	Pts	Junior	Pts	Senior	Pts
Basic Core—Cultural and scientific foundations for professional education and responsible citizenship	English Mathematics Laboratory Science Social Science (History, Government, Sociology, Psychology) Classics	3 6 4 12 3 3	Economics Literature	6 6	Philosophy	6		3
Electives			Liberal Studies Electives	6	Liberal Studies Electives	4	Liberal Studies Electives	4
Professional Studies								
Business Base—Professional foundation for the effective organization and operation of business and other enterprises			Accounting Statistics	6 6	Management Banking & Finance Business Law Marketing Written Communication Oral Communication	6 6 3 6 3 3	Business Policy	3
Department Core—Integration of the cultural and professional foundations and their application to specific decision making areas.							department Core	12
Professional Electives							Professional Electives	6
Free Electives							Electives	8

SOURCE: NYU, *Dean's Annual Report*, School of Commerce, 1965–1966, 11.

advanced courses comparable to that for the "A" courses. Otherwise, scheduling became complicated.

The educational rationale underlying the proposal was similar to that put forward in Commerce when the 2-credit course module gave way to the 4-point and 3-point ones; namely, the reduction in number of courses taken per semester would reduce the fragmentation in the degree program, enhance student study in individual courses, and enable broadening and deepening of each course's scope and substance. But a major difference existed between Dean Buckler's proposal and the earlier actions at Commerce. *Dean Buckler wanted to keep the prevailing three contact hour arrangement for courses offered, but grant 4 credits.* Students would get about 20 percent less classroom contact hours in their baccalaureate. But the tuition "price" of the degree would not be cut. To offset the contraction in contact hours, Dean Buckler argued that additional work would be required in the courses offered, and that faculty would provide additional tutorial and other consultative service. These assurances led the New York State Board of Regents to approve the new arrangement.

The four-course plan had another feature that probably loomed large in Dean Buckler's mind. Since faculty teaching loads were calculated in terms of credit hours per week, the traditional undergraduate full-time teaching load of 12 hours per week would now require only three 4-credit courses instead of the old four 3-credit courses. This was a basic, not a nominal change. The faculty teaching load would be reduced from 12 contact hours per week to 9. It was argued that this change would have several potent advantages: (1) it would free faculty time for reworking course offerings; (2) provide time for additional student counseling; (3) provide time for more faculty research and publication (a major consideration in developing a research-oriented school); and (4) enhance the attractiveness of NYU in its efforts to recruit new faculty (especially those holding PhDs by offering the promise of significant research and publication output). Possible conflict of priorities between improving teaching and the educational content of the baccalaureate degree, on the one side, and freeing faculty time for research, on the other, apparently did not become significant in the final decision to approve the plan.

But problems developed for the School of Commerce. One has already been noted, that is, the impact of the plan on evening students, who would be charged as full-time students when they took 12 credits per semester. Although that impact was overcome in money terms after a couple of years (i.e., Commerce evening students did not pay as full-time people until they registered for 13 points), its short-term effect increased the difficulties of the school in trying to preserve a viable program of evening studies. Those difficulties would perhaps not have seemed so large were it not for the perception in Commerce that an evening program remained an important part of its mission and purpose as a school of opportunity, albeit at a high level of academic excellence.

Another problem and the subject of intense debate in Commerce was the view among a substantial portion of the faculty that offering four credit hours for three contact class hours somehow lacked honesty, because the alleged increase in out-of-class work and faculty tutorial and counseling help seemed unlikely, in practice, to offset the cutback in classroom contact hours. This feeling was most intense among the Accounting faculty, who argued vehemently that they could not cover the work necessary to prepare for the profession and the CPA exams with fewer classroom hours. And so the four-course plan in Commerce came to involve four contact hours per four-credit hour course. No doubt the Commerce faculty felt virtuous, and believed that their decision reflected educational integrity. The Science departments in Washington Square College came to the same conclusion, interestingly enough, and generally maintained their traditional contact hour-credit hour relationship. In any case, the change involved another reworking of courses and curriculum in the School of Commerce.

There was also a problem in figuring proper teaching loads for faculty teaching both undergraduate and graduate courses. The Graduate School of Business had continued to adhere to the two-contact hour-two-credit hour module. If teaching loads were figured in terms of courses instead of credit and contact hours, then a two-credit hour-two-contact hour graduate course became equal to a four-credit hour-four-contact hour undergraduate one. Such a calculation made undergraduate teaching relatively undesirable. Keep in mind that to a faculty member, preparation, teaching, paper grading, and student counseling in a 2-credit hour course can be as great as in a 4-credit hour one. So, seeing a course as a course is not a silly or indulgent exercise. This problem has proved to be persistent, and will probably never go away completely until an equivalence of effort and reward is achieved between undergraduate and graduate teaching. Achieving such equivalence is not easy, for any action taken at the undergraduate level to move its teaching load closer to the graduate level stimulates a graduate-level reaction to restore the prior

TABLE 3.2
*School of Commerce, Degree Requirements,
1970–1971*

Liberal Studies (60 points)	
Core:	
Computer Science	4
Economics	8
English Composition	4
Mathematics: (8 points)	
Analytic Geometry & Calculus	4
Linear Algebra	4
Psychology	4
Science	4
Sociology	4
	36
Electives:	24
Professional Studies: (60 points)	
Professional Core:	
Accounting	4
Banking and Finance	4
General Business	4
(any one of Business Communication,	
Business Law, Business Policy)	
Management	4
Marketing	4
Quantitative Analysis	4
	24
Department Core:	12
Electives	24
Free Electives:	8
	128

Note that *only one* course was now required from Communication, Law, or Business Policy. That change was associated with the dismantling of the Department of Business Administration, which had been created only six years before in 1964, to pick up the remnants of the former departments of Business Writing and Speaking, Real Estate, Business Law, and Public Utilities and Transportation. I wrote about this action earlier, but it is, once again, a reminder of the massive and traumatic reforms which occurred in the School of Commerce. We were winning respect, but it was neither easy nor painless.

difference in load. Thus, when Commerce moved, after adopting the four-course plan, to reduce the basic teaching load for productive research faculty from 12 hours to 8 hours per week (the prevailing teaching load at GBA), the graduate school moved to reduce its teaching load to 6 hours per week. This whip- sawing pattern can be explained partly on grounds of educational philosophy, that is, equivalence of courses rather than hours. Perceptions of pecking order and relative status are probably also significant keys to understanding such arrangements. In terms of curriculum reform, after interim adjustments in 1969–1970, the Commerce faculty adopted the curriculum design, shown in Table 3.2, effective in the 1970–1971 academic year.

Note that *only one* course was now required from Communication, Law, or Business Policy. That change was associated with the dismantling of the Department of Business Administration, which had been created only six years before in 1964, to pick up the remnants of the former departments of Business Writing and Speaking, Real Estate, Business Law, and Public Utilities and Transportation. I wrote about this action earlier, but it is, once again, a reminder of the massive and traumatic reforms which occurred in the School of Commerce. We were winning respect, but it was neither easy nor painless.

The Undergraduate College: Resurgence in the Seventies and Eighties

Perhaps one of America's most extraordinary academic turnarounds occurred at N Y U's School of Commerce, known in the seventies and eighties as the College of Business and Public Administration. That turnaround became obvious in the seventies, but signals were already seen in the late sixties. They included the glowing AACSB accreditation report in 1969, remarkable increases in student admission credentials, significant improvement in faculty working conditions (office facilities, teaching loads, research assistance), salaries, academic credentials (doctorates), and research productivity, as well as approval to construct Tisch Hall as a new home for Commerce. Also, the curriculum was further revised and broadened. One major factor, enrollment, continued negative in the late sixties, a depressant which held hostage the positive developments. The crucial question was: Would the positive developments turn the enrollment tide? If they failed, then the future of the School remained in doubt. Fortunately, the tide turned in Fall 1973 and enrollments more than doubled in the next ten years (from 1,082 in Fall 1973 to some 2,408 in Fall 1983). The transformation just outlined was accompanied by several organizational changes, which can be described before we turn our attention to the other developments.

Organizational Changes

Joseph Taggart, dean of GBA and executive dean of the Schools of Business, retired in 1970. He was succeeded by William Dill as dean of

GBA. But Dean Dill was not made executive dean. Consequently, GBA and Commerce reverted to their prior status as two independent entities, with co-equal deans.

In 1972 New York University found itself in a major financial crisis. President Hester appointed a special Task Force of six deans to study the situation and recommend solutions. The members were: Dick Netzer, dean of the Graduate School of Public Administration, chairman; Sidney Borowitz, dean of the University College of Arts and Sciences; Daniel Griffiths, dean of the School of Education; Robert McKay, dean of the School of Law; Bayley Winder, dean of Washington Square College of Arts and Sciences; and Abraham Gitlow, dean of the College of Business and Public Administration (the new name for the old School of Commerce).[1]

Shortly after the Task Force began its work, Dean Borowitz left the group, having been asked by President Hester to become Chancellor of the University. (His predecessor, Chancellor Allan Cartter, had resigned and taken a position elsewhere.) The remaining five deans carried on with the difficult job confronting them. One thing was clear; politically inspired recommendations would fail.

The Task Force made a number of radical recommendations. Among them were: (1) sale of the University Heights campus of NYU to City University of New York; (2) merger of University College and Washington Square College at the Washington Square center; (3) merger of the School of Engineering with the Polytechnic Institute of Brooklyn, thereby forming a new Polytechnic Institute of New York; and (4) vertical mergers of the graduate and undergraduate faculties in both Business Administration and Arts and Sciences.

The last recommendation was consummated in Fall 1973 in Business Administration, and the faculties of GBA and BPA (College of Business and Public Administration) were merged. Dean Dill was designated as dean of the merged faculty, recognizing the stronger position of the graduate school in 1973. However, the reality was that Deans Dill and Gitlow continued to function as co-equal partners in planning for and administering the schools and the faculty. Collegiality and congeniality count for more than organizational structures in such cases.

Dean Dill resigned in 1980 and was replaced by William May, just retired as board chairman of the American Can Corporation. Dean Gitlow's relationship with Dean May was no different from what it had been with Dean Dill. Again, the functional reality was one of co-equals, and it was so perceived by the faculty and the central administration. Thus, Dean Gitlow continued to be called upon by the central administration to serve as a member or chairman of major all-university committees; for example, the Fiscal Review Group in 1975, the Committee on Faculty Benefits, and the Committee on Computer Services.

When Dean May retired in 1984 and was succeeded by Dean Richard West, an organizational change was agreed upon and recommended by Deans West and Gitlow. Dean Gitlow had been asked to postpone retirement for one year, to 1985, and he had agreed. While West and Gitlow continued to function in 1984–1985 as had earlier been the case, both thought the relationship between the deans of GBA and BPA had to be spelled out for Gitlow's successors. They agreed that a simple adjustment would set things straight for the future; namely, the undergraduate dean would assume the title of vice-dean of the faculty. The primacy between the two deans would thereby be clarified. The graduate dean would continue as dean of the faculty, but the undergraduate dean would now have formal status and empowerment as vice-dean. Gitlow had preferred to eschew that title, liking better the organizational fuzziness which enabled him to function essentially as a co-equal dean. To set the change in place, Dean Gitlow accepted the title of vice-dean for the remaining months of his 20-year tenure in office. The reality of the conduct of affairs continued as it had, but the organizational structure was firmed for the arrival of Daniel Diamond as Dean Gitlow's successor in BPA. That structure prevails to the time of this writing, in 1994.

The foregoing description of decanal relationships would have no substantive place in this history if it was concerned only with an interplay of personalities and egos. The underlying reality is that profoundly important educational and financial issues are involved. They center on faculty perceptions of the extent and power of the undergraduate dean's influence over curricular and other matters. Remember that Dean Taggart had been appointed executive dean to give him power. Remember also that Dean Prime's retirement and his replacement by Dean Gitlow was part of the plan. Since Dean Taggart and Gitlow agreed on curricular, faculty staffing profiles, teaching loads, and other basic educational issues, they were able to function well together. In fact, the essential nature of their relationship was settled in Acting Dean Gitlow's first week on the job. He felt it was imperative to signal to those resisting change in Commerce that their resistance was doomed. To that end he asked the then chairman of the Management department to resign. The reason: The department chairman had become the lead figure in the group resisting change. The chairman appealed Acting Dean Gitlow's demand to Dean Taggart, who indicated he would like to avoid so drastic a step. Acting Dean Gitlow explained his belief that the proposed action was critical to moving matters ahead quickly. With that, Dean Taggart accepted Gitlow's decision, the resignation was received, and reform moved ahead at full speed. From that point on, and for the next five years, until Dean Taggart's retirement in 1970, the two deans functioned as partners, without any serious substantive issue between them.

The arrival of Dean Dill re-opened the matter of the relationship between the GBA and Commerce deans. Dean Gitlow, concerned about his ability to press ahead with plans to continue improving faculty compensation, teaching loads, and other qualitative but expensive aspects of the undergraduate operation with an as-yet-unknown decanal partner, was leery of the existing executive dean arrangement. When Chancellor Cartter was apprised of Gitlow's concern, and presumably President Hester too, he dropped the executive dean's title, and both Dill and Gitlow became formal co-equals. Their relationship quickly developed into the same collegial, congenial pattern that had existed between Taggart and Gitlow.

The 1972 Task Force report, and its recommendation that the graduate and undergraduate faculties be merged, reopened the decanal question. With a merged faculty, who should be its dean? Although Dean Gitlow was a member of the Task Force, his conviction that the merger was a necessary step overrode any thought he may have had as to his personal position thereafter. Indeed, he was equally convinced that the position of dean of the faculty should go to Dean Dill, as dean of GBA. Dean Gitlow, unwilling in 1970 to accept a less than co-equal structure, discussed the situation with Dean Dill. He told Dill about his concern over being able to preserve and enhance the quality of the undergraduate program. Dill, respecting Gitlow's views, agreed to a de facto partnership. And so the GBA dean became also dean of the merged faculty, while the BPA dean, with no title relative to the faculty, functioned as his co-equal, and was so perceived by the faculty and others. It was a case where form and substance were at variance. But underneath was a desire to maintain the academic quality and student services of the undergraduate program, as well as those of the graduate programs.

Gitlow's tenure as dean extended over a period of 20 years, and involved his working with four GBA deans. When Dill resigned in 1980 and May succeeded him, the de facto decanal relationship continued. It continued also throughout Dean Gitlow's last year in office, 1984–1985, when he worked with Dean West. But the issue of the undergraduate dean's ability to mitigate any tendency to exploit the undergraduate program for the benefit of the graduate ones came once again to the fore. It was in that context that Deans West and Gitlow worked out the solution which involved the undergraduate dean assuming the title of vice-dean of the faculty. While it indicated number one and number two, it also indicated that the undergraduate dean possessed power and influence over the faculty. Other organizational arrangements might have sufficed as well, but this one seemed the simplest solution. In any case it appears to have worked satisfactorily in the nine years that have passed since Dean Diamond succeeded Dean Gitlow. How things will develop between Dean Diamond and Dean George Daly and their successors remains to be seen, but this writer hopes ardently that any arrangement made will preserve the qualitative integrity of the undergraduate program.

Faculty Compensation, Teaching Loads, and Class Size

Deans Madden and Collins, especially the former, complained bitterly about the exploitation of Commerce as a "cash cow." Madden warned, over and over, that failure to reinvest a portion of the surpluses generated would one day be disastrous. The warning was to no avail, and finally disaster did strike.

The three variables emphasized in the heading above are the keys to the generation of cash surpluses, assuming a reasonable enrollment base. Too few students spell financial catastrophe despite clever operational devices. Yet, in a research-oriented university like N Y U, an undergraduate B-school enrollment of a full-time equivalent of 2,000 students should generate cash surpluses. The real issue is the size of the surplus which is sought. If it is too large, then serious issues of educational quality arise. Let us take a look at the arithmetic.

Large *class size* means few faculty relative to the number of students; put differently, the tuition dollars generated per faculty member are large. The opposite is true in the case of smaller class sizes. High *teaching loads* compound the effect of large class size, increasing further the proportion of students to faculty and the tuition dollars generated per faculty member. It also reduces the possible faculty time available per student for counseling, and, perhaps more important, for students and faculty to spend time together outside the classroom.

Faculty compensation is a trickier business, for it involves more than the level of faculty salaries and benefits. Of course the level is important, but equally significant is the staffing profile. This latter factor involves the distribution of full-time faculty among the several professorial ranks, that is, full professor, associate professor, and assistant professor. It involves also the relative numbers of full-time and part-time instructors. The greater the use of full-time faculty and the larger the proportion of higher to lower ranks, the more expensive the staffing pattern. A fairly common arrangement is to schedule huge sections in basic courses, with hundreds of students. Such sections hear lectures by senior professors, and are then broken down into much smaller tutorials led by graduate teaching assistants. The usual rationale supporting the arrangement is that many more students get to hear top professors, while the assistants get teaching experience in the tutorial sessions. Questions can be raised about the competence with which most assistants teach, but that concern is often overridden by the attractive financial aspects of the arrangement. Also, wider exposure of students to top professors can be lost if the teaching loads of the senior professors are concurrently reduced below the level prior to the adoption of the pattern described.

I remember clearly the situation at Commerce in the late forties, when the tidal wave of returning veterans inundated the school. Most classrooms held 65 seats, and some could accommodate 100 or more. All were filled, with waitlisted students ready to fill in should anyone drop out of a class. The normal teaching load was 12 contact and credit hours per semester (meaning six separate 2-credit sections). Very few faculty had released time, usually for administrative duties. The use of part-time teachers and of untenured instructors and assistant professors was heavy. Full-time faculty were commonly allowed to teach overloads (as much as 16 contact-credit hours per week, i.e., 8 sections) and the "overtime" payment was small. It is no wonder that the School was an enormous cash cow.

The situation had improved significantly by the mid-sixties, mainly because the drop in enrollment was substantially greater than the contraction in faculty. This did not translate as much into reduced teaching loads as it did into reduced class sizes. Yet, great improvement did occur in staffing between 1965–1966 and 1969–1970. In the former year one-half of Commerce's classes were taught by nonterminally degree-qualified faculty (according to AACSB accreditation standards). Some 17 percent of the classes were taught by part-time faculty. By 1969–1970 the situation had changed greatly. Three-quarters of the School's classes were staffed by terminally degree-qualified faculty and only 9 percent by part-timers.

Subsequent events reveal how difficult it can be to sustain relatively costly staffing profiles at the undergraduate level. Thus, I wrote in my 1973–1974 annual report:

> The increased flow of faculty between BPA and GBA prior to the merger of September 1973 and since that merger has had the unintended effect of: (1) reducing the proportion of BPA classes taught by terminally degree qualified faculty (to 62 percent in Spring 1974); and (2) increasing the proportion taught by part-time instructors (to 20.7 percent in Spring 1974).
>
> The foregoing trends are not healthy and will require positive action in the recruitment efforts of the Schools of Business. We do *not* think the data reflects a deliberate scheduling policy among departmental chairmen to staff classes at the undergraduate level at a lower qualitative level than at the graduate one. We are of the opinion rather that overall recruitment activity and decisions have been less effective than they should be, so that we have gradually accumulated last-minute staffing deficiencies. (Pp. 31–32)

No matter how and why the situation deteriorated as it did between 1969–1970 and 1973–1974, the inescapable fact is that staffing preference went to the graduate level as against the undergraduate. That is the root problem which persists across the decades, and which reflects the psychology inherent in the academic pecking order. It necessitates an ever-vigilant administration to offset, or at least mitigate the problem. The simplest but costliest solution is to hire additional full-time faculty. That solution requires negotiation with the central administration to win authorization. An easier and faster short-run answer is to cut back the number of sections, which increases class size. But that course is constrained by the course availability needs of the curriculum (so students can take the courses required by their degree programs). While an increase in teaching loads for full-time faculty would help reduce the need to employ part-timers, such a course of action is sure to produce powerful faculty opposition. Also, it is inconsistent with efforts to advance research output. These pressures help explain in part the enormous pressure to raise tuition fees in the last decades of the twentieth century.

A scan of faculty compensation records back to 1929–1930 indicates very little change in salary structures between that year and 1947–1948. Generally, full-time instructors appear to have received annual base salaries of $2,500–$3,500; assistant professors $3,500–$4,500; associate professors $4,500–$5,000; and professors $5,000–$8,000. The high end involved long-service, senior professors, often with additional duties as department chairmen or assistant deans. Thus, Professor Edward J. Kilduff, who was chairman of the General Course department and an assistant dean, received $8,250 in 1929–1930, while Professor George Burton Hotchkiss, a pioneer in developing the field of marketing and onetime department chairman, received $8,000. Professor Willford I. King, a pioneer in the development of national income analysis, was paid $7,500. And Dean Madden, as we noted before, received $10,000.

The depression of the thirties, and the wage and salary regulations of the World War II years, kept the structure pretty much intact into the postwar years. In 1947–1948 the minimum base salary for full-time instructors was $2,950. Higher ranks were not markedly different from the earlier period. However, things did move up during the fifties and early sixties. But salaries tended to bunch about the minimum of the range for each rank.

Major changes occurred between 1964–1965 and 1970–1971:

1. In 1964–1965, some 68 percent of all full professors earned between $12,000 and $12,999. In 1970–1971 only 9.4 percent earned less than $16,000 and 37.5 percent received $20,000 or more. *In 1964–1965 no professorial salary exceeded $16,000 per year.*

2. In 1964–1965, some 66 percent of the associate professors received less than $10,000 per year, but in 1970–1971 some 79 percent received $12,000 or more, and slightly more than 42 percent received salaries of $14,000 or more per year.

3. Assistant professors enjoyed the greatest relative improvement, reflecting the extraordinary market conditions during the 1960s and the School's decision to build the faculty by hiring promising junior faculty rather than aging stars. In 1964–1965 slightly over 92 percent of the assistant professors received salaries between $7,000 and $8,999. But in

1970–1971 none of them were below $12,000 and 80 percent received salaries between $13,000 and $14,999.

4. Finally, in 1964–1965 two-thirds of the instructors were below $7,000, while in 1970–1971 two-thirds were in the $12,000–$12,999 bracket.

Bunching or clustering about the minimums had broken down for full professors and associate professors by 1970–1971. That tendency still existed, however, in the junior, nontenured ranks (assistant professor and instructor), probably because strict adherence to the tenure rules mandated an up-or-out decision no later than the sixth year in nontenured status.

No doubt, the 1970–1971 salaries look meager today, when the salary structure is probably four to five, or more, times higher. Of course, the intervening decades saw double-digit inflation in the seventies and a general upward movement of academic salaries in America (especially in those faculties where a strong external market demand buttressed the internal academic one). Also, the central administration, trustees, school administrators, and faculty in NYU were determined to improve the university's relative position, partly by offering competitive salaries.

Whatever the reasons, the absolute and relative financial position of the Business faculty underwent a profound change for the better in the seventies and eighties. That change was accompanied by a substantial overall reduction in teaching loads, as well as a shift in the staffing profile in favor of full-time faculty.

Tisch Hall

The completion and occupancy of Tisch Hall by Commerce-BPA in Fall 1972 was an enormously important symbolic and substantive development. Designed by famed architect Philip Johnson, it was a large physical symbol of confidence in the future of the School. It could not have come at a more timely moment, for Fall 1972 was the nadir of Commerce's enrollment. The building gave the School a beautiful new face to the world, and it undoubtedly helped attract new students. Everyone's spirits rose. Faculty had comfortable private offices in which to work and meet students. Comfortable lounges for faculty and students were provided. Tisch Hall had a conference center, a computer center, and office suites for the Ross Institute of Accounting Research and the Institute of Retail Management. The ambience was pleasant and energizing. Alumni interest in and fund-raising for the School were stimulated. In fact, fund-raising for the building was reported as $7,426,096 in the dean's annual report for 1969–1970 (page 75), representing some 83 percent of the total cost of the building chargeable to the School of Commerce. In addition, fund-raising for scholarships and unrestricted use also hit levels unknown in the earlier years of the School.

Another aspect of Tisch Hall had perhaps the greatest long-term significance. The building was built on the basis of a carefully constructed plan of the future College of Business and Public Administration. Central to that plan were assumptions as to target enrollment (2,100 full-time equivalent students), average class size (50 in business core courses and 25 in advanced ones), and an average teaching load of 2.5 sections per faculty member, per semester. Reflecting these assumptions, numbers of faculty offices and numbers and capacities of classrooms were computed. Spaces for lounges, conference rooms, institutes, computer center, and such, were added. In short, the structure had a qualitative underpinning, intended to set some physical constraints on any future plans to generate large cash surpluses through a debasement of the quality of the undergraduate program. Of course, that goal could still be pursued, but it became somewhat more difficult than used to be the case.

New Programs and Promotional Efforts

A broad spectrum of new programs and promotional efforts were undertaken by Commerce, beginning in 1964 and expanding rapidly from 1965. The academic year 1964–1965 saw the production of a *filmstrip,* distributed to 500 selected high schools around the country.[2] Designed to tell the story of Commerce's new educational program, it sought in sound and pictures to transmit a sense of excitement and challenge. The hope was that guidance counselors and students would gain a new outlook toward education for business in general, and toward pursuing it at NYU in particular. A companion pamphlet published in Spring 1966, entitled *Is It For You?* buttressed the filmstrip's message. Five thousand copies were printed and distributed to high schools and two-year community colleges. Also, the School's bulletin was thoroughly revised. Judged by enrollment results these efforts were not successful, for aggregate enrollments continued on a downward path until 1972.

The following seven efforts, however, seemed to have an impact in slowing the decline: (1) development of automatic student transfer agreements with two-year colleges; (2) a tuition-free summer computer program for outstanding high school students who had completed their junior year; (3) creation of a new major in computer applications and information systems, and later a new department to provide the courses; (4) compensated business internships for Commerce students in cooperating firms; (5) a certificate program for full-time people engaged in business and the media, called the Professional Program in Business (PPB); (6) interschool degree programs, including a 5-year BS-MBA program and a program in Science Administration; (7) a major and continuing drive to raise money for scholarships.

Automatic Student Transfer Agreements.[3] The rapid growth of two-year colleges in the late fifties and sixties was one reason for the disastrous decline in Commerce enrollments. Assuming that relationship had validity, it made sense to develop transfer agreements between Commerce and two-year colleges. The underlying concept, from the Commerce side, was that students would pursue an Associate in Arts degree at the two year college, and thereby satisfy almost all of the liberal arts and sciences core requirements of the BS degree. In place of SAT scores and high school grade point averages, students eligible for automatic transfer would have to present a cumulative grade point average of 2.5 on a 4.0 scale in the two-year college.

The concept was attractive to two-year colleges, and by Spring 1967 11 community and private junior colleges had entered into agreements with Commerce (Bronx, Queensborough, Rockland, Staten Island, Suffolk, Westchester, and Farmingdale in New York; and Trenton, Union, Wesley, and York in New Jersey). Also, agreements were subsequently arrived at with Dutchess and Nassau Community Colleges, as well as a number of other schools.

A significant problem arose in developing the agreements. It involved students taking Associate in Applied Science (AAS) degrees at the two-year schools. The AAS degrees were relatively light in liberal arts content and heavy in professional courses, that is, Accounting, Marketing, and so on. Understandably, the faculty teaching the professional courses in the two-year institutions desired Commerce to "validate" their professional courses with its BS degree, leaving Commerce to provide most of the liberal arts core requirement. The collision of preferences was both financial and philosophical. The former aspect is obvious, in terms of tuition revenues to Commerce as against Arts and Sciences at NYU, and in terms of revenues to the Business departments at the junior colleges. Philosophically, Commerce had adopted an essentially layer cake curriculum, with the Liberal Arts and Sciences concentrated in the freshmen and sophomore years. The reason was the resulting greater maturity and educational background of the students when they took the professional course work in the junior and senior years. From the Commerce standpoint, to have accepted the arrangement desired by the professional faculty in the junior colleges would have resulted in an "inverted" BS degree, and would have been contrary to the educational philosophy underlying the Commerce curriculum.

The outcome was that Commerce accepted *only* work done in *basic* professional courses, and only then on the basis that the student achieved a satisfactory grade in advanced courses taken on arrival at Commerce. No transfer credit was granted for advanced professional course work taken at the junior college. Based on this arrangement, agreements were consummated with the two-year colleges noted above.

The actual negotiation of the agreements involved invitations to the top administrators of each junior college to visit Washington Square, have lunch, examine our facilities, and discuss our curriculum and how it might mesh with their own. Prior to their departure, they were asked to identify 5 to 10 of their outstanding students who might have an interest in education for business. Since these students usually faced financial constraints, Commerce's director of advisement and scholarship scheduled visits to each of the 13 two-year colleges, to interview the students.

Summer Computer Program. It may seem odd, but the undergraduate School of Commerce became involved with the educational use of computers before GBA did. Actually, as is so often the case, the intense interest of a single individual appears to account for what happened. The individual was Assistant Dean Harry M. Kelly, who pushed vigorously and successfully for budgetary approval for Commerce to acquire an IBM 1620 computer in 1965.

This hardware was in place when I took over administrative responsibility in August 1965. Discussions with Assistant Dean Kelly, Associate Dean Raymond Buteux, and Professor Ernest Kurnow, chairman of the Statistics department, brought agreement to initiate a tuition-free summer computer program of six weeks' duration, during the summer of 1966. Thirty-five superior high school students from 12 states (as far west as Colorado and as far south as Florida) were accepted. They and their parents were welcomed at a reception and taken on a tour of the Commerce Academic Computer Center. Twenty-five out-of-state participants resided in the Joe Weinstein Residence Hall. The others, residents of New York City, lived at home.

The program of instruction was designed for high school students who completed the eleventh grade. With an IBM 1620, they were taught programming and use of computers. Instructed in Statistics and Operations Research techniques with emphasis on computer applications, the students were exposed to such techniques as: regression analysis; analysis of variance; queuing theory; inventory models; and linear programming. The applications were in the experience range of high school students. For example, Operations Research techniques were used to determine the number of check-out counters needed in a school cafeteria; a plan was designed for scheduling student programs at a high school; a model was developed for forecasting attendance at football or basketball games.

Two housemothers resided in the Joe Weinstein Residence Halls and accompanied students on the varied activities scheduled for selected afternoons, evenings, and weekends. Included in the program of activities were trips to a variety of cultural and athletic events, and scenic and historic places around New York. Students participated in as many of these activities as they chose, or they used their free time to work individually in the Academic Computer Center.

So that no qualified students would be barred from participation because of financial need, the School of Commerce, with the help of a gift from Mr. Charles C. Moskowitz, Commerce '14, awarded scholarships of $200 each to nine students in the program. These awards were distributed to cover the expense of dormitory, breakfast, and lunch, as well as other activities.

The success of the 1966 Summer Computer Program resulted in 358 responses and 291 applications for admission to the 1967 Summer Program. The applications came from 38 states, Puerto Rico, and Washington, D.C., as compared with 90 applications for the 1966 program.

The 1967 program was attended by 26 students (13 boys and 13 girls), coming from 12 states and Puerto Rico. Almost all had preliminary SAT scores in the 600–700 range in Mathematics, and several were at the head of their high school classes. It should be noted that by 1967 Commerce had already outgrown its IBM 1620 and had acquired an IBM 360–30 and peripheral equipment.

The Major in Computer Applications and Information Systems (CAIS). The smashing success of the Summer Computer Program stimulated Commerce to create a new CAIS major in 1968–1969 (originally called Computer Science). A marketing niche was discerned which seemed in complete harmony with the School's direction. But Commerce did not have a department to offer the program. Not wishing to lose time or market position, a deliberate decision was taken to package existing relevant courses offered by the Statistics and Management departments with those offered in Computer Science by the Washington Square College of Arts and Sciences.

The program was successful in achieving its initial objective, reaching an enrollment level of 173 majors by Fall 1970. It helped moderate the overall decline in enrollments. But there was a fundamental problem. The program, despite good intentions, was a jerry-built educational package, and did not coalesce conceptually or in substance. The student consumers, bright and perceptive, recognized the weakness, and they complained. There was also adverse word-of-mouth from them to prospective students, so that the initial upsurge in majors was not sustained, declining to 72 by Fall 1975.

The complaints were met by corrective actions. The first significant step was a thorough review of the program by Professor Gerald Glasser. He recommended: (1) the program should focus on information systems and computer modeling, and thereby distinguish itself from the computer science programs offered by Arts and Sciences and Engineering Schools; (2) new courses should be created and offered by Commerce that were consistent with the conceptual reorientation of the program; (3) the program and its courses should be identified with distinct numbers, in a separate section of the School's bulletin; (4) administrative control over the program should be placed in the Department of Quantitative Analysis (former Department of Statistics), with the future probability of creating a new Department of Computer Applications and Information Systems; (5) faculty who had primary interest in CAIS should be hired to obtain top-quality instruction and research in the area; and (6) to the degree Commerce continued to rely on Washington Square College to serve its students, there should be insistence on a reworking of the courses required there so they became consistent with the philosophical orientation of the new Commerce program.

Professor Glasser's recommendations were well conceived and were implemented in 1972–1973. They were followed later by the creation of a separate CAIS department which became well known, highly respected, and successful in attracting top quality students. By Fall 1983 the number of majors had expanded to 265, due also to the prestige achieved by the program. But there was a lesson well learned by the experience. Do not be blinded by perception of a market niche and clever marketing into offering a program or product that is not well conceived to satisfy the consumer's need. This is not a case of *caveat emptor,* but rather of *Seller Beware.*

Internships. In my 1965–1966 Annual Report, I described a plan to establish close ties between the School and leading business and accounting firms in New York City. The plan envisaged providing internship experience for selected students and, simultaneously, facilitating the recruitment of desirable students by the firms.

Cooperating enterprises would finance four full-tuition scholarships with a value of $2,000 each per annum, or a total of $8,000 per enterprise per year. Under one arrangement, scholarship money would go to selected students of high quality, who would carry a distinctive designation indicative of the uniqueness of their award. Under another arrangement, scholarship money would go to selected black or Hispanic youngsters who, while they did not meet the usual standards for admission to the School of Commerce, showed such promise and had such recommendations as to warrant admission to a specially designed program of study, leading ultimately to completion of the regular Commerce curriculum. In the latter instance, the essential idea was to do something constructive at the input end about the scarcity of qualified people from disadvantaged groups available for managerial roles in commerce and industry. These students would carry a designation indicative of their sponsorship, and would also have some sort of internship arrangement to facilitate their movement into business management, as well as to stimulate their motivation.

The plan, implemented in 1967–1968, won support only in the accounting profession, with Ernst and Ernst the first firm to participate. As implemented, the plan envisaged the identification of interns at the time they matriculated in Commerce (whether as freshmen or as transfer students). Up to their junior year, they received partial tuition scholarships from the general financial aid resources available to the School. During their junior and senior years they received $2,000 per year, the money being provided by the participating accounting firm sponsoring the internship. The interns worked for the sponsor for a seven-month period, beginning July 1 following the junior year and ending January 30 of the senior year. During this period, they received a weekly salary of $125.

The seven-month work period did not delay graduation for the interns. By taking 33 credits each in the freshman and sophomore years, 8 credits in the summer session following the sophomore year, 36 credits in the junior year, and 18 credits in the Spring semester of the senior year, the interns could graduate within the normal four-year time span. The proposed program imposed no excessive intellectual burden on the interns, who were top-quality students. To the contrary, it afforded them extraordinary exposure to the work of the accountant, and to the realities of business organizations and activities. It did so at a generous level of remuneration, designed to reflect the importance attached to the intern status by sponsors and School.

To guarantee the educational integrity of the program, a senior professor, Eli Kushel, was designated to work with the interns. Relatively frequent and regularly scheduled seminar meetings were held with them. These meetings discussed work experiences and cases, so that the interns benefited from each other's exposure as well as from the knowledge of the professor-in-charge. If a sponsor employed an intern in activities not considered consistent with the educational aims of the program, such a sponsor was to be dropped. The last point was made clear in the first discussions with potential sponsors.

Despite the attractive conceptual character of the plan, its success was small. Even in the Accounting profession, it never attracted as many as a half dozen firms, and it was dropped after several years. This writer continues to think that the concept is a good one, and knows that variations of it have apparently been successful elsewhere.

Professional Program in Business (PPB). This is a certificate program created for college graduates engaged in a business career, or seeking to embark on such a career but lacking a relevant formal educational background. It was created also for people possessing such a background, but wishing to update their knowledge. The PPB enabled students to participate in a program of concentrated, integrated study of particular professional areas, rather than a scattered sampling of courses. While the program was neither a prerequisite for entry into an MBA program, nor a guarantee of admission to such a program, it did encourage a number of students who completed it to continue successfully toward completion of an MBA. But no credits earned toward the PPB certificate could be counted toward an MBA degree's required credits.

As it developed over the years, the PPB offered nine area specializations, or "modules." Each module consisted of a cluster of three to four carefully selected courses. The courses were drawn from the advanced undergraduate offerings of the School. Students selected the module best designed to suit their educational and professional needs. The program could be completed in one year of intensive part-time study. Where the substance of certain course modules required prior exposure to quantitative, economic, social science, or other academic disciplines, it was the student's responsibility to obtain the preparation necessary for enrollment. Individual counselling for each student was provided to ensure enrollment in the appropriate module and normal progress to completion. Participants in the program could elect to be graded on a pass/fail or a letter grade basis, depending on their plans for future academic studies.

The PPB was a success and continues to be offered by the undergraduate division of the Stern School, enrolling some 50 students per year. As of 1993–1994 it offered modules in nine areas: Accounting; Economics; Finance; General Business; Information Systems; International Business; Management; Marketing; and Statistics, Operations Research, and Actuarial Science. Accounting and Marketing each offered two module variations, while Finance offered three module variations.

International Business Program. In Fall 1974 a new major was introduced in International Business, with an initial registration of 20 majors. The program grew, reaching an enrollment level of 107 majors in Fall 1981. It has since hovered at that level, or somewhat below, generally drawing between 4 and 4.25 percent of the School's total majors. The program is regarded as moderately successful in enrollment terms, and the Department of International Business, which administers it, is one of the most distinguished in the College.

Interschool Degree Programs. Of the several interschool degree programs considered in the early seventies, only one developed and continued, albeit in modified form, over the next two decades. That was a combined five-year BS-MBA program between Commerce and GBA, which enabled highly qualified Commerce graduates to move directly into the MBA program, count the equivalent of almost one year's credit toward the graduate degree, and complete the MBA program with a fifth year. Accepted students had to meet minimum grade point average and GMAT (Graduate Management Admissions Test) scores.

The minimum requirements were stiffened over the years, most particularly with the added requirement that participating students acquire two years of full-time work experience between receiving the baccalaureate degree and beginning the MBA program; that is, students admitted to the program begin graduate study the fifth term after graduation from the undergraduate school. Students who wished to matriculate in the MBA program earlier than the fifth term after receipt of the baccalaureate could do so only after an interview with a member of the Graduate Admissions Committee. The student's essays, recommendations, and work experience would be evaluated, as well as his or her level of maturity, interpersonal and communication skills.

As of the 1993–1994 academic year, the academic criteria for admission to the program were:

1. Completion of 108 points of undergraduate study with at least 32 points of course work at the Stern Undergraduate College. Grades of "Pass" were not acceptable in this 32-point minimum. A student had five Fall and Spring terms within which to apply, be accepted, and begin studies at the Graduate Division.

2. The GMAT (preferably in the Junior year).

3. Meeting the standard elucidated by the following formula: (GPA x 200) + GMAT Score $\geq$ 1300.

Examples of GPAs and GMAT scores that would be required with those GPAs are:

$$(3.2 \times 200) + 660 = 1300$$
$$(3.4 \times 200) + 620 = 1300$$
$$(3.6 \times 200) + 580 = 1300$$
$$(3.8 \times 200) + 540 = 1300.$$

The minimum GPA considered is 3.2, regardless of the strength of the GMAT score. The GPA considered is the average on the *Stern transcript*. Additional conditions applied with regard to course equivalencies between undergraduate and graduate courses.

Among other interschool programs, none of which came to fruition, were a possible combined BS-JD program with the Law School. While the law school did not favor that combination, it did later agree to a combined MBA-JD program with GBA. Another program envisaged a degree in Science Administration. Developed with the Arts and Science college it attracted one student and then died.

Enterprise. Enterprise was a student-inspired and developed magazine, supported by the School financially and through the provision of a paid faculty advisor (Professor Lawrence Brennan). It published scholarly articles by students, selected from outstanding research papers done in advanced courses, as well as speeches by prominent speakers at School affairs (such as Dean's Day and Student honorary societies). *Enterprise* sought to project an improved image of the School to other B-schools and to high school guidance counselors and their counterparts in junior colleges. The publication was continued for some half dozen years, finally dying because student interest waned. During its publication, however, it was well received.

Renaming the School

Great hope was attached to a newly created undergraduate major in Public Administration, which was worked out with the Graduate School of Public Administration and which paralleled conceptually the 5-year BS-MBA program. The program seemed a natural, reflecting a belief that there was a solid base of knowledge common to the governance of both private and public organizations. This philosophical belief was held also at Yale University when it created its Graduate School of Management. Yale claimed that it was unique in embracing the management of both private and public organizations. At N Y U, where two separate graduate schools existed, one in Business Administration and one in Public Administration, common elements were recognized as residing in a basic core of knowledge and theory. But it was recognized also that profound differences distinguished the two forms of organization, and those differences warranted division at the graduate level.

In any case, the two areas of organizational governance were joined at the School of Commerce. To recognize and reflect that fact, the School's name was changed to the College of Business and Public Administration in 1971, and the first majors in the field were registered in the Fall of that year. They were seven in number. The number of majors reached a peak of 42 in Fall 1978, falling off thereafter. The sad reality is that the program and its underlying concept did not attract a significant number of students.

Enrollment Trends, Student Quality, and Other Factors

Enrollments in Commerce began a sharp decline after the veteran crush which followed World War II and the Korean War. That decline approximately halved the student population *per semester* from a bit above 8,000 to the 4,364 of Fall 1962 (see Table 4.1), and was concentrated in the seven-year period 1955–1962. Also, until 1960 the decline was not associated with major cutbacks in full-time faculty staffing, so there was some decline in average class size, and it was possible to abandon the "block" system of assigning students to classrooms and having professors rotate to those rooms.

In Fall 1963 another factor became operative. It was then that the more selective admission standard demanded by the 1956 NYU Self-Study report was imposed by President Hester's new administration, and implemented by the School in a really significant way. The ensuing collapse in enrollments was huge, reducing them by more than half within the four years between Fall 1962 and Fall 1966, from 4,364 to 1,909. The bodily transfer of the Journalism department and its majors from Commerce to Arts and Sciences also occurred at that time, and it should not be forgotten. The decline continued thereafter, but at a slower pace, finally ending in Fall 1973. By then, drastic changes had taken place in the School and its programs, and Tisch Hall had opened in Fall 1972. Commerce, now BPA, was a transformed School, and a true rebirth became evident, with enrollments climbing steadily to a new peak of 2,576 in Fall 1984. Enrollments hovered at that level until Fall 1986, after which a deliberate decline was begun toward the 2,100 level envisaged in the planning for Tisch Hall. A profoundly important point must be made. Between 1975 and 1985 much larger enrollment levels were possible, if the school had been willing to revert somewhat to the standards and practices of an earlier period. But it did not do so.

TABLE 4.1
Undergraduate Enrollments, Fall 1960–Fall 1988,
by Sex and by Part-Time Status

Year	Total	Women	% Women	Part-Time	% Part Time
1960	4,813	428	8.89	1,922	39.93
1961	4,624	436	9.43	1,811	39.17
1962	4,364	413	9.46	1,764	40.42
1963	3,488	324	9.29	1,465	42.00
1964	2,908	293	10.08	1,270	43.67
1965	2,352	238	10.12	933	39.67
1966	1,909	204	10.69	694	36.35
1967	1,838	218	11.86	658	35.80
1968	1,732	182	10.51	581	33.55
1969	1,582	185	11.69	493	31.16
1970	1,422	189	13.30	371	26.1
1971	1,278	183	14.32	388	30.36
1972	1,106	201	18.17	333	30.11
1973	1,082	225	20.79	309	28.56
1974	1,137	292	25.68	379	33.33
1975	1,237	397	32.09	378	30.56
1976	1,455	514	35.33	467	32.10
1977	1,756	693	39.46	457	26.03
1978	1,989	849	42.68	510	25.64
1979	2,259	975	43.16	536	23.73
1980	2,349	1,020	43.42	485	20.65
1981	2,414	1,082	44.82	475	19.68
1982	2,351	1,126	47.89	462	19.65
1983	2,408	1,171	48.63	474	19.68
1984	2,576	1,294	50.23	458	17.78
1985	2,555	1,298	50.80	458	17.93
1986	2,519	1,266	50.26	409	16.23
1987	2,374	1,194	50.29	352	14.83
1988	2,184	1,061	48.58	290	13.28

SOURCE: School of Commerce, College of Business and Public Administration, Dean's Office Statistical Records, 1960–1988.

It must be said that this decision was respected by the university's central administration, perhaps not always with great joy, but respected nonetheless. *The decision to sustain a high admissions standard was ruling.*

An odd and perhaps perverse aspect of the high academic standard of NYU's undergraduate business college is a reversal in the attitudes and relationship between it and the Arts and Sciences college. For years the former was regarded as inferior, and not without some grounds. By way of example, the Arts and Sciences college would not count grades achieved by its students in Commerce courses in computing their grade point averages for determining graduation with honors. Also, there were students who, being unable to gain admission to the Arts and

Sciences college, would matriculate in Commerce and then attempt an intra-university transfer after the freshman or sophomore year. Today, some students unable to gain admission to the undergraduate business college matriculate in Arts and Sciences and then seek an interschool transfer after the first or second year. In the early eighties there were over 100 students per year following that path. Also, the B-school now requires a grade point average of 3.0 in Arts and Sciences courses to effect a transfer. Further, in Fall 1990, 79.2 percent of the freshmen entering the Stern School were in the top fifth of their high school graduating class, compared to 67.0 percent for the university as a whole. In Fall 1992 the Stern percentage was 79.4 while the overall university percentage had improved to 70.7. Academically and otherwise, the undergraduate business school is no longer at the base of the pecking order, looked down upon with no respect. We have achieved the status so long sought by comedian Rodney Dangerfield—respect!

The opening of Tisch Hall and the achievement of academic quality and respect did not entirely explain the resurgence in enrollments. Another major factor was a remarkable movement of young women into business. No doubt, this was part of a larger societal transformation, but N Y U's business school was alert to this change and eager to encourage it. We noted earlier that women comprised a significant minority of the Commerce student population from the early years of the School. We noted also that Gladys Reutiman, advisor to women students, recorded their numbers at over 600 in 1937. The data of Table 4.1 show their number at over 400 in the early sixties, when they constituted some 9.5 percent of total enrollment. But, while their numbers declined as total enrollment went down, it did not drop as rapidly. Consequently, the proportion of women in the student body rose. What's more striking is the fact that the enrollment trend for women turned upward five years before total enrollment did (Fall 1969 as against Fall 1974). Also, the data make clear that the increase in the enrollment of women between Fall 1968 and Fall 1985 was remarkable, going from 182 to 1,298 and, proportionately, from 10.51 percent to 50.8 percent of the total. It has declined since as the school's total enrollment has been reduced, both absolutely and relatively. Is this a portent of a reversal in recent societal trends? Is it a response to a growing awareness of the so-called glass ceiling, which is allegedly a barrier to women seeking top management positions? Or, is it a reflection of a new order of priorities among younger American women? The phenomenon seems significant and bears watching.

Table 4.1 demonstrates another aspect of the School's transformation; the large reduction, both absolutely and relatively, in the presence of part-time (essentially evening) students. The N Y U Self-Study report of 1956 called for such a change in Commerce, probably reflecting some doubts about the quality of evening educational programs. But the School's part-time evening program was at the core of its founding philosophy and culture. It was also integral to its self-perception as a school of opportunity. Consequently, even as the School was transformed qualitatively in the sixties, it was not a deliberate policy to jettison or markedly reduce the part-time student population. In fact, the introduction of the Professional Program in Business was a contrary action. Thus, the proportional presence of part-time students did not decline below 30 percent of the total, on a continuing basis, until Fall 1977. No doubt, part of the reason is that part-time students are in stream over a longer span of years than full-time students. Ultimately, however, the academic dynamics of the school and the general university disinterest in part-time evening undergraduate students had that effect, with the result that today the undergraduate evening program is small. But I detect no discernible bias against continuing the evening program. In fact, the movement of the graduate division to Washington Square may well help sustain the undergraduate evening program, for the graduate division maintains a large evening MBA program, and insures the presence of significant numbers of students and faculty at Washington Square during the evening.[4]

Financial Aid

The subject of financial aid is attended by controversy across the broad spectrum of American educational institutions. If financial aid is perceived as a scholarship, then it implies an award or grant in recognition of some special ability or merit, academic or athletic. Even those two criteria invite intense argument, for the very term "scholarship" is solely derivative of academic or intellectual ability. And one need only read the daily papers to become aware of the oftentimes scandalous awarding of so-called athletic scholarships where the last and least requirement is academic competence. But athletic scholarships as a source of disputation practically disappeared from NYU after it abandoned "big-time" football in the early fifties, followed by "big-time" basketball in the late sixties. After those steps, internal debate on financial aid focused on financial need, academic merit, and ethnic (minority) criteria. The last criterion became especially prominent after the tragic assassination of the Reverend Martin Luther King, Jr., in 1968.

The desire to increase the enrollments of African-American students inspired NYU in 1968 to announce its Martin Luther King Scholarship program, at a funding level of $1,000,000 per year. The program was attended by some initial success in all the undergraduate colleges, including the business school, but eventually failed due to a lack of external funding. Its place was taken by government financial programs like Higher Education Opportunity Grants (HEOP).

Academic merit, on the other hand, gradually achieved success because it won outside financial support from private donors. Thus, the university instituted its University Scholars program for the undergraduate colleges. That program made substantial tuition grants, plus additional grants for enrichment activities such as annual trips abroad and special arts events involving theater and the opera. The University Scholars awards went to academically outstanding students, and were distributed among the undergraduate schools in accordance with the relative number of applications of such students to the several colleges. At least, that was the original concept.

Commerce-BPA, in addition, was especially successful in the 1965–1985 period in winning scholarship funding from wealthy alumni, who were grateful for the school of opportunity philosophy which had enabled them to start their careers. Two named scholarship programs were and are of a magnitude requiring special mention. These are the John Ben Snow and Theodore R. Racoosin Scholarships.

John Ben Snow, a 1903 Commerce alumnus, came from upstate New York. After graduation he went to work for the Woolworth Company, attracted the attention of top corporate executives, and was sent to England to build up the Woolworth chain in that country. His success was phenomenal and he acquired the sobriquet of "Sure-Fire" Snow, because his business decisions were certain to be successful. He remained in England until just before World War II, when he retired from Woolworth and returned to America. Here, he joined Merritt C. Speidel, an old friend who was a journalist, and began a second career as an owner of a chain of newspapers (bearing Speidel's name). Ben Snow had become an avid horseman during his stay in England, and moved to the area around Colorado Springs, Colorado, where he purchased a ranch and maintained an office. Also, he acquired a magazine, the *Western Horseman,* which became successful. A life-long bachelor, he showed interest in N Y U after his return to America, and contributed funds for rooms in several new university buildings (Vanderbilt Hall, Tisch Hall, and the Bobst Library). I visited him in Colorado Springs at the time of the dedication of Tisch Hall, to present personally the John T. Madden Award of the School of Commerce. The Madden Award was given annually to outstanding Commerce alumni. A congenial relationship developed between us, followed by increasing interest by John Ben Snow in his school. When he died, this interest was known to the trustees of the Snow Foundation, and they initiated annual grants to the School in the amount of $75,000 for merit scholarships in the name of John Ben Snow. The Ben Snow scholarships have been very important in attracting top-quality scholars to Commerce-BPA.

Like the Ben Snow Scholarships, the Theodore R. Racoosin grants are merit-based. Their magnitude, however, has become greater. Further, they are permanently endowed in the sum of $1.5 million, comprising an original gift of $500,000 during Racoosin's lifetime, and a bequest of a further $1 million following his death in 1985. An ardent supporter of a homeland for the Jewish people, Ted Racoosin also felt a deep sense of gratitude to the School of Commerce. An extraordinarily charitable man, his benefactions embraced a host of educational and religious institutions, non-Jewish as well as Jewish. Sharing his sympathies, his widow, Edlyn Racoosin, continued to show a keen interest in the projects initiated and supported by her husband.[5] Ted Racoosin had become an accountant, but he made the bulk of his wealth through investment in real estate and an insurance company. In this respect, he was similar to other Commerce alumni in the accounting profession who acquired capital through wise business investments. Ted's uniqueness was in the scale and breadth of his charitable donations.

The John Ben Snow and Theodore R. Racoosin Scholarships enabled Commerce-BPA to campaign vigorously for top-quality students. The substantial numbers of them who attended the School and are alumni, along with increased numbers of University scholars in the School, have been a significant source of word-of-mouth testimony about the superior quality of N Y U's undergraduate college. In fact, I cannot overstate the importance of privately donated funds to merit-based financial aid. Unfortunately, a strong body of opinion exists in educational institutions toward granting so called scholarships *entirely* on the basis of need, a criterion that is best weighted in favor of ethnically based grants. Those holding this opinion favor the term "financial aid" over scholarships, recognizing the implicit meaning of the latter term. The clash of opinions is not as extreme as the foregoing language may suggest, for neither side means to exclude entirely the criterion of need or academic merit from its respective award decisions. But it is still real, for the need-oriented group accepts a minimal level of academic ability as a threshold beyond which aid grants reflect *only* financial need. Candidly, the merit-oriented group sees such a policy as endangering efforts to upgrade and sustain academic quality. The N Y U Self-Study report of 1956, the Ford Foundation Proposal of 1963, and a series of painful actions over a period of years in the undergraduate business school were all directed toward raising academic quality. We wanted to remain a school of opportunity, but in the best sense of opening doors for able students who were willing to work hard to achieve success. We were anxious to open those doors for poor people, but not for poor, unmotivated students.

The issue focuses most sharply on the awarding of unfunded financial aid, and its packaging. Unfunded aid is not externally financed, either by government or private donors. It's a direct charge on the school's budget, and is justified in economic terms by providing partial aid for students who will make up the difference between the aid and total tuition through borrowing available government guaranteed funds and/ or using their own family resources. Consequently, they bring some outside funding to cover the cost of their education. The issue becomes the extent to which the unfunded aid is packaged in favor of student applicants with greater need and weaker academic records, as against those showing less need and greater academic merit. The right or wrong of the matter is not easy to resolve, and the feelings of those on both sides of the issue are strong. It took years, but the resolution in Commerce-BPA was weighted in favor of academic merit.

The economic aspect of unfunded financial aid warrants additional explanation. The important underlying reality is that unfunded partial tuition aid does not increase actual operating costs significantly until the additional students it brings in cause an increase in faculty numbers and/or plant (classroom) needs. For example, the only increase in cost associated with additional enrollments is the inconsequential one associated with classroom supplies. On the other hand, unfunded partial tuition aid which expands average class size from, say, 25 to 35, increases revenue by the average tuition funds actually paid by the partial aid recipients times the number making the payment. Consider the reverse. If enrollment is declining, unfunded partial aid cushions the decline in real revenue by the degree it reduces the rate of decline in enrollments. However, there is an important caveat. At some point, so many students may receive unfunded partial aid that aggregate losses force the termination of the program. Remember the old story about the businessman who told a friend that he would solve his problem in a failing business by building volume. Enough additional volume at a loss per each additional unit sold eventually guarantees bankruptcy. But, within limits, the policy permits a multitier pricing (tuition) arrangement and is convincing. In any case, then Chancellor Allan Cartter, a labor economist, "bought" the argument in 1968 and unfunded financial aid was expanded by the School of Commerce.

The School's financial aid policy which finally took shape in the late sixties emphasized these three aspects: (1) a basic shift in emphasis from grants to students already enrolled to those of high quality who were likely matriculates (freshmen and transfers); (2) a sharp increase in packaging, with student financial aid considered *in toto,* that is, including loan and work-study arrangements with direct grants of money and/or tuition remission; and (3) a strong insistence on the maintenance of a high level of academic performance as a prerequisite to continuing financial aid. This policy was associated with a large and continuing expansion in the School's financial aid-scholarship awards.

The record reveals the remarkable increase which occurred in financial aid funds beginning in 1965. Thus, in 1966–1967 total aid amounted to $322,320, of which $62,320 was funded ($22,320 income from endowed funds and $40,000 from current contributions by Commerce alumni).[6] Although a small level of scholarship aid had been available in the School from its earliest days, it had never been substantial. In 1965, when I became acting dean, scholarship aid did not aggregate more than $100,000. Reflecting an increase in 1965–1966 of $145,520 in endowed scholarship funds and a large increase in unfunded monies (based on the economic logic of partial tuition paid by recipients of financial aid), the 1966–1967 aid figure was $322,320. By 1982–1983 total financial aid provided by the School amounted to $2,140,719.[7] Of that total $612,600 was funded and $1,528,119 unfunded. By 1993–1994 the total had grown to $5,725,000, of which $975,000 was funded and $4,750,000 unfunded.

The real growth in these numbers is remarkable. Put into dollars of 1982–1984 purchasing power, the 1965 dollar is worth 4.44 times the 1992 dollar (3.166 ÷ .713 = 4.44).[8] Thus, the 1964–1965 financial aid of $100,000 becomes $444,000, and the $5,725,000 of 1993 aid is 12.9 times as great, in real dollars, as the level of aid was almost 30 years before. Put the other way around, the $5,725,000 of 1993 aid is worth $1,288,125 in 1965 dollars (.713 ÷ 3.166 = .225), or 12.9 times the $100,000 of 1965.

Attention must be directed to the huge increase in unfunded aid over the period, which was even larger that the great growth in funded aid. Perhaps of greatest significance for the future is the expansion in endowed scholarship funds. As of March 31, 1993, the corpus of endowed undergraduate scholarships amounted to $10,406,689, and the income balance available for financial aid grants equaled $827,323. A further $645,386 was available for award in 1993–1994 from current Stern School endowment income.

The endowment data raise a question: Why is an income balance of $827,323 allowed to accumulate, rather than being spent? A prudent regard for past history and the vagaries of interest rates provide the answer. If *all* income is expended as received, then at some future time not enough may be available to take care of prospective and desirable matriculates. Such an inability could have severe long-term effects on recruitment and enrollments. The matter of striking a sensible balance is sensitive, for central officials will likely be prepared to commit income at a higher rate than the college administrators.

Faculty: Dominance of the Doctorate and Other Observations

Earlier chapters pointed out the emphasis on practical experience in enriching the teaching competence of faculty. That emphasis was associated with a lesser degree of importance attached to possession of a doctoral degree. The earliest years of the School of Commerce saw no faculty with doctorates. Also remember Professor George Burton Hotchkiss's story of the advice he received from Dean Joseph French Johnson; namely, to get a job on a newspaper in preference to continuing graduate work toward completion of his PhD. Yet, the inexorable trend over time was to the professionalization of the faculty, so that it gradually came into conformance with the academic standard characteristic of quality Arts and Sciences faculties. That standard almost universally required the PhD for promotion to the rank of assistant professor, with work on the doctorate to be "all but dissertation" (ABD) as the usual prerequisite to employment as a full-time instructor.

Table 2.1 in Chapter 2 showed the operation of the trend in the half-century from 1910 to 1960, during which period the percentage of all professorial ranks possessing an earned doctorate rose from 28.6 to 55.6. The final triumph of the trend is seen in Table 4.2. It shows the full-time and part-time faculty of the merged Stern School of Business since the merger occurred in 1973. The particular point of the table is the dominance of the doctoral degree. Thus, in a period of 17 years, when the size of the faculty more than doubled, possession of earned doctorates by all ranks of full-time professors ranged between 88.5 percent in 1980–1981 and 93.9 percent in 1973–1974. Typically, the figure hovered around 90 percent. The slight reduction in the percentage since 1973–1974 is probably due to the appearance of full-time *clinical professors,* of whom there were 10 in 1990–1991. The concept of the clinical professor was borrowed from the medical faculty. It involves the employment of *outstanding practitioners* as teachers. But they are not placed on the faculty rolls as tenure track appointees, because they usually lack the doctoral and published research credentials of tenure track faculty. The aim is not unlike that of the School's founders, and is intended to sustain inputs from the practical and real world of business alongside the theoretical and research-oriented inputs of academicians.

Note that while possession of the PhD was unusual among instructors, it ran around 40 percent among part-time faculty. It seems plain that even among the part-time staff, possession of the doctorate is considered a significant plus.

The present dominance of the doctorate among the B-school faculty has brought it into conformance with the academic standard of *quality institutions of higher learning,* and has brought it academic respect. That is an important development, for it was a necessary element in winning acceptance of the business school as an appropriate unit in the university. But there was a cost, we hope only temporary, in a lessening of faculty attention to the teaching function of the university.

Some other characteristics of the faculty of the Stern School warrant note, especially against the background of observations on student enrollment trends. For example, when I came to Commerce in 1947 the

TABLE 4.2

Full-Time and Part-Time Faculty, by Doctoral Degree Status, 1973–1974 to 1990–1991, Selected Years

Bulletin Year*	Total No. Faculty	Full-Time by Rank							Part-Time (Adjuncts, Lecturers)			
		Tot. # F.T.	All Professorial Ranks			Instructors			Total No.	# PhD	% PhD	% Part-Time
			Tot. #	# PhD	% PhD	Tot. #	#PhD	%PhD				
1973–1974	161	103	98	92	93.9	5	0	0	58	22	37.9	36.0
1975–1976	185	137	113	101	89.4	24	0	0	48	18	37.5	25.9
1980–1981	240	163	148	131	88.5	15	1	6.7	77	24	31.2	32.1
1985–1986	370	236	204	184	90.2	32	0	0	134	60	44.8	36.2
1990–1991	377	240	184	165	89.7	56	6	10.07	137	55	40.1	36.3

SOURCES: NYU Bulletins, *Graduate School of Business Administration,* 1973–1974, 1975–1976, 1980–1981, 1985–1986, 1990–1991, Faculty listings, by name, rank, and degrees.

*Faculty listed are as of year prior to year of publication of bulletin.

faculty had only a few women, mainly in Secretarial Studies. On the other hand, in 1990–1991 there were 35 full-time faculty women (25 of professorial rank and 10 instructors) and 21 part-time faculty women (19 of professorial rank and 2 lecturers). But the full-time women faculty represented only 14.6 percent of all full-time faculty,[9] and the part-time women accounted for only 15.3 percent of the part-time faculty. Contrast these proportions with those showing that in the eighties almost half of the undergraduate student enrollments were women. It seems reasonable to expect the proportion of women among the faculty to grow.

Observe also that enrollments of substantial numbers of Asian students occurred during the 1980s. There is, again, a counterpart development among the Stern School faculty. Thus, in 1990–1991 there were 33 full-time professorial faculty of Asian origin (23 Indian and 10 Oriental), plus another 10 full-time nonprofessorial faculty. In Fall 1989 and Fall 1992 the percentage of Asian students among freshmen matriculates to the undergraduate school rose from 36.7 to 53.9. Although I do not have data as to the breakdown between Indians and Orientals in the Asian enrollment, my observations on campus indicate that Orientals greatly outnumber Indians among undergraduate students.

We should not leave this topic without remarking on the continuing substantial reliance on part-time faculty. Over the 17-year period covered by Table 4.2, part-time faculty, in terms of nose count, approximate 36 percent. Of course this is not a full-time equivalent figure, but it is significant. Some reliance on part-timers has the advantage of providing staffing flexibility, enabling adjustment to enrollment changes to be most immediately absorbed by the part-timers. Perhaps most remarkable is the relative stability in the proportion of part-timers, considering the enormous expansion in the numbers of total faculty over the period. With such a build-up one could have expected an even greater use of part-timers. That it did not occur reflects an earnest commitment to avoid repeating past practice. However, that commitment may require a proportion of part-timers significantly below 36 percent.

Distinguished Adjunct Professor Seminars

Reflecting a strong desire to preserve important classroom inputs by outstanding business leaders, the Distinguished Adjunct Professor Seminar Series was introduced in 1968. Major executives were invited to team teach seminars in specific subject areas of their experience and competence with full-time faculty members. The first seminar brought together the late William Bernbach, a founder of Doyle, Dane, Bernbach and an advertising genius, and Professor Kit Narodick of the Marketing department. They taught a seminar on "Persuasion." A second concurrent seminar brought together the late Gustave Levy, managing partner of Goldman, Sachs, and Ernest Bloch, Charles W. Gerstenberg Professor of Finance, who conducted a seminar on "Investment Banking." Later seminars teamed Ray Hagel, chairman and CEO of the Macmillan Company, with Professor William Berliner, and Moses Shapiro, chairman and CEO of General Instrument Corporation, with Professor Ralph DiPietro. The two last seminars were in Management. These seminars, in addition to exposing students and faculty to leading businessmen, exposed the businessmen to our School and its best students. There was gain all around.

Variations on the concept continue to be used by the School, but the purposes are the same. Thus, individual lectures by business leaders are arranged every year, and significant numbers of them come to the school, meet with students, and discuss topics of current interest to business and the economy. Also, since my retirement as dean in 1985, I have conducted a seminar entitled "The Chief Executive." Students who apply for the seminar must have completed at least a year of graduate studies, and must explain what they expect to learn. Enrollment is limited to 25 students, of whom four to five may be specially selected seniors who are University Scholars. A dozen of America's major CEOs are invited to meet with the students, speak for 20–40 minutes on some specific aspect of the chief executive's job and responsibility for leading his or her organization, and then engage in a free and unfettered discussion. Two substantial essays are required of each student which, coupled with class participation, become the basis for a grade. Executives who have participated include Lawrence Tisch, of CBS and Loew's; Allan Murray, of Mobil Oil; John Whitehead, of Goldman, Sachs and former Deputy Secretary of State; Moses Shapiro, of General Instrument; Abraham Krasnoff, of Pall Manufacturing; John Creedon, of Metropolitan Life; Walter Shipley, of Chemical Bank; Kay Koplovitz, of USA Network; Martin Lipton, of Wachtell, Lipton; William May, of American Can; Arthur Imperatore, of APA Trucking; Henry Taub, of Automatic

Data Processing; David Margolis, of Coltec Industries; Eugene Cartledge of Union Camp; and Richard Rosenthal of Citizens Utilities, among others.

Both students and executives continue to display enthusiasm for these opportunities to meet and engage in substantive discussions.

Curriculum

By 1976–1977 the undergraduate business curriculum reached its zenith, in terms of exposure to Liberal Arts and Sciences and program flexibility. In broad terms, it required 56 credits of professional courses, 52 credits of Arts and Sciences, with 20 credits of free electives (which could be used by the student in either professional or Liberal Arts and Sciences courses). That structure permitted as many as 72 credits in Arts and Sciences, as well as making possible double majors. The philosophical ideal of the professional undergraduate baccalaureate was achieved; namely, a broad intellectual exposure to the humanities, the social sciences, and the natural sciences. The Commerce-BPA baccalaureate had become one with which the School's graduates could face the world as broadly, rather than narrowly, educated people. Further, the Arts and Sciences work was concentrated in the freshman and sophomore years, enabling the professional course work to be conducted on a more mature level than might otherwise be the case. Also, the liberal arts and professional requirements allowed 20 credits *each* for elective work. Coupled with the 20 credits of free electives, this curricular structure thus permitted a total of 60 credits of electives.[10]

It took half a century, from the introduction of the 128-credit BS degree program in 1926 to the 1976 curriculum described above, to achieve the goal of a truly broad professional program of studies. It is a striking and remarkable fact that since the late seventies, a partial reversal has occurred. By 1982, the curricular structure had become somewhat more restrictive.[11] First, required professional courses were expanded from 56 credits to 60 credits, by increasing the required professional core from 24 to 32 credits (courses in Computers and Information Systems and in Operations Research for Industry and Government were added). Second, the amount of professional electives required was increased from 20 to 28 credits. The relatively small increase in the required professional component of 4 credits should not obscure the greater prescriptiveness of the 1982 program. Finally, the amount of free electives was reduced from 20 to 16 credits. The program was still broad and flexible, but a new direction was evident. Later, we shall see further movement in that new direction.

Other Developments

The undergraduate school's prestige was significantly enhanced in the sixties and seventies by two lecture series, the Charles C. Moskowitz Lectures and the ITT Lectures. The former was funded by Charles C. Moskowitz, an alumnus who had achieved prominence in the motion picture industry. The Moskowitz Lectures, which ran for some 20 years (1960–1980), brought Nobel laureates, leading academicians, outstanding industrialists, and prominent politicians to the school. No less important, the lectures were published variously by the N Y U. Press and the Free Press, and were widely distributed to AACSB members, prominent alumni, and others. The ITT Lectures were funded by the ITT Corporation, also attracted outstanding speakers, and were published and widely distributed. The Joseph Lubin Lecture Series followed and was a successor to the Moskowitz lectures, beginning in the early 1980s.

The Graduate School: Breaking Free and Broad Trends

The Beginnings

The Graduate School of Business Administration was a creation of the School of Commerce, having begun its existence as the Graduate *Division* of Business Administration. It was in its initial few years an arm of Commerce, launched at the Wall Street Division location, and under the direction of Professor Willard C. Fisher. Archibald Wellington Taylor, director of the Commerce Wall Street Division, became dean and administrative head of the new graduate entity in 1921.

The graduate program was an offspring of Commerce, and was nurtured by its mother. It operated in the same facilities, with the same faculty and administration. As might be expected, it was a cultural offspring too, sharing the overall educational philosophy of the parent. However, almost immediately following its creation as a legally separate entity in 1921, when the so-called division became an "independent" school in New York University, new and different priorities and "cultural" directions became evident. Thus, while GBA was a minnow compared to the Commerce whale for many years following its founding, eventually it was weaned and emerged as a truly independent force. Today it is the inescapable truth that the overall reputation and academic status of the Stern School's undergraduate programs rest to a considerable extent on the standing and prestige of the graduate operation. Not completely by any means. Poor quality and repute at the undergraduate level would significantly compromise the entity. Put differently, quality is indivisible and must be maintained in all parts of an institution.

The dependence of GBA on Commerce at its inception and for years after emerges with crystal-like clarity from a reading of Chancellor Elmer Brown's *Annual Report* for 1919–1920, as well as from Dean Taylor's annual reports in later years. Chancellor Brown's report tells at length about the conceptual and philosophical foundation which undergirded the decision to establish GBA as a separate and distinct entity in N Y U. Noting that the university's acquisition of the old Trinity Church School building at 90 Trinity Place facilitated the action taken, the Chancellor commented that: "The step was taken on the recommendation of Dean Joseph French Johnson, of our School of Commerce, Accounts, and Finance."[1] The context is amplified in the same report by Dean Johnson's observations that, while there was some increase in enrollments at the Graduate *Division* of Business Administration between 1919 and 1920 (from 49 to 91), *"there was no evidence that the division was appealing to the best type of eligible student,* and it is probably well that the history of that division is closed in favor of our new Graduate School of Business Administration" (italics added).[2]

Chancellor Brown's perception of purpose in establishing GBA is remarkable in its prescience. He envisaged the new entity as a component in N Y U's objective of attacking "with unfailing initiative the whole problem of higher education for commercial pursuits, in this capital of the commercial world."[3] The Chancellor foresaw: (1) *an undergraduate college,* "for the training of men and women who will, for the most part, go directly from their high school graduation to enter upon a three year or a four year course of standard commercial studies of college grade"; (2) *a graduate school* for "graduates of regular American Colleges, who purpose entering upon a business career"; (3) *executive programs,* that is, "conferences made up of small groups of men, themselves the active heads of large concerns, who are obliged to avail themselves of the wisdom of specialists of the highest grade in new subjects which are assuming practical importance"; (4) *research programs and facilities;* (5) *cooperative educational arrangements* between the business school and major corporate educational programs (Brown mentions National City Bank, Guaranty Trust Company, W. R. Grace and Company, etc.); (6) provision of *evening and part-time courses;* and (7) a specialized *library* of commerce and industry. The concept is full-blown, and grand in its reach and scope. Thus, GBA was begun as "a fully organized school for graduates of standard American Colleges, having a two year course leading to the degree of Master of Business Administration." And Chancellor Brown added, *"From the outset, emphasis will be laid upon organized research"* (italics added).

Many years would pass before the grandness of the scheme would be realized. One reason was probably that sufficient private endowment and other financial support did not come from business groups and organizations. In this respect the Chancellor's explicitly stated hope and expectation was frustrated. His words were: "The full development of this undertaking in all of its parts, in a manner appropriate to the prestige and the practical requirements of this city, will require large expenditures in the years immediately before us. I cannot think the University that is rendering such service is to be left so largely as it has been left in the past to struggle on without material encouragement, in the richest commercial center the world has ever known."[4] But it was left to struggle! That the struggle was ultimately successful is a testimonial to the conviction and persistence of the faculty and administration of Commerce and GBA. It is a reflection also of the enormous demand for undergraduate and graduate business education which the schools served, and which provided huge tuition revenues that sustained the university and enabled the survival of the schools themselves (although their qualitative transition to today's peak had to wait on a redirection of internal university resources, coupled finally with the external support of which Chancellor Brown spoke).

The chronic inadequacy of funding which bedeviled Commerce and GBA is revealed again in Dean Taylor's annual report for 1936–1937, fifteen years after the founding of GBA. The dean wrote:

> In the interest of the larger social good, even more than to the school, it would seem that the time had come to press the responsible leaders in business to provide more adequate financial support in order to realize in larger measure the opportunities for service which are presented to the school and the University. . . . No school offering graduate instruction in the broad field of economics and business started under less favorable conditions financially. Other efforts of similar nature have had from the beginning ample private or public support. *The Graduate School of Business Administration from the time it was organized has been, with some help from the School of Commerce, self-sustaining.* That this has been possible was due largely to the enthusiasm, devotion, and physical energy of the faculty. (Italics added)[5]

A contemporary statement by Dean John T. Madden of Commerce indicates that Dean Taylor's comment about GBA's being self-sustaining, albeit with some help from Commerce, overstates its financial independence. Thus, Dean Madden said:

> The University at no time has received from Wall Street firms any financial aid in this work [that is, support for GBA]. It has been supported entirely from student fees. At first, the losses of operation were paid out of the educational surplus of the School of Commerce at Washington Square. Today, the Wall Street Division is practically self-supporting on a computed cost basis, *if we leave out of consideration the fact that the main load for instructors' salaries is borne by the School of Commerce at Washington Square.* That is to say, that if instructors of the present high calibre had to be employed solely for the work in Wall Street, the educational income would not meet the total cost. (Italics added)[6]

An interesting side note is the fact that the N Y U Treasurer's Report for 1927–1928 didn't even list GBA as a separate unit of the university, including its financial data in that for Commerce.

The close cooperation which characterized the Commerce-GBA relationship, and which sustained the latter as it slowly developed and generated independent strength, was not without problems.

Important differences of educational purpose and priority emerged, and with them went problems of divided loyalty and preferences among the faculty. It is no surprise therefore to read in Dean Taylor's 1936–1937 report that: "I have mentioned in previous reports the problems of a joint faculty with the School of Commerce and the added responsibilities arising out of membership in both faculties, and also the heavy teaching load required of those giving graduate instruction."[7] Dual citizenship could not forever continue to mask emergent and growing divisions of preference and educational priority.

I think it appropriate to interject a difference of opinion with one expressed by Robert E. Gleeson, Steven Schlossman, and David Grayson Allen in their article "Uncertain Ventures: The Origins of Graduate Management Education at Harvard and Stanford, 1908–1939."[8] Discussing the origins of collegiate business education, the authors point out that two mutually supportive environmental factors were important: first, willing students; and second, "recent changes in the scope and organization of business." I find no fault with those points, and found them richly supported by experience at N Y U. But I take exception to their sweeping assertion that "the principal impetus for university based business education came from inside the academy." This notion, while it is attractive and has some credibility at the graduate school level, especially at Harvard, is not supported by the evidence and experience across the American higher educational scene, especially at the undergraduate level. Of course there were individuals in the academy who were supportive and made possible the establishment of B-schools. But there was also a large and skeptical body of opinion of a contrary kind, especially in the traditional Arts and Sciences faculties. And they had support outside the academy as well. At least the NYU experience supports that view.

Even experience at Harvard supports that view, for the B-school there was a failure under the guidance of its original academic founders (President Charles W. Eliot, Professor A. Lawrence Lowell, Professor Frank Taussig, and Professor Edwin Gay). Professor Gay became the first dean, and the School was on the verge of extinction when he took a leave of absence in December 1917. Thus Gleeson, Schlossman, and Allen observe: "Dean Gay's effort to legitimate business education at the graduate level was not a success. He clearly failed to satisfy his two principal audiences (beyond his academic colleagues): students and businessmen."[9] The eventual success of the Harvard B-school was achieved by its second dean, Wallace Donham, who came into office in 1919 after a two-year interregnum under Acting Dean Lincoln Schaub. Donham had no experience as an educator. He was a lawyer, a successful banker, and he had been the court-appointed receiver of the financially troubled Bay State Railway Company. But he had strong convictions about professional education for business. As a man of practical experience and pragmatic inclination, he sought a realistic and relevant program of study. To that end, he hit on the case study method, which became the hallmark of Harvard and the key to its future success.

Cultural Shifts

We turn back to NYU and GBA. For decades GBA shared most of the major cultural characteristics of the School of Commerce. It was an evening school, devoted to mature students who worked full-time, practical in its orientation, a school of opportunity, and congenial to large-scale admission of students and the swollen enrollments which resulted. But two profoundly contrary tendencies became manifest: an emphasis on *research activity* and, as an understandable handmaiden, an ongoing interest in the introduction and development of a *doctoral degree program*. Both tendencies emerged at the first two meetings of the newly established GBA faculty. At the first meeting, on November 9, 1920, almost the entire time of the assembled faculty was devoted to discussion of the thesis required for the MBA degree. It is most revealing that the standard of quality expected of the thesis was that it be *publishable*. That standard is the one traditionally associated with the PhD degree, not the master's. But it was the one to which the GBA faculty was drawn. The lack of realism inherent in the expectation quickly became apparent, for at the faculty meeting on November 21, 1921, the faculty agreed "that our present standard of a publishable thesis was higher than could be realized on account of the relatively small training and short time of the graduate student."

The underlying predilection for publishable research being frustrated at the MBA level, the faculty "went on record as authorizing steps to be taken towards the granting of the Ph.D. degree in the Graduate School of Business Administration; first, in the arrangement of a schedule of courses and requirements; and second, petitioning the University for permission to grant such a degree." But first the MBA program had to be worked out, an exercise brought to rapid completion. Thus, Professor de Haas wrote to Dean Taylor on January 16, 1922, and reported that the faculty committee considering the matter agreed that the plan for the MBA degree should comprise: (1) four core survey courses; (2) three other basic courses in Statistics, English Law, and Cycles; (3) four additional courses, one of which had to be a seminar; (4) solution to a problem put to the students by Dean Taylor at the beginning of the first semester of their graduate work; (5) a "carefully prepared report upon a subject to be approved by a 'Report Committee' "; and (6) a formal oral examination of at least one hour by a minimum of three professors on the "entire field of business administration." Given the extensiveness of the last requirement, the student could submit a list of at least 12 topics upon which he felt prepared to be examined, but the topics were subject to the approval of a faculty committee. Also, reports were required in the seminar course, as well as in the courses in Statistics and Cycles, and examinations were required at the end of each semester in each course.

But the School's 1921–1922 bulletin did not conform exactly to the recommendations of the faculty committee.[10] The only requirements specified by the bulletin were: (1) a minimum of one full year of study at GBA; (2) satisfactory completion of approved courses equivalent to

48 points (12 full courses of 60 hours, or four points each (up to one-half of which might be transferred from acceptable outside institutions); (3) *a thesis* reflecting original and independent study of some important problem in a field of business in which the student is interested (subject to the approval of a faculty committee); and (4) employment during the summer vacation months in some business of interest to the student. However, the bulletin for 1923–1924 conformed more closely in its description of the MBA requirements with those recommended by the faculty committee. *In particular, the thesis requirement was withdrawn in favor of a report.*[11] Later, the report requirement was apparently watered down in favor of an oral examination, in concept not unlike the oral examinations associated with the PhD degree.

The MBA program was substantial and required a significant amount of writing. Plainly, despite its drawing back from the original requirement of a *publishable* thesis, the faculty continued to show its interest in some form of research activity that resulted in a written product. The faculty minutes reveal how seriously this aspect of the program was taken, for detailed reviews of *unsuccessful* theses were placed in the minutes, along with brief statements about successful ones.

Having got the MBA settled, the faculty turned to the doctoral degree. The faculty minutes contain rather extensive committee reports summarizing the arguments for and against the award of a doctorate. Essentially, five arguments were put forward in favor: (1) student demand; (2) business demand; (3) demand for business educators (teachers of business in colleges and universities); (4) "granting of the Doctor's degree would tend to establish *the reputation of the Graduate School* on a higher plane than would be true if they grant only the Master's degree" (italics added); and (5) enhancement and advancement of NYU's "duty" to do *research in the field of commercial education.* Of more than passing interest is the consideration given to status. Even then, the academic pecking order was a factor to be considered. On the negative side of the case were these considerations: (1) practical businessmen looked with distrust on holders of doctorates, presumably as too theoretical; (2) GBA lacked the "equipment" to do successful doctoral work; (3) the effort given to a doctoral degree program would depreciate the MBA degree; and (4) the PhD degree was not as appropriate as a technical degree would be.

No surprise should be aroused by the outcome of the deliberations; namely, a doctoral program and degree should be approved, and it should be the Doctor of Commercial Science rather than the PhD. To that end, the above objections were overcome by: (1) offering a practical applied doctorate (the DCS rather than the PhD); (2) examining the faculty resources, course offerings, and research capability available at GBA and concluding that they were ample in the fields of Finance, Management, and Marketing; and (3) modifying the MBA degree to reduce its extensiveness. In the third connection, it was recognized that the MBA degree requires of all candidates two years of graduate work and yet is to all intents and purposes a Master's degree. It was believed that recognition of work done in Commerce in undergraduate work should be taken and that students who have completed a certain amount of commerce work as undergraduates should be allowed to finish the MBA in one year. This practice would conform to the usual Master's degree practice. With such action, the Doctor's degree would normally cap the Master's degree with two years of additional work.[12] This was certainly a prescient comment, for the Master's arrangement anticipated N Y U's five-year combined BS-MBA program by half a century, although the present program contains more rigorous conditions.

The decision in favor of the DCS degree over the PhD was not based entirely on the considerations put forward. A considerable factor appears to have been the attitudes in the Graduate Faculty of Arts and Sciences, which had final jurisdiction and control of the PhD degree. Thus, the GBA faculty committee report states: "the Graduate School [of Arts and Sciences] has cooperated so far as possible, [but] the work required for the Doctor of Philosophy degree is sufficiently different from that of the Graduate School of Business Administration to make it difficult and impracticable in many cases for advanced students working in applied economics to meet the requirements of the Doctor of Philosophy degree. *Moreover the difficulty of the Graduate School accepting credits from the Graduate School of Business Administration over which they have no control*" (italics added). The committee went on to add that it preferred the PhD degree, but, as we have seen, they settled on the DCS.

An additional and fascinating insight into the deliberations attendant to the decision on the doctoral degree is afforded by a reading of the annual bulletins of the newly established GBA. Thus, while its first bulletin, for the 1921–1922 year, describes only the MBA degree and its requirements, the second bulletin, for 1922–1923, describes the availability of the Doctor of Philosophy degree, adding that the degree is given in the Graduate School of Arts and Sciences with work done for the MBA degree counting toward the course requirements for the PhD.[13] In the following year's bulletin, for 1923–1924, the availability of the PhD degree was repeated as was the way MBA course work could count toward partial fulfillment of the requirements.[14] *But in the 1924–1925 bulletin, minus any explanation, all reference to the PhD is dropped and the requirements for the DCS degree are described.* Imagine the disappointment and consternation which must have existed! The desire for the PhD and the confidence that it would be approved were so high that its availability was published in two successive bulletins; then it was abruptly dropped for reasons hinted at in the faculty minutes cited above.

The Council of N Y U approved the DCS degree at GBA in 1923, and its action was appended to the faculty minutes of the meeting of April 20, 1923. The purposes of the degree were to: (1) prepare teachers of commercial subjects; (2) train researchers; and (3) develop executives. The Council specified these conditions for granting the degree: (1) a minimum of three years of graduate work, comprising five courses or their equivalent per year (for full-time students); (2) a minimum of one year during which the major portion of the student's time was devoted to study (for students employed in business); (3) dean and faculty approval of a plan of study immediately following matriculation; (4) student selection of a major department after one year of study, choice of a thesis subject in the department and taking at least four advanced courses in the department; (5) knowledge of the techniques of business research (gained through possible work for at least one year in the School's Bureau of Business Research); (6) a basic course in Economic Theory, Economic History, and Statistics; (7) at least one advanced course in Accounting, Banking, Corporation Finance, Transportation, Foreign Trade, Management, and Marketing; (8) passing a preliminary examination at the end of the first year following matriculation, consisting of a written part in Economic Theory, Economic History, and Statistics, and an oral part covering the general field of business; (9) a thesis demonstrating research and analytical ability; (10) competence in written English expression and command of one modern foreign language (the language requirement to be satisfied prior to matriculation); (11) at least two semesters in residence and 20 points of course work at GBA; and (12) a written final examination covering courses taken in the field of the thesis, plus an oral examination on the thesis and courses taken in other fields.

The first two DCS degrees were awarded by GBA at Commencement in 1928, and the last one at Commencement in 1948. During the 20-year period a total of 45 DCS degrees were awarded.[15] But in 1938 GBA awarded its first PhD degree, finally turning to the doctorate it had so clearly preferred from the beginning. In so doing it had the approval of the university. The PhD degree had finally triumphed as *the* graduate research degree in professional as well as Arts and Sciences faculties. N Y U's old Doctor of Pedagogy degree also died after a short life, being succeeded by the PhD and EdD (Doctor of Education). But in the academic pecking order the EdD does not have the cachet of the PhD. Even Harvard's DBA (Doctor of Business Administration) degree was questioned some years ago by Derek Bok, Harvard's then president. Bok questioned also the Harvard B-school's extensive reliance on the case method, as against some other and more traditional graduate modes of instruction. The resultant outcry from alumni and others seemed to still that controversy. Yet, the July 19, 1993 issue of *Business Week*[16] contained a prominent article and cover on the question: "Harvard B-School: Is It Outmoded?"

Another aspect to GBA's introduction of the doctoral degree program must not be overlooked because it reveals so clearly the expensive arrangements which commonly accompany the doctoral program. (Perhaps I should not be reticent, and should say bluntly *always* accompany the doctoral program.) I refer to the matter of faculty teaching loads. Three major points were involved: first, only full professors would be involved in the doctoral program; secondly, they "would be required to do less undergraduate teaching in order that they may devote more time to advanced work"; and third, "the work of these faculty members should be adjusted so as to enable them to give the time required to direct graduate students." These points were made in the reports of the Committee on the Doctoral Degree which were appended to the faculty minutes of January 16, 1923. The next report of the Committee, appended to the minutes of the faculty meeting of April 20, 1923, added: "The teaching load of certain professors should be lightened so as to enable them to give the time necessary to direct the work of graduate students. *For such professors the maximum should be eight hours*" (italics added). That limit represented a one-third reduction in the standard 12 hour teaching load, and, as stated, the policy allowed for larger reductions.

Please do not misconstrue my remarks. I am a product of the Arts and Sciences, a holder of a PhD, and a person devoted to the importance of research and scholarly productivity. I recognize the appropriateness of a reduction in teaching load and number of courses for faculty involved in research and graduate teaching. I accept and support the appropriateness of some number of *research professors,* people of outstanding scholarly reputation and ability, having minimal or even no formal teaching assignments to courses as such. But I question the sweep and commonness with which major and not so major American universities have adopted broadly applied contact hour teaching load schedules of six or fewer hours per week. I question also the readiness of faculty to shy away from undergraduate teaching, a readiness apparent at the inception of GBA's doctoral program.

The awarding of the PhD degree by GBA was finally authorized and then published in the School's bulletin for 1937–1938.[17] By then all candidates for the PhD degree were under the supervision of the *Graduate Commission of the University,* a body no longer exclusively controlled by the Graduate Faculty of Arts and Sciences. Significantly, the bulletin's description of the requirements for awarding the PhD degree differed most importantly from that relating to the DCS in the language used to describe the PhD dissertation as against the DCS thesis. The most important stated differences were: (1) in the PhD at least half the students undergraduate work had to be in *academic* subjects; and (2) at least two years had to be spent in residence at N Y U. In the case of the DCS, the undergraduate requirement did not include the reference to academic subjects, and the residence requirement was two terms of residence and a minimum of 20 points of work at GBA. The most important substantive difference probably resided in perceptions that the quality of the PhD dissertation was superior to that required in the DCS.

The interest in and emphasis on research activity which characterized GBA from its inception was reflected by its taking over the Bureau of Business Research at the Wall Street Division of the School of Commerce.[18] The bureau was under the supervision of Professor Lewis H. Haney, its director, and a well-known neoclassical economist and free market advocate. The stated purpose of the bureau was to make available to businessmen and public officials "trained minds of professors and graduate students of economics to the end that economic principles may be applied in the solution of practical industrial problems." The GBA bulletin emphasized that the work of the bureau would be done principally by graduate students and expert accountants and statisticians, under the direction of Professor Haney. The bulletin added that the research work would be done on a nonprofit basis, reflecting only the costs associated with the research.

Before leaving our review of graduate degrees, we must return to the Master of Commercial Science (MCS) degree. That degree, originally created by the undergraduate School of Commerce and published in its bulletin for 1906–1907, was transferred to GBA's control in 1929–1930. The MCS was no longer available at Commerce after October 1931.[19] As described in the GBA bulletin of 1929–1930 it did not appear substantively less rigorous than the MBA, yet it was discontinued in 1931.

Conflict between Ambition and Reality

Even a cursory examination of the record reveals that the ambition of the GBA faculty initially outran reality. We see this in connection with the desire to award the PhD, and the original expectations associated with the MBA. In both cases the faculty had to draw back. In place of the PhD, the DCS was adopted. And reports and an oral examination took the place of a publishable thesis in the MBA.

There were other manifestations of the conflict between ambition and reality. In the doctoral program, the faculty decided that only full professors should offer instruction and guidance at that level, and that they should have reduced teaching loads and be free of undergraduate teaching. Yet, some graduate classes in the doctoral program were permitted to co-mingle undergraduate and graduate students. This interaction of academic and economic considerations is not and was not manifested only at GBA or NYU. This phenomenon existed elsewhere in higher education. What is amazing is that some people behave as though it was not so. Similarly, at the MBA level, the faculty decided that no faculty below the rank of assistant professor should be assigned teaching responsibilities. Yet, a significant number of faculty of higher rank did not themselves possess doctoral degrees. Ambition outreached reality also in the academic standards set for MBA oral examinations. Students were originally required to pass *all* four parts of the oral examination, that is, all of four subject areas. Too many students must have had difficulty, because the faculty voted that strong passes in three areas would be sufficient. In favor of this decision, it was argued that three strong passes out of four were superior as an index of intellectual ability to four weak passes.

And so pragmatism conditioned policy, an outcome which should occasion far less surprise that it sometimes seems to do.

Enrollments

Table 5.1, despite some discontinuities in the data, shows in broad outline some significant enrollment trends in the Graduate School of Business Administration. As to the discontinuities in the nature of the data, these points need to be made: (1) the figures for the years 1921–1922 through 1944–1945 represent *average enrollment* and are internally consistent; (2) the figures for the years 1945–1946 through 1952–1953 represent *cumulative enrollment* and are internally consistent; (3) the figures for the years 1953–1954 through 1959–1960 seem to be *Fall semester enrollments* but their internal consistency seems suspect, especially in the three-year period 1957–1958 through 1959–1960; and (4) the figures for the years 1960–1961 through the last year shown are for *Fall semester enrollments,* and are internally consistent. I believe that the total enrollment numbers are a fair representation of reality, except for the latter years in the decade of the fifties. Despite the noted shortcomings of the total enrollment numbers, I believe the percentages shown for evening and women students are accurate indicators of proportions.

What conclusions may be drawn from the data of Table 5.1? First, from its inception to the early sixties GBA was an evening school catering to part-time students. In this regard the character of the school and its culture was like that of its parent, the undergraduate School of Commerce. But it persisted in its dedicated and practically exclusive concentration on being an evening school long after Commerce had developed a large full-time day student program. That orientation changed significantly after the early sixties, when Dean Joseph Taggart introduced a day program. The change was facilitated by GBA's construction of two buildings to replace the ancient structure (the Trinity Church School building) which had been its quarters since 1921. The first of these buildings was Nichols Hall, opened in 1960, while Merrill Hall, opened in 1973, was the second. Construction of these two facilities emphasized GBA's commitment to the downtown Manhattan location, and reflected a kind of umbilical connection to an area long associated with the nation's and the city's financial center. It reflected also GBA's established strength and reputation as a center for educating

TABLE 5.1

GBA Registration, by Academic Year, 1921–1922 to 1992–1993 Total and Percent Evening and Percent Women

Year	# Students	% Evening	% Women	Year	# Students	% Evening	% Women	Year	# Students	% Evening	% Women
1921–22	181	100.0	3.3	1945–46	2,273	99.4	17.7	1969–70	3,184	84.9	8.8
1922–23	178	100.0	1.7	1946–47	2,748	99.7	8.6	1970–71	3,415	83.0	9.8
1923–24	192	100.0	4.7	1947–48	3,176	100.0	7.9	1971–72	3,306	82.3	11.6
1924–25	212	100.0	5.2	1948–49	3,502	99.3	6.5	1972–73	3,358	82.2	13.6
1925–26	347	100.0	5.5	1949–50	3,891	98.7	5.7	1973–74	3,524	84.5	17.7
1926–27	345	100.0	6.4	1950–51	4,386	100.0	4.0	1974–75	3,520	83.5	22.5
1927–28	396	100.0	4.5	1951–52	4,644	100.0	5.0	1975–76	3,773	82.3	28.0
1928–29	564	100.0	7.8	1952–53	4,783	100.0	5.5	1976–77	4,147	77.7	31.9
1929–30	773	100.0	8.7	1953–54	4,692	na	5.1	1977–78	4,217	75.9	41.5
1930–31	678	91.2	8.0	1954–55	4,992	na	5.1	1978–79	4,100	77.4	40.1
1931–32	743	96.8	6.2	1955–56	5,206	na	5.5	1979–80	4,115	82.3	43.5
1932–33	915	97.1	9.3	1956–57	5,392	na	5.8	1980–81	4,045	78.8	43.4
1933–34	731	96.3	7.3	1957–58	5,973	na	5.2	1981–82	4,414	71.4	44.2
1934–35	863	96.3	7.5	1958–59	6,370	na	3.9	1982–83	4,336	76.2	43.8
1935–36	1,043	98.3	7.9	1959–60	6,596	na	4.4	1983–84	4,323	75.8	42.8
1936–37	1,194	98.4	8.0	1960–61	5,176	100.0	4.1	1984–85	4,199	77.4	41.6
1937–38	1,396	98.5	8.5	1961–62	4,795	na	4.9	1985–86	4,084	72.3	41.1
1938–39	1,308	98.1	7.8	1962–63	4,507	na	4.8	1986–87	3,927	69.7	40.2
1939–40	1,318	99.1	8.0	1963–64	4,173	na	5.4	1987–88	3,889	69.0	40.3
1940–41	1,196	99.3	8.7	1964–65	4,121	95.5	5.8	1988–89	3,609	65.8	38.2
1941–42	1,001	99.6	10.4	1965–66	4,199	93.8	5.9	1989–90	3,799	64.5	37.2
1942–43	656	99.4	22.6	1966–67	3,871	na	6.7	1990–91	3,885	64.9	35.0
1943–44	707	99.6	23.9	1967–68	3,904	85.9	6.6	1991–92	3,885	64.0	34.5
1944–45	1,012	99.2	25.8	1968–69	3,267	85.7	8.1	1992–93	3,925	67.0	34.0

SOURCES: NYU, Annual Reports of the Registrar, and Stern School's Registration Records.

future financial leaders. But, as electronic technology advanced and the dominance of lower Manhattan as a financial center diminished, GBA's location was open to reexamination. We will return to this matter later.

Second, GBA did not achieve enrollment levels like those at Commerce until the late fifties, when each school had an aggregate enrollment of some 5,000 students. However, since about one-half the Commerce enrollments were day students, who registered for more points of instruction per semester than evening students, Commerce continued as a larger producer of tuition revenues. Of course this situation changed by the early sixties, when Commerce enrollments collapsed. Since then, GBA enrollments have fluctuated between some 3,200 and 4,400, with a decline between 1960–1961 and 1969–1970, a subsequent build-up between 1969–1970 and 1981–1982, and finally, a contraction in the late eighties and early nineties.

Third, the enrollment growth between 1969–1970 and 1981–1982 appears to be explained mainly by an upsurge in the enrollment of women. That phenomenon parallels a similar one at the undergraduate level. The enrollment declines in the late eighties and early nineties appear to reflect a shift in the attractiveness of business careers to women. We observed this possibility before, when discussing the undergraduate data. The GBA numbers appear to confirm the points. This writer's impression is that the time and attention demands of business careers are being perceived as too burdensome by women who desire motherhood and nurturing children. Also, the financial attractiveness and time flexibility of more traditional careers for women, like teaching and nursing, appear to have become more attractive. In short, our data probably reflect the tip of a deeply submerged psychological and cultural iceberg.

Finally, Table 5.1 reveals the persistent growth in GBA's day programs of study; or, from the reverse side of the coin, the proportional decline in the evening character of the school. Thus, in the early nineties the School is roughly one-third day and two-thirds evening. Continuation of this trend may be expected, for the shift in GBA's geographical location from downtown Manhattan to the new Management Education Center at Washington Square added university facilities (residence halls, Student Center, Bobst Library, Coles Recreation Center, etc.) which enhance the physical attractiveness of the graduate business school to full-time day students.

TABLE 5.2

PhD Candidates Enrolled and Degrees Conferred by Year, 1937–1938 to 1992–1993

Year	Number* Enrolled	Number Degrees Conferred	Year	Number* Enrolled	Number Degrees Conferred
1937–38		1	1965–66	457	31
1938–39		1	1966–67		25
1939–40		0	1967–68		18
1940–41	96	2	1968–69		20
1941–42		5	1969–70		21
1942–43		2	1970–71	297	28
1943–44		3	1971–72		31
1944–45		1	1972–73		42
1945–46	86	1	1973–74		36
1946–47		5	1974–75		30
1947–48		2	1975–76	201	27
1948–49		9	1976–77		19
1949–50		5	1977–78		16
1950–51	na	6	1978–79		14
1951–52		11	1979–80		16
1952–53		8	1980–81	154	15
1953–54		6	1981–82		14
1954–55		17	1982–83		15
1955–56	512	20	1983–84		17
1956–57		12	1984–85		13
1957–58		21	1985–86	122	22
1958–59		21	1986–87	122	23
1959–60		5	1987–88	116	30
1960–61	687	18	1988–89	90	27
1961–62		14	1989–90	88	20
1962–63		21	1990–91		15
1963–64		20	1991–92	80	21
1964–65		16	1992–93	158**	27

SOURCE: NYU, Annual Reports of the Registrar.
  * Selected years
  ** Stern School Graduate Division data
  na Not available

The PhD Program

The demise of the Doctor of Commercial Science degree coincided with the conferring of the first PhD degree in 1938. The latter degree had been authorized for GBA ten years before, and by 1940–1941 96 students were enrolled. Table 5.2 presents the statistical record of the program, for degrees conferred and students enrolled. The data for enrollments are shown for five-year intervals, while those for degrees conferred are shown annually. Several observations seem relevant: (1) the number of students enrolled reach a remarkable peak of 687 in 1960–1961, a very large figure for a doctoral program; (2) since 1960–1961 the number of students enrolled has declined sharply and steadily to a current level of some 150; (3) in marked contrast to the large number of students enrolled, a modest number of PhD degrees were conferred annually; and (4) the number of PhD degrees conferred annually ranged between 30 and 42 only in the period 1965–1966 through 1974–1975, being less since then.

The huge disconformity between the number of students enrolled and the number of degrees conferred until 1970–1971 requires explanation. Essentially, the explanation is that the students were permitted to enrol without much difficulty, and then allowed to maintain their status as PhD matriculates by paying a modest annual fee of some $10 until 1975–1976, when the fee was raised to $100 per year and a maximum period for staying in that status was set at three years. As the data indicate, significant tightening began earlier, and especially so after Professor Ernest Kurnow took over as director of the PhD program in 1976. A central factor in the transformation was a drastic contraction in the number of evening students who matriculated in the PhD program, with the dream of obtaining the degree on a part-time basis. Fueled by hope, they maintained their enrollment status by paying the annual fee, continuing that way year after year so long as their dream did not dim and fade away. That dream proved to be persistent. But in the decade of the sixties and especially after 1970, steps were taken to compel enrollees either to complete the degree requirements or face the reality of dropping out.

Dean William Dill's recollections of the transformation of the PhD program are relevant and pointed.[20] Dean Dill recalls his conclusions about the program when he arrived at GBA in mid-1970. They were, principally: (1) the doctoral program was, at the time, the weakest link in GBA's academic chain; (2) too many doctoral candidates were carried "on the books," without really measuring up in qualitative terms; and (3) the actual numbers of eligible doctoral candidates greatly exceeded the numbers shown in Table 5.2, possibly aggregating as many as 1,200, if one included all those not enrolled in a particular semester but eligible to return and attempt completion of the degree.

Dean Dill, with Professor Ingo Walter, whom he had appointed as an associate dean, and a representative faculty committee, planned the changes needed in the doctoral program: higher admissions standards; time limits for completion; greater faculty monitoring of candidates; full-time attendance by some (but not all) candidates; and measures to clear the pipeline of candidates who were unlikely to complete the program, but in ways fair to them. Professor Ernest Kurnow was chosen as the doctoral program director, to carry out the changes. He was a felicitous choice; for, as Dean Dill comments: "he knew how to bring the old guard along with him." He knew also the human sensitivities of the candidates. On both counts, Professor Kurnow proved particularly effective as an agent of change.

An important governance lesson is involved in the transformation of the PhD program from one swollen with part-time students to one peopled overwhelmingly by full-time candidates. Part of the transformation was effected through *changes in regulations:* (1) an increase in the annual fee for maintenance of matriculation; (2) establishment of a limited number of years between entry into the program and completion of the degree requirements; and (3) establishment of check points along the way when certain requirements had to be satisfied in order to continue.

Professor Ernest Kurnow, during the seventies, applied *an additional set of actions* which proved effective, and which did not spread an odor of heavy-handed autocratic and bureaucratic authority. These actions included, successively: (1) an initial letter sent to all students enrolled in the PhD program asking whether they were still interested in continuing and informing them that if an affirmative reply was not received by a specified date, they would be automatically dropped; (2) a follow-up letter to those indicating no interest in continuing and to nonrespondents informing them that they were officially dropped; (3) for those students remaining in the program and having passed the orals (and with no official limit on the time they could remain in the program) a letter from the faculty advisor on their research progress on the dissertation, followed by semester-by-semester interviews and discussions of progress (serious candidates were pressed to complete, while others dropped out); and (4) students who had not completed the orals had a six-year time limit within which they had to complete the program, with a semester by semester follow-up of student progress.

The result of the changes in regulations, the letters enabling a graceful and voluntary withdrawal, and careful monitoring and follow-up of student progress was the development of today's essentially full-time PhD program comprising about 150 candidates and 15–30 degree conferments per year. The ill-fitting mantle of a PhD diploma mill has been cut off. In its place raiment of prestigious quality has been donned.

The quality story entails more than so far set down. Professor Kurnow tells of the steps taken to build today's full-time quality program. Most significant are probably these actions: (1) an increase in the number of paid graduate assistants and in their compensation; (2) an upgrading in the substantive rigor of the program (shifting to a major/minor combination in place of two fields of major concentration); (3) an overall strengthening in faculty quality; and (4) more intensive and extensive efforts by individual faculty and the school to do a better job of placing PhD graduates in both academic and nonacademic jobs, especially the former. Successful professional placement builds the school's reputation. Probably of equal importance was reaching out by Professor Kurnow to the directors of other prestigious doctoral programs in business. Thus, annual meetings of the directors of the top 20 doctoral programs in the country were arranged, with N Y U acting as occasional host. These meetings allowed N Y U to publicize the changes made in its PhD program, and to expose our doctoral students to the directors of other top programs. Since quality had become our handmaiden, such exposure was beneficial and yielded important positive results.

Table 5.3 shows the field of concentration of PhD candidates, classified according to dissertation topic, for the periods 1938–1959 and 1960–1985.

Table 5.3 reveals the *real* growth in the PhD program since 1960. It also shows the continuing importance of Finance, Management, and Economics. But the emerging importance of the other functional areas in generating doctoral research and achieving greater balance in the *overall* quality of the school's faculty demands recognition. Including recent growth in CAIS, the doctoral output of the departments is substantial, and contributes to the school's present reputation.

Professor Kurnow observed an additional phenomenon as worthy of note; that is, as the PhD program became predominantly full-time, the proportion of foreign-born students rose from approximately one-fifth to about one-half of the total enrollment. This relationship is not a cause-and-effect one, but rather a concurrence of disparate trends. Also, it is not peculiar to N Y U, but is observed as well in the doctoral programs of other prestigious B-schools. In the absence of any conclusive evidence to explain it, one is compelled to fall back on sophisticated speculation. Having confessed that small foundation for my opinion, I speculate that in the seventies and eighties American-born students perceived more remunerative and rewarding careers in business, coupled with possession of an MBA degree, than they did in academic careers,

TABLE 5.3
PhD Fields of Concentration, Classified by Dissertation
1938–1959 and 1960–1985

Field of Concentration	1938–1959	1960–1985
Accounting	6	59
Computer Applications and Information Systems	0	5
Economics	33	98
Finance	56	123
International Business	0	46
Management	17	106
Marketing	40	46
Statistics	7	69
Total	159	552

SOURCE: Professor E. Kurnow's records.

coupled with a PhD degree. Alternatively, careers in law and medicine appeared more attractive. Put differently, the nonmaterial qualities of an academic career suffered in the face of the material differences between academic and other careers. But the comparison was not like that for foreign-born students, who assumed greater importance in doctoral enrollments in B-schools (in particular, Asian-born students). It appears likely that their perception of the relative attractiveness of academic and nonacademic careers was quite different from that of American-born students. Perhaps also their perception of ethnic barriers, in business as against the Academy, whether real or not, may have influenced their actions. One result is a gradual growth in the absolute and relative presence of Asians in the faculties of American B-schools.

A look at data from 1993 completes the picture of the Stern School's doctoral program. It comprised 158 students, of whom 73 percent were full-time and 27 percent part-time. Forty-eight percent were foreign and 52 percent domestic, with 78 percent male and 22 percent female. Finance continued to be the most popular field of specialization (26 percent), followed by Information Systems (14 percent), Accounting (12 percent), Management and Statistics/Operations Research tied (11 percent each), Economics and International Business also tied (9 percent each), and Marketing slightly behind (8 percent). The cumulative grade point average of the enrolled doctoral candidates was 3.66, with the international students doing slightly better at 3.685. The average age was 32. All candidates received some form of financial aid. Thus, of the 158 total, 72 were research assistants, 72 more held NYU fellowships, and 6 had scholarships. Of the foreign students some 40 percent were from India, with Korea, China, and Taiwan representing approximately 28 percent more. Europe was the origin of some 10 percent, with the rest scattered among other Asian, Middle Eastern, and South American countries. Canada was the source of about 4 percent. Finally, in the period from January 1, 1988, through May 1993, there were 127 graduates of the doctoral program, and 79 percent of them went into university and college faculty positions.

Other Graduate Degree and Certificate Programs

Table 5.4 shows the inception and subsequent development of various master's degree programs and the Advanced Professional Certificate Program (APC) in selected years since 1935–1936.

These observations are worthy of note: (1) the MBA program is overwhelmingly dominant; (2) the MBA is large, with enrollments ranging roughly between 2,800 and 3,700 in the near 40-year period since 1955–1956, but it has had a relatively stable enrollment level of some 3,500 since 1980–1981; (3) the executive MBA program, which was initiated in 1982–1983 with a minuscule enrollment of 19 participating students, has developed strongly with a current enrollment of 170; (4) the one-year Master of Science programs (in Accounting, Mathematics/Statistics and Operations Research), begun in 1972–1973, started slowly, showed promise, faded, and then revived in the early nineties; and (5) the Advanced Professional Certificate Program showed significant strength after its beginning, also in 1972–1973, but slipped badly in enrollments after 1980–1981. We will revisit these programs in the next chapter, when we look at them in substantive terms. We should note that the School also has several joint MBA degree programs with other divisions of the university: (1) the Juris Doctor with the law school; and (2) the Master of Arts with the Graduate Arts and Sciences departments in French Studies, Journalism, and Politics.

The International Management Program

Among the educational initiatives undertaken by GBA in the early seventies was the International Management Program (IMP). An international student exchange program, it was begun in 1973 by GBA,

TABLE 5.4
GBA Enrollments, Master's and APC Programs, Selected Years, 1935–1936
to   1992–1993*

Year	MBA	Executive MBA[a]	MCS	Master of Science (MS)	Advanced professional Certificate (APC)
1935–36	1060	ne	63	ne	ne
1940–41	692	ne	29	ne	ne
1945–46	1030	ne	5	ne	ne
1950–51	na	ne	d	ne	ne
1955–56	3615	ne	d	ne	ne
1960–61	3741	ne	d	ne	ne
1965–66	2770	ne	d	ne	ne
1970–71	2855	ne	d	ne	ne
1972–73	na	ne	d	36	88
1973–74	na	ne	d	58	158
1975–76	3059	ne	d	101	260
1980–81	3549	ne	d	73	217
1982–83	na	19	d	na	na
1985–86	3490	79	d	98	154
1990–91	3547	170	d	72	73
1991–92	3601	na	d	118	65
1992–93	3638	170	d	126	59

SOURCE: NYU, Annual Reports of the Registrar and *Stern School Registration Records.*
   [a] These enrollments are included in the MBA data.
   d Discontinued program
   ne Nonexistent program
   na Not available

*Note that the School had numbers of *unclassified students* enrolled. They are not in the data of Table 5.4, but are included in the total enrollment figures shown in Table 5.1

L'Ecole des Hautes Etudes Commerciales (near Paris), and the London Business School. As originally conceived, students from each school would spend one semester at each of the other two schools, making two semesters of study abroad. The program has since grown considerably, now involving over 20 schools in 16 foreign countries. Programs similar to GBA's have spread among major American B-schools, but GBA's is among the earliest and most extensive. I shall discuss this program in detail in the next chapter, as well as such other programs as the Urban Business Assistance Corporation (UBAC) and the Management Game.

The Graduate School, 1960–1990: Three Transforming Decades

1960: The Turning Point

Two events at GBA marked the opening of the century's seventh decade, and both were of major importance to the School. The first was the beginning of Joseph H. Taggart's tenure as dean. Joe Taggart had been associate dean for several years, and succeeded George Rowland Collins as dean in 1959. But he was different from his two long-service predecessors, George Rowland Collins and Archibald Wellington Taylor. The latter had been dean of GBA from its inception in 1921 to 1946, while Collins, although dean only from 1946 to 1959, had served on the faculty and in administrative positions from the early days of the school. Both Taylor and Collins were "old school," steeped in the traditions and culture of Commerce and GBA. Neither had an earned doctorate. Taggart was out of another and academically more elite tradition. A 1924 Bachelor of Philosophy from Yale, Taggart had earned an MBA at Harvard in 1927, and a PhD at Columbia in 1938. He was not wedded to the tradition of evening part-time education, and had strong feelings that a full-time day program at the master's and doctoral levels would yield large academic benefits to GBA's quality. Similarly, his views with respect to the importance of the doctorate as an academic credential, and of research productivity as a leading criterion in promotion and tenure decisions, were not like those which characterized the earliest traditions of Commerce, and to a lesser degree of GBA.

The second major event was the dedication and opening of Nichols Hall in 1960. To appreciate the significance of this facility to the transformation of GBA, we must comprehend the conditions before its dedication. Probably no better description of those conditions can be found than this one penned in February 1937 by Commerce Dean John T. Madden:

> A visit to the Wall Street Building on any evening from 4:30 to 9 p.m. would reveal the paucity of facilities for the work accomplished. In fact, it may be said that if the students were not convinced of the value of the instruction which they receive there would be no other incentive to attend. The congestion is almost as bad as the subway at rush hours. Library and recreational facilities are primitive. Classrooms are overcrowded. Ventilation is miserable. Every conceivable disadvantage is present.[1]

Madden's description seems devastating. Yet it is inadequate to the full reality. The old Trinity Church School building, which served as GBA's home for the four decades between 1921 and 1960, regularly shook as the subway trains of the BMT (Brooklyn-Manhattan line) rumbled by on their tracks beneath Trinity Place. One block west, on Greenwich Street, the Seventh Avenue Interborough (IRT) subway line contributed its noise and vibration to the area's ambience. And prior to the IRT subway, Greenwich Street had been the location along which the old Ninth Avenue elevated railway line ran. When the elevated railway was dismantled after World War II, the IRT subway remained as a contributor to the panoply of static producing factors affecting GBA. The building itself was unprepossessing. Madden mentioned the poor ventilation among other deficiencies. Professor Emeritus Ernest Kurnow recalls his days as a faculty member at GBA. During the summer, windows were opened and large fans in the back of every classroom were needed to circulate air. Add the noise of those fans to the subways and street static, and some notion of the physical effort required of faculty to be heard, let alone understood, begins to come into focus. Professor Emeritus Michael Schiff recalls times, at the end of two-hour no-break summer class sessions, when students rising from their seats had paint from the chair backs sticking to their shirts.

Despite these adversities, a vital, productive, and important educational enterprise existed at 90 Trinity Place. Thousands of students attended, learned, earned degrees, and, subsequently, became leaders of American business, both financial and industrial. For example, in 1964–1965, students attending GBA were drawn from over 300 American colleges and universities, and some 70 foreign collegiate institutions.

Among the American institutions and apart from N Y U, these colleges and universities sent over 100 students each. City College of New York (236); Columbia University (259); Cornell University (117); Fordham University (165); Howard University (118); Manhattan College (104); University of Pennsylvania (177); Rutgers University (127); St. John's University (123); and Yale University (128).[2]

It would be a travesty of large proportions to ignore, in this description of conditions at GBA prior to 1960, the critically important fact that the faculty included people of unusual quality and prominence. Among them were such giants as Marcus Nadler, a financial guru whose words were avidly followed by the leaders of the investment and banking community; Jules Bogen, also a leading authority in the field of finance; Peter Drucker, whose seminal writings on management have been eagerly read by generations of industrial chief executives around the world; W. Edwards Deming, whose work in quality control played a large part in the postwar emergence of Japan as a major economic power; Lewis Haney, spoken about earlier and a widely known and respected economist; Ludwig Von Mises, an internationally famed economist of the Vienna School; Herman Kroos, an outstanding economic historian; Darrel Lucas and Arnold Corbin in Marketing; Solomon Fabricant, internationally known as an authority in national income analysis; and Arnold W. Johnson and Michael Schiff in Accounting. In 1976, W. Edwards Deming conducted a survey of GBA alumni, inquiring as to the faculty they remembered as having had a lasting impact on them. He noted that "although several hundred teachers have entered and departed the GBA during the past 30 years, . . . only a handful turned up in the responses for lasting impact. . . . The following names stand out with prominence," and he listed: Peter Drucker, Marcus Nadler, Herman Kroos, Jules Bogen, W. Edwards Deming, and Michael Schiff. Deming added this observation: "All the men in the above array were (and are, if living), heavily engaged in the practice of their professions. This fact may be an important indicator of the requirements in a professional school."[3]

That was the context at the opening of Nichols Hall. The fund-raising campaign to finance the building had been launched in 1954, was announced in the *New York Times* of November 7, 1954, and was headed by John M. Schiff of Kuhn, Loeb and Company. The naming gift of $800,000 in securities announced in the *New York Times* of October 1, 1957, was made by C. Walter Nichols, chairman of the board of the Nichols Engineering and Research Corporation. Originally estimated to cost $3.5 million, but finally costing slightly over $4.0 million, the naming gift represented 23 percent of the original cost and 20 percent of the final cost. According to a September 4, 1962 memorandum from Vice President Daniel Robinson to Dean Taggart, additional contributions covered the final cost of the structure. Among these contributions were those which resulted in the naming of the building's 500–seat Arthur K. Salomon auditorium and John Ben Snow Executive Dining Room. Nichols Hall is a ten-story structure, fully air-conditioned. It included modern classrooms, seminar rooms, a two-story library, a bookstore, and administrative offices. Nichols Hall radically changed the ambience and physical quality of the Graduate School of Business Administration.

One major consequence of the opening of Nichols Hall was that it facilitated Dean Taggart's initiative to introduce a full-time day student MBA program, as well as to "beef up" the school's doctoral program. We saw in the last chapter's statistical data that both these initiatives were fruitful. Also, a major help was the funding made available by the $25 million Ford Foundation grant to NYU, a portion of which was allocated to GBA to establish a full-time day MBA program.[4] In the next three decades, the full-time student body grew to about one-third the school's total enrollment. If part-time students may be assumed to represent one-half a full-time student, then the full-time student enrollment would represent about 40 percent of the full-time *equivalent* student enrollments. In the case of the PhD program, the number on the books dropped from about 1,200, mostly inactive, to some 150, of whom about half are active candidates.

Merrill Hall

While we're discussing GBA's physical development and transformation in its downtown location, we might as well fill in the picture by speaking of the construction of Merrill Hall, which was completed by 1975. Made possible by a naming gift from the Charles E. Merrill Trust, the building memorialized the founder of Merrill Lynch, Pierce, Fenner and Beane, otherwise occasionally referred to as the "thundering herd." The building made possible a large expansion in GBA's library, provided computer facilities for faculty and students, and enough additional office, classroom, and lounge space to increase markedly the School's capacity to offer quality support for its education and research programs. Patently, Merrill Hall enhanced GBA's ability to expand the full-time day MBA program, as well as to institute other programs. On the research side, Merrill Hall made possible the establishment of the Salomon Brothers Center for the Study of Financial Institutions. The Salomon Brothers Center, funded by a gift of $3 million, occupied the twelfth and thirteenth floors of the 14 story, $8 million structure. The Center absorbed the former C. J. Devine Institute of Finance, and became a major research arm of the School under its longtime director, Professor Arnold W. Sametz. A student lounge, with food service capability, occupied the fourteenth floor, while the 200–seat Samuel and Esther Gitlow Auditorium was located on the second floor. Concurrent with the construction of Merrill Hall, substantial renovations were made in Nichols Hall. A bridge at the seventh floor of Nichols Hall connected that structure with Merrill, so that the two buildings served as an integrated facility.

In the long-standing debate as to whether bricks and mortar or programs and people are more important in fund-raising for educational institutions, the record of Nichols and Merrill Halls, as with Tisch Hall at Washington Square, is that both are equally necessary to long-run viability. At both GBA and Commerce, new, modern, and attractive buildings were enormously important to the development of high-quality research and learning centers.

In light of later developments, namely GBA's 1993 relocation to Washington Square, some retrospective questioning of the wisdom of investing in two major structures at 90–100 Trinity Place would seem reasonable. But such questioning is subject to the wisdom embedded in the old cliché that hindsight is superior to foresight; or, as President Harry S Truman is reported to have remarked "Any 9 year old child is smarter than the greatest statesman after the event." I well recall debate on this very issue at the time that Merrill Hall was being considered. There was real consideration of relocating GBA to the Square at that time. But the sentiment of a significant portion of the faculty opposed it, for many of them liked the autonomy afforded a satellite operation removed from the university's central administration. Others undoubtedly still had concerns about being too close physically to the undergraduate school. Also, there was concern that student enrollments would be adversely affected by a move away from GBA's traditional and long-established location in the heart of the New York financial community, a community perceived as the unique market niche of GBA.

The decision about the construction of Merrill Hall at Trinity Place, as against relocating the school to Washington Square, was still pending when Dean William Dill arrived in 1970. Dean Dill recalls the factors which finally weighed in favor of building Merrill Hall at the downtown location.[5] They were, principally: (1) the core group of GBA's students still came from locations more accessible to Trinity Place than to Washington Square, although the movement of financial firms to the midtown area had already begun; (2) the Washington Square area offered little possibility of housing for full-time students, whose enrollment GBA was anxious to enlarge, while the prospective development of Battery Park City and the Washington Market area seemed to hold out future housing possibilities; (3) the planning for Merrill Hall was far advanced, substantial funding was in hand, and a university trustee, Charles Nichols, was excited about and supported the project; (4) there was some question about how the graduate and undergraduate schools and facilities would co-exist, when their eventual merger was still unclear and in the future; (5) the financial firms in the downtown area were able to observe at first hand the powerful progress toward greater academic quality at GBA; and (6) the distance from central administration was useful, enabling GBA to develop its computer and registration facilities and capabilities independent of similar, but laggard, efforts at Washington Square.

The die was cast for Trinity Place, and two decades would pass before the grand vision of the Stern School would be realized at Washington Square. In the meantime, GBA proceeded apace to enhance its reputation through a variety of educational initiatives, some representing enhancement of existing programs and others entirely new thrusts.

Industry-Specific Training

While Dean Taggart was eager and enthusiastic in his desire to enhance the MBA and PhD programs, his feelings were contrary with respect to industry-specific training. Both Commerce and GBA had a long tradition of providing such educational preparation, and had developed degree programs in Real Estate, Insurance, Advertising, Public Utilities, and Transportation. Dean Taggart, anxious to shed the aura of vocationalism and narrowly focused descriptiveness so harshly criticized in the Gordon-Howell and Pierson studies published in 1959, worked to cut back majors, minors, and their associated courses in such specific areas, replacing them with fewer and more broadly conceived courses.

Consider these examples: GBA's bulletin for 1960–1961 showed seven courses in Advertising, six in Industrial Relations, two in Insurance, six in Personnel Administration, seven in Public Utilities and Transportation, and five in Real Estate and Land Economics. But the 1972–1973 bulletin showed one course each in Public Utility Economics, Transportation Economics, Advertising, Management, and Sales Management. No courses were offered in Insurance. There was one course in Retail Marketing (Merchandise Management), a particularly significant change from 12 years before. In 1960–1961, the GBA bulletin made available four courses offered in the School of Retailing at Washington Square. But the School of Retailing was converted into the Institute of Retail Management in the Schools of Business in 1963, consistent with a recommendation of the 1956 N Y U Self-Study report. Nine years later, at the graduate level, all that remained of its graduate degree programs (Masters and PhD) was the single Retail Marketing course noted.

The content and sweep of GBA's courses had been reworked in the dozen years between 1960 and 1972. New courses and departments had been added; for example, Computer Applications and Information Systems, and International Business. In general, the mathematical and computer-related work required of students had been greatly expanded. New degree and certificate programs were developed in the seventies. We will examine them shortly.

But new industry-specific programs were carefully eschewed. The result was fascinating and possibly illogical, for the university did not abandon these educational market niches. Struggling to offset Commerce's shrinking enrollments, I had some interest in and explored several possible certificate programs, as well as one master's degree program to be developed jointly with a major corporation in the metropolitan area with a substantial educational program and facility of its own. The last program failed almost immediately because of faculty opposition to substantive educational content input by the prospective corporate partner. The certificate and other possible degree programs fell before Dean Taggart's concern over the vocationalism issue. My interest was not so great as to inspire me to try to change Dean Taggart or other minds, and so I accepted, and indeed worked to shed the aura of vocationalism, where I strongly shared Dean Taggart's sentiments.

Of particular interest is the fact that the School of Education and the School of Continuing Education picked up and avidly pursued both degree and certificate programs that were industry-specific. Thus, the Sunday *New York Times* of August 1, 1993, in its section 4A (Education Life) had almost a full-page ad by NYU's School of Continuing Education offering three programs: Master of Science in Tourism and Travel Management; Master of Science in Real Estate; and Master of Science in Hospitality Industry Studies. For its part, the School of Education has a degree in Hotel and Restaurant Management. There is more, but these illustrations should suffice to make the point that educational elitism in one section of the university does not necessarily mean that market niches are abandoned by the entire university.

This discussion has so far avoided the question of Accounting: Is that an industry-specific program? If one sees it only as a distinct, licensed profession, then one might argue affirmatively. But, if one has the broad intellectual insight of Charles Waldo Haskins, then one perceives the Accounting profession as providing the data analyzing ability absolutely essential to everyone who wishes to understand the organizational operations central to modern society. I have the latter view, and believe Accounting to be an essential element in the B-school's programs—all of them.

Before leaving this topic, I should note that I have lived long enough to revisit, and rethink the issue of industry-specific programs. Rethinking is no doubt made easier by the fact that the charge of narrow vocationalism no longer clings to America's top business schools. Indeed, major criticism is now levied against them for having lost touch with the realities of the practical day-to-day business world. The real issue is *how* industry-specific educational programs are designed and taught. They can be done on a highly demanding, rigorous intellectual level and so qualify truly as belonging in institutions of higher learning. Or, they can be done in narrowly descriptive ways which simply convey a picture of existing practices minus any analytical aspect. If done the latter way, they do not belong. If done the former way, they do belong.

The PhD Program

GBA's doctoral curriculum underwent significant changes between the early sixties and the late seventies, but by then it was essentially shaped in form and substance for the following decades. The overall requirements for the degree[6] as of 1960–1961 were: (1) work in five fields of study out of 14 specified, with *two fields required* (i.e., Economic and Financial History, and Economic Theory and History of Economic Thought) and *three fields selected* from the remaining 12 areas; (2) a minimum of three years of graduate study (a minimum of 40 points had to be taken at GBA); (3) a written examination in a foreign language; (4) a written examination in statistics; (5) completion of all course work listed on the final approved program of study; (6) written examinations in two fields of study selected as minors; (7) an oral qualifying examination in the three major fields of study selected in accordance with item 1 above, to be done *after* completion of all required course work except the dissertation; and (8) the dissertation and its defense in a final oral examination. As we have observed before, the dissertation is a major element in obtaining the PhD. The bulletin specified that its subject had to be in one of the candidate's five fields of study, and it "must demonstrate the candidate's ability to do independent and scientific research and must contribute to the advancement of learning in the selected field."

By 1965–1966, these changes appear: (1) the number of fields of study were reduced from 14 to 8, to 7 if Corporation Finance and Investments are considered as one field (as in 1960–1961) rather than two (as in 1965–1966); (2) fields such as Advertising, Personnel Administration and Industrial Relations, Public Utilities and Transportation, and Real Estate and Land Economics were gone; (3) the fields remaining were of broad scope namely Accounting, Banking, Economics, Corporation Finance, Investments, Management, Marketing, and Quantitative Analysis (Statistics and Operations Research); (4) *interfield programs,* such as international business, were now possible, drawing on courses across the functional department lines; (5) the number of required points of advanced graduate work was reduced from 66 to 64, of which a minimum of 38 points had to be taken at GBA; and (6) the work on the dissertation was enhanced by the provision of special doctoral seminars and workshops. Significantly, the 1965–1966 bulletin stated the goals of the doctoral program as being the education of: (1) teachers of business administration; (2) researchers in the area of business; and (3) personnel in business organizations desiring advanced, integrated knowledge in business. Of the three goals the first was emphasized in this added statement: "The need for qualified teachers is critical and many openings each year go unfilled."

By 1972–1973 the central goal of the doctoral curriculum emerged with great clarity and focus, and its language has changed by hardly a word in the two decades since. The language bears on earlier discussion of the PhD degree and its importance in today's academic culture. The 1972–1973 GBA bulletin says:

> The Doctor of Philosophy degree is awarded for scholarly attainment and represents the highest honor that the University may bestow on a student. *It is essentially a research and teaching degree; it is this that distinguishes the doctor's from the master's degree.* The disciplined work required is designed to prepare the student for a professional career in research and teaching through the development of the student's critical understanding of his fields of study and of his capacity to pursue independent investigation. The doctoral dissertation, as the culmination of each student's scholarly efforts, is expected to be a contribution to knowledge in the student's special field. (Italics added)[7]

In place of the five fields of study specified in earlier bulletins, there was now a requirement to take core courses or to demonstrate competence in five areas; namely, Quantitative Analysis (two courses, one in Mathematics and one in Statistics); Economics (two courses, one in Microeconomics and one in Macroeconomics); Behavioral Science (1 course); Accounting (1 course, by passing a proficiency exam, or providing evidence of adequate previous study in accounting); and Computer Usage (passing a proficiency examination). There was also the requirement for the student to select *two fields of specialization* out of these eight: Accounting; Economics; Finance; Management; Behavioral Science; Marketing; Quantitative Analysis; and International Business. Reference was made also to interdisciplinary fields available through cooperation with other schools in NYU. And there was a possible additional requirement for the student to take up to two courses in Quantitative Analysis, plus a course in "Applied Empirical Analysis," depending on requirements determined by the individual department in which the student was taking his or her two fields of specialization. Interestingly, the modern foreign language requirement had now become optional, subject to determination by the individual department in which the student was working (but, in any case, no more than one foreign language could be required of a student). As to the dissertation, the student now had to enroll in six dissertation seminars, presumably to sharpen his or her research and writing skills.

The general format of the program is depicted in Figure 6.1. The

FIGURE 6.1
The Doctoral Program, 1972–1973

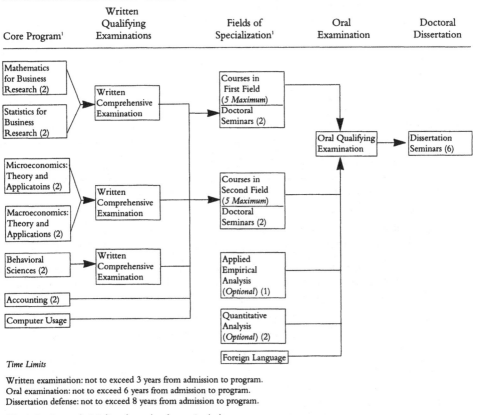

Core Program[1]	Written Qualifying Examinations	Fields of Specialization[1]	Oral Examination	Doctoral Dissertation

Time Limits

Written examination: not to exceed 3 years from admission to program.
Oral examination: not to exceed 6 years from admission to program.
Dissertation defense: not to exceed 8 years from admission to program.

The numbers in parenthesis indicate the number of courses involved.

[1]Courses may be waived in appropriate circumstances

SOURCE: NYU Bulletin, *GBA*, 1972–1973, 59.

major expansion in the quantitative and computer areas is clear, as is the reduction in areas of specialization and the general intellectual broadening of the program. Above all, the nature and purpose of the doctoral program are now sharply defined.

Few changes appear in the GBA bulletin for 1982–1983. One change worthy of note is that the eight fields of study, while remaining the same in number, have been changed in composition. Behavioral Science is now embraced in the Management field, and the new field of Computer Applications and Information Systems is added. Also, *the two fields of study selected by the student for concentration are now specified as a major and a minor, with selection of the minor subject to consultation with an advisor in the major field.* The earlier requirement for two doctoral seminars in the second (minor) field of concentration is reduced to one seminar. There is no longer any reference to the need to take six dissertation seminars, and the requirement that the student maintain a minimum 3.0 grade point average to remain in the doctoral program is changed to a minimum of 3.3. But this change was later abandoned and the minimum grade point average reverted to 3.0. Professor Emeritus Ernest Kurnow, commenting on the shift from two fields of specialization to a major/minor combination, with the advisor in the major field, reflected the difficulty our PhD graduates were then facing in competing for faculty positions in top-quality schools. They discovered that their preparation lacked sufficient depth and sophistication to compete in their major functional field of interest. That problem compelled the eventual reduction in the number of fields of specialization required of doctoral candidates. Professor Kurnow speculates that departmental "turf protection" may have been a factor delaying the eventual reduction in the required number of fields of specialization.

A particularly interesting development is the automatic award of a Master of Philosophy degree to all PhD candidates following successful completion of the doctoral comprehensive examination. At that point the candidates are ABD (all but dissertation), so the Master of Philosophy might seem a consolation prize for those who do not complete the dissertation. The idea of awarding the MPhil degree had been discussed for years, but approval to do so apparently did not come immediately. However, by the late eighties it was an established practice.

The MBA Program

Although faculty have a profound cultural affinity to the doctoral program, the MBA program is the backbone of the graduate school in terms of student enrollment, number of degrees conferred, tuition revenues generated, faculty and staff employment, and plant facilities needed. Its nature and fulfillment are therefore of fundamental importance, as are the educational and other issues encountered in its operation. It is consequently imperative that we exercise patience in our examination of its development at GBA since 1960.

One MBA issue has been chronic over the decades and still dominates discussion of the nature of the degree. It is the *generalist* versus *specialist* issue, a persistent source of debate. The title of the degree itself implies a broad, general command of knowledge and insight into the administration of business organizations. The holder is presumably a master of the administration of business organizations—all such organizations. Yet, lack of in-depth knowledge of particular fields suggests the creation of a "jack of all trades and master of none." The issue usually manifests itself in argument over the scope and content of the *basic core* required for the MBA (the general component) as against the scope and content allowed for *major and minor fields,* as well as *electives.* Changes over time in the MBA program reveal also shifts in emphasis. One hesitates to call them fads, but that word comes to mind because of the way in which their popularity ebbs and flows. Thus, Economics remains a constant and basic curricular component over the decades, as do Accounting, Finance, Management, and Marketing, while Production, Labor Relations, Organizational Behavior, Strategy, and Ethics seem to shift. But Quantitative Analysis became a basic requirement as did Computer Applications, and they show lasting power. With Accounting, they are the cornerstones upon which rest the student's information-handling and analytical ability.

Before turning to the specifics of the MBA program, we should note also that the generalist-specialist issue is reflected in the development in the early seventies of one-year specialized Master of Science (MS) programs. They raise this significant issue: Do specialized MS programs "cannibalize" the MBA program by drawing enrollments away, and thereby undermine the school's backbone program? I suggest that, if and when MS programs achieve significant size, this issue could become contentious. But not in all cases. The MS in Accounting program, to be discussed later, was symbolic for GBA, having positive spillover effects in the MBA program.

A valuable insight into the generalist-specialist issue is provided by Professor Michael Schiff. He wrote in "Ends and Means in Business Education":

> While business education is similar to all other professional education in its relationship between ends and means, it differs drastically from the old professions and their schools in the relationship between specialist and generalists.

In all the older professions the beginner is the generalist. As the practitioner and the scholar in law and medicine advance in the profession, they become increasingly specialized. In business, however, the beginner works of necessity, as a specialist, in one "function," or in one skill area. As he advances in business and becomes a "manager," he is concerned increasingly with wholes, with the interrelationships between specialties, disciplines, and techniques, and with building and maintaining an "organization" that is a complex human community in which individual specialists work together for joint performance and results. Increasingly in business, advancement means moving from "specialist" to "generalists."

The reason for this is, of course, that the older professions have traditionally been practiced alone or in small partnerships. Business is practiced in and through an institution. It is the purpose of this institution to make specialists productive—and this is its strength. But this means that the progress of the business executive is almost exactly the opposite of the progress and professional education of the past assumed for its practitioners.

This has, of course, been known all along. But it has not been taken into account in the business school. This explains, in large measure, the confusion that has been so prevalent in American business education and the dissatisfaction of business educators with their own work, despite their impressive success, both within academia and in the business community. For the distinct and different relationship between specialist and generalists in business has profound implications for business education—its publics, its structure, and its subject matter.[8]

Professor Schiff goes on to identify four distinct "student bodies," perhaps we should say markets, for professional business education: namely, (1) senior managers, who benefit from executive management programs and could benefit also from "real world" research by B-school faculty; (2) people entering middle management, who need the broader perspective provided by quality graduate schools of business through the MBA; (3) specialists, who need to improve their command in their specialty, and who can do so through some form of continuing education (e.g., GBA's and Commerce's certificate programs—APC, PPB or Professional Program in Business, etc.); and (4) the Liberal Arts and Science graduate who needs education for a first job in business. In the last connection Professor Schiff takes an implicit stance against the MBA degree as being appropriate, arguing that the newly minted Arts and Sciences baccalaureate needs to "be trained as a *specialist*." Of course his view is controversial, but it was written in the late sixties, a quarter of a century ago, before it became common practice for quality B-schools generally to require two to four years of full-time work experience prior to admission to the MBA program. Also, the growth of Master of Science (specialist) degree programs in B-schools takes on added meaning in terms of Professor Schiff's analysis. The same is true of the popularity of executive management programs. One market remains inadequately tapped by B-schools. That market is the one for "real world" research, *as viewed by business leaders and managers who consume it.* All too often, faculty research in the B-schools is directed at other faculty and of little or no perceived relevance to business people.

W. Edwards Deming, in the survey of GBA graduates referred to earlier in this chapter, asked whether a student who specialized in his studies would have a better chance to get a job interview, and, having gotten an interview, would receive more serious consideration than a student who had spread his education over a wide variety of fields. Slightly over half reported that they thought the specialist would do better. However, for economic achievement at the end of ten years after graduation, the proportion of replies shifted to slightly over half (54 percent) in favor of the nonspecialist.[9]

With that background we turn to the development of GBA's MBA program in the three decades from 1960 to 1990. We begin with the program described in the school bulletin for 1960–1961. That program continued the two contact hour-two credit hour course module which dated to the School's early years. It required 24 courses representing 48 credits of work of a student having no undergraduate study in Economics or Commerce. Students presenting satisfactory evidence of such study could get up to 24 credits waived, making the MBA a one-year degree for them. *Fundamental (*i.e.*, core) courses in each of three fields of study were required, in addition to which the student had to complete a *major* (including a seminar in which a written report was completed) and a *minor* (comprising at least four points of advanced course work). The minor *had to be* in an area or field distinct from the area in which the major was taken, no doubt a recognition of the danger of excessive specialization. Remaining credits could be used as electives. Nine fields of study were presented in the bulletin, including Political Economy, Public Utilities, and Real Estate. These last three were dropped by 1965–1966, and replaced by International Business. Finally, *a written* *report* "embodying the results of an independent study of some important problem in the student's major field of interest" was required of all candidates for the degree.

Professor Emeritus Ernest Kurnow recalls that the pre 1965–1966 MBA program revision was weighted 2:1 in favor of breadth over depth in courses required; that is, 15–16 courses from several departments (the core plus electives), and 8–9 courses (the major-minor combination plus theses). Philosophically, the MBA program aimed at educating managers having a broad knowledge of the several functional areas important to the successful operation of a business organization. Yet, it was felt that the manager also needed deeper knowledge in some specific area of the organization's operations.

Figure 6.2 shows graphically the essential features of the MBA program that existed from 1965-1966 through 1973-1974. The most significant changes were: (1) the establishment of a *12–course 24–credit core* (some courses could be taken intensively in one semester as double courses) covering Accounting, Banking, Corporation Finance, Economics, Management, Behavioral Sciences, Marketing, and Quantitative Methods (with double courses in Accounting and Economics and a triple course, i.e., six credits in Quantitative Methods); (2) *24 credits of advanced work* (12 more courses) comprising a *major, electives,* and a *thesis.* As Figure 6.2 shows, the thesis requirement allowed the options of a *project* or GBA's *management game.* The project involved participation in a managerial task within an organization, whether business or government. The student had to solve an actual problem and write a report that embraced analysis of the problem, examination of relevant literature, a record of the experience, an evaluation of procedures followed, and a description of the solution. The *management game* involved student teams operating a computerized simulation of a multimillion-dollar enterprise. The team had to make pricing, production, and organizational decisions, interact with businessmen, bankers, and labor leaders constituting a board of directors, implement decisions, and be responsible for the results. The figure also shows the fields and numbers of courses permitted in the major and elective segments of the program. But one could not exceed nine courses in the combination (if six major, then three elective; or if five major, then four elective), with three course equivalents reserved for the thesis and its options. Day students were required to take an integrating capstone course in business policy, a reflection of AACSB (American Assembly of Collegiate Schools of Business)

1. The American Book Co. building, now N Y U's Main Building, constructed in 1894. In 1900, the top 3 floors were occupied by the Law School, the School of Pedagogy, and the new School of Commerce, Accounts, and Finance. The structure is at the southeast corner of Waverly Place and Washington Square East, the original 1831 site of New York University.

2. *Left:* Charles Waldo Haskins, first dean of School of Commerce, Accounts and Finance, 1900–1903. *Right:* Joseph French Johnson, Dean, School of Commerce, Accounts and Finance, 1903–1925.

3. Cafeteria, Main building, about 1947.

4. Commerce building, occupied in 1926, viewed from Washington Square
Park looking southeast, early 1950s. Buildings on right are garage and Fountain
Luncheonette, on block now site of Elmer Holmes Bobst Library.

5. John T. Madden, Dean, School of
Commerce, Accounts, and Finance,
1925–1948.

6. Violet owl, one of 2 atop entry to Commerce building. The Commerce
building is now Leon Shimkin Hall, and is part of the 3-building complex comprising today's Stern School (the other 2 buildings are Tisch Hall and the Management Education Center).

7. Commerce building, front view, late 1960s, when present site of Bobst Library had been cleared and was temporarily a park.

8. Cutting anniversary cake, 50th Anniversary of School of Commerce, Accounts, and Finance. Dean George Rowland Collins, second from left. Collins was dean of the Graduate School of Business Administration, 1946–1959, and concurrently dean of the School of Commerce, 1948–1954.

9. Dean's office staff, 50th Anniversary School of Commerce, Accounts, and Finance. Dean John H. Prime (1962–1965), then Associate Dean, first left, standing.

10. Room 826, Commerce building, later renovated as Charles Waldo Haskins Accounting classroom.

11. Lassman Hall, student lounge on lobby floor of Commerce building.

12. Thomas Norton, dean, School of Commerce, 1954–1962.

13. Daniel Diamond, dean, BPA, 1985–1989; dean, Undergraduate Division, Stern School, 1989–1995.

14. Excavation and construction site for Tisch Hall, looking south at Washington Square Village, Warren Weaver Hall on left and rear of Commerce building on right.

15. President James M. Hester, Preston Robert Tisch, and Lawrence Tisch, left to right, setting sealed lead box containing memorabilia into foundation of Tisch Hall. Box is set below stage of Schimmel Auditorium.

16. Tisch Hall, with the Founders' Monument on Gould Plaza. The Monument is now relocated to Bobkin Lane between Leon Shimkin Hall and the Bobst Library. The monument is a segment of N Y U's original Gothic building, which was located where the Main building is now situated.

17.1.

17.2.

17.3.

17.4.

17.5.   17.6.

17. Photos 1–3 are views of the
Dean Edward Kilduff Faculty
Lounge, 8th floor, Tisch Hall. Pho-
tos 4–6 are views of the Surdna Con-
ference Center, 3rd floor, Tisch
Hall. Photo 7 is a view of the
Michael Schimmel Auditorium, Up-
per Concourse, Tisch Hall.

17.7.

18. Platform party, dedication of Tisch Hall, 1972. Left to right, Robert Mc-
Kenzie, dean, Pennsylvania State University Business School and president
American Assembly of Collegiate Schools of Business, Philip Johnson, architect, Preston Robert Tisch, donor, Abraham L. Gitlow, dean, College of Business and Public Administration (formerly School of Commerce), Lawrence A.
Tisch, donor and Chairman, N Y U, Board of Trustees, and James M. Hester,
president, N Y U.

19. The Trinity Church School building, original home of the Graduate School of Business Administration, 90 Church Street (site of Merrill Hall). Building on the left is New York Curb Exchange, (later site of American Stock Exchange). Horizontal structure in forefront is old elevated railroad line. View is from Trinity Church graveyard.

20. Archibald Wellington Taylor, founding dean, Graduate School of Business Administration, 1921–1946

21. Joseph Taggart, dean, GBA, 1959–1970.

22. Students at entry of original GBA building. This building served originally as the site of the Wall Street Division of the School of Commerce, Accounts, and Finance. Between 1916 and 1921, GBA was the Graduate Division of the School of Commerce, Accounts and Finance. It became the graduate school in 1921.

23. 100 Church Street, present site of Nichols Hall, just north of old Trinity Church School building, mid 1950s.

24. Nichols Hall, 100 Church Street. Old Trinity Church School building on left.

25. Right to left, Nichols Hall, Merrill Hall, and American Stock Exchange.

26. William Dill, dean, GBA, 1970–1980.

27. William May, dean, GBA, 1980–1984.

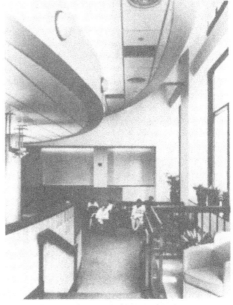

28. Present home of the Leonard N. Stern School of Business, at Washington Square. Left to right, Tisch Hall, Management Education Center and Leon Shimkin Hall. Student lounge in the MEC building.

Above: 29. Dedication of the MEC building and the 3 building management center of the Stern School. Left to right, Richard West, dean, Stern School, L. Jay Oliva, president, NYU, Leonard N. Stern, Mrs. Stern, and Lawrence A. Tisch, chairman, board of trustees. Richard West was dean of GBA, 1984–1988, and dean of the Stern School, 1988–1993.

Left: 30. Leonard N. Stern, right, cutting cake at dedication of Management Education Center. Dean Richard West at left.

31. George Daly, dean, Stern School, 1993–

32. NYU Commencement ceremonies, Washington Square Park. Arch at right, fountain in center, official platform party at center rear. Faculty, graduates, and guests completely occupy park.

FIGURE 6.2
MBA Program, 1965–1966 to 1973–1974

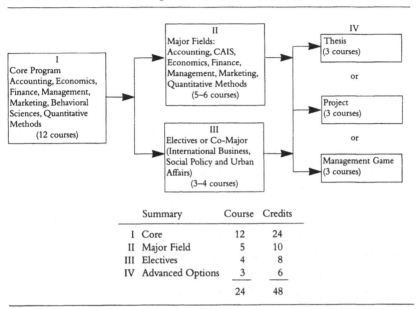

Summary		Course	Credits
I	Core	12	24
II	Major Field	5	10
III	Electives	4	8
IV	Advanced Options	3	6
		24	48

SOURCE: NYU, GBA, *Faculty Minutes*, Special Meeting October 24, 1973, Appended Report of Faculty Committee on the MBA Program. Also, NYU Bulletin, *GBA*, 1965–1966, 10–14; and 1972–1973, 43–48.

accreditation requirements. It should be noted that the thesis was also regarded at GBA as an integrative experience, but this was a view which was later challenged (as were the options to the thesis). Finally the minimum amount of course work which had to be taken at GBA was increased from 24 to 30 credits.

Commenting on the 1965–1966 revisions to the MBA program, Professor Emeritus Kurnow observed[10] that the basic philosophy with respect to breadth-depth was as before. The goal of the change was to raise the level of sophistication and analytic content of the program, without an increase in the number of courses required. Since Dean Taggart and the faculty shared these goals, the new program was readily adopted. The most significant changes were: first, in the core; and, second, in the options to the thesis. The changes in the core: (1) increased the required Quantitative courses from two to three; (2) decreased the required Marketing courses from two to one; and (3) split the Management Process course into two courses, i.e. Behavioral Science in Business and the Management Process.

The new Quantitative courses replaced the two Statistics courses previously required with a single course in Statistics, another in Calculus, and a third in Operations Research. These actions reflected the post-Sputnik belief that quantitative methods would be of increasing importance in business and other decision making. Further, there was a widespread conviction that increased quantitative skills would enable increased sophistication and analytic content in the School's courses in other substantive areas. The reduction in the number of marketing courses reflected the belief that a single course was sufficient to present the coverage of the two prior courses, with the level of the intellectual challenge to students elevated. The division of the Management Process course into the Management Process and Behavioral Science in Business reflected the growing recognition of the importance of organizational behavior, in addition to business strategy. It was inherent that the coverage of the two courses would be much greater than the old Management Process course. The appearance of options to the thesis foreshadowed the dropping of that requirement in a later revision of the MBA program.

William Dill became dean in 1970. During his 10-year tenure a major, perhaps even a radical, redesign of the MBA program was put in place. Discussed extensively in 1973–1974, it was approved by the faculty and implemented in 1974–1975. Figure 6.3 shows the program graphically. The older, traditional format of a core, followed by major, minor, and electives is replaced by six so-called tiers of courses. Tiers I and V are especially noteworthy because they reflect an attempt to force an interdisciplinary, broader, and more general approach to the core (i.e., the knowledge base) and to several overarching societal issues (i.e., social, economic, legal, and political). Even tier II seeks to stretch the traditional functional departments to address problems in their organizational areas from a wide viewpoint. In broad terms, the concept of a core, a major, and a capstone experience (thesis, project, and management game, or the new added option of policy studies) are retained. But they are subject to stress in the new structural framework. Note should be taken that, while the number of courses required was reduced from 24 to 20, the point value of the program was increased from 48 to 66. This outcome was achieved by the simple expedient of increasing the point value of a *standard* GBA course from two to three points, minus

FIGURE 6.3
MBA Program, 1974–1975 to 1986–1987

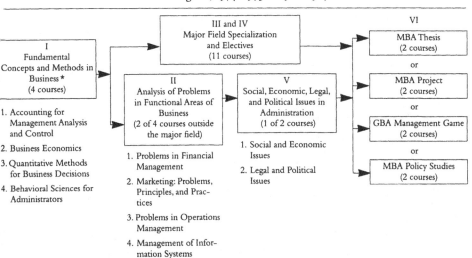

*Courses that meet twice weekly.

	Summary	Courses	Total Points
I	Fundamental Concepts and Methods	4	16
II	Analysis of Problems in Functional Areas	2 (of 4)	6
III	Major Field	6 or 7	18-21
IV	Electives	5 or 4	15-12
V	Social, Economic, Legal, and Political Issues	1 (of 2)	3
VI	Advanced Professional Options	2	8
		20	66

SOURCE: NYU Bulletin, *GBA*, 1974–1975, 39.

any change in contact hours. Also, the minimum number of courses taken at GBA was set at 15, with waivers obtainable only in tier I and II courses. Thus, only 25 percent of the 20 required courses could now be waived, as against 50 percent of the 24 courses earlier required.

In addition to the effort to strengthen the interdisciplinary aspect of the MBA program, the 1974–1975 program's achievements in reducing the use of waivers and in enlarging discussion of social responsibility of business are noteworthy. Also, the development of additional options to the MBA thesis strengthened the tendency toward eventual dropping of the thesis. And the nature of the options, in particular the management game, policy studies, and the MBA field project was made even more

148 Three Transforming Decades

consistent with a capstone, integrative experience, even though there was some debate with AACSB about that point.

Oddly, as Professor Emeritus Kurnow observes, the 1974–1975 MBA program revision decreased the required breadth of the curriculum in one significant respect; that is, a student could now get the MBA degree by taking only two of the four courses in tier II. The Operations Management course was a response to growing criticism that attention to production had slipped to the point of disappearance. He recalls also that the adoption of the program by the faculty was accompanied by much contention, with Economics, Finance, and Quantitative faculty strongly opposed. At the crucial faculty meeting that voted to adopt the revisions, Professor Kurnow recalls an impassioned speech by Professor Robert Kavesh of the Economics department as having turned the tide in favor of the proposal.

Another feature of the 1974–1975 program requires note. A probable outgrowth of faculty complaints that the MBA thesis supervision was an onerous, burdensome chore, the 1974–1975 program involved adoption of a released time policy allowing one released course for every eight theses supervised. Probably inadvertently and certainly unfortunately, there was no constraint on the number of released time courses a faculty member could accumulate. In other words, it became possible for a faculty member active in supervising MBA theses to "save-up" the equivalent of two-three years of released time. Such accumulations soon threatened, if used, to upset significantly staffing and sabbatical leave arrangements. Within a decade (i.e., by 1984–1985), the problem could no longer be ignored or side-stepped, and had to be confronted. It was, with the redesign of the MBA program in 1985–1986, implemented in 1986–1987. There was no cash buyout. Instead, faculty with accumulated release time were given a period of two-three years within which to apply it against their usual teaching loads. In practice relatively few faculty did so, probably because most of the time was held by department chairmen who were busy with their regular duties and felt they could not reduce those commitments. So an ill-designed, inadequately conceived, policy disappeared without lasting damage. But it was for a time a source of contention and ill-will.

By 1985–1986 there was another source of dissatisfaction with the 1974–1975 MBA design. It had become somewhat more complicated structurally, increasing to 21 courses and 71 credits, partly due to increasing the point value of the tier I courses from 4 to 4.5 points each.

In place of one out of two required tier V courses, came two required mini-courses of 1.5 points each, all in addition to the standard 3-point courses. And a fifth tier VI option (the International Business Negotiation Exercise) had been added to the four already in existence. Given these complications, plus the added one of equating graduate courses to undergraduate ones, the important task of assigning faculty to both graduate and undergraduate courses, and designing sensible teaching loads, became difficult. In short, the program's structure became ponderous, and administratively and educationally counterproductive.

An Ad Hoc Review Committee for the MBA Program was appointed in 1983, chaired by Professor Gerald Glasser. It submitted its report for faculty review and discussion on November 20, 1984. Although the Committee report was presented in the framework of the existing tiered program, it effectively revamped that structure and reverted to the simpler and more traditional concept of a core of courses, with a bundle of advanced courses comprising a major and electives. As finally adopted for implementation in 1986–1987, the program called for *39 credits of required courses* (33 credits of *core* courses and a 6-credit *strategy and policy* requirement), *plus 33 credits of advanced courses,* consisting of six courses (18 credits) in a *major,* and four courses (12 credits) *of advanced electives* outside the core and major. That arrangement left one course (3 credits) which could be taken in any area, to complete a total requirement of 72 credits. Note that the new program consisted of 24 courses of 3 credits each, almost equally split between core courses and advanced courses. This was a reversal with a vengeance.

The 6-credit strategy and policy requirement consisted of the old tier VI options (i.e., the Management Game, the Management Advisory Project, the Policy Studies option, and the International Business Negotiation), *minus the thesis.* The thesis was finally dropped and replaced by a capstone integrative Business Policy course coupled with a Legal and Social Issues course. This action was taken to satisfy the AACSB accreditation requirement of a capstone, integrative policy course.

The composition of the required 33-credit core is of interest relative to the generalist-specialist issue, for it provides the multidisciplinary foundation of the degree. The 1986–1987 core embraced 6 credits each (two courses) in Accounting, Economics, and Statistics, with 3 credits each (one course) in Finance, Marketing, Operations Management, Information Systems, and Organizational Behavior. The "new" program represented a substantial reversion to an older, more traditional pattern, with students still required to be proficient in writing, computers, and analytical methods and calculus.

The Ad Hoc Committee, in its November 20, 1984 report, made a number of significant points: First, the Committee emphasized its belief that GBA's distinctive strength was its ability "to provide more in-depth training in areas of specialization" than other schools could. The Committee saw this strength as reflecting the size of the faculty and student body, which enabled the school to "offer more sections of more courses in more semesters with more diverse faculty specialties." But the Committee added that this capability should be used "without erasing the important cornerstone of any MBA curriculum: broad, diverse and general business education." Obviously, the Committee was acutely conscious of the generalist-specialist issue.

Second, these pertinent and significant comments were made: (1) "some of the hopes for the tier system, . . . have, . . . not materialized"; (2) "virtually every other leading business school . . . has a simple structure"; (3) "we see advantages, . . . in recasting the structure of our program in these simple terms;" (4) "we . . . propose . . . we move back in the direction of a more standardized course. Point count, at present, is a bookkeeping device for pricing rather than a measure of course content"; (5) "many of our faculty, and students too, perceive class time per course at GBA as a problem," because the contact hour content of the program at some 588 hours falls significantly short of Columbia's 620–640 and Wharton's 665; and (6) "we believe that an integral part of the (proposed changes) is to make the normal teaching load *6 courses per year* for regular full time faculty."

Observe that the suggested 24 course, 72-point program involved 672 contact hours, that is, 24 courses x two contact hours each = 48 contact hours x 14 weeks for each course = 672 contact hours, making a favorable comparison with Columbia and Wharton. *Note also that a six course per year teaching load reduced itself to three courses per semester x two contact hours per course and equalled six contact hours per week. The teaching load transformation from three to four decades earlier is substantial.* No doubt it was associated with an enormous increase in faculty research output, but some doubt exists about benefits accruing on the teaching side of the educational ledger. That requires continuing attention.

The last chapter pointed out that there were several MBA joint degree programs with other graduate N Y U divisions; namely, MA-MBA (French Studies), MA-MBA (Journalism), MA-MBA (Politics), and JD-

MBA (Law). Of the four programs, the Law-Business combination is the most significant in terms of student enrollment. Thus, in the Fall 1992 semester 13 full-time and one part-time students were enrolled in the JD-MBA program, five in the French Studies program, two in Journalism, none in Politics. In fact, the Politics program had only one student registered over its entire existence. The JD-MBA program was initiated in Fall 1970, Journalism in Fall 1976, Politics in Fall 1977, and French Studies in Fall 1981.

The essential elements making the JD-MBA program attractive are: (1) the achievement of joint professional training in two inextricably interrelated fields; (2) the accomplishment of that training in one year less than it would take if done separately; and (3) the fact that it would be accomplished in two of the country's best programs. To be accepted in the program, students must apply to both the Stern School and the School of Law, and be accepted by both. Requiring four years instead of the five involved when done separately, the JD (Juris Doctor)-MBA program involves alternate periods of full-time study in each school, with selected courses in each accepted for credit toward the other school's degree. Typically, the first two years and the last year of the program are spent in the law school, with the third year in residence in the business school.

A review of these programs, limited to their curricular aspects, is inadequate. They were created and offered by the School to provide a limited range of students a chance to cross school boundaries, and also to encourage faculty bridges across school lines. In the last connection, Professor George Sorter's teaching activity in the School of Law is noteworthy.[11]

Two special MBA programs deserve note. They are: (1) the executive MBA program; and (2) the satellite MBA program in Westchester County. The executive MBA program was begun in 1982, to provide advanced management study for middle-level managers of outstanding promise. Participants are usually managers whose careers have been specialized in production, engineering, or marketing, and who can advance their careers by acquiring broad management knowledge. The MBA program provides an excellent solution, but it has to fit the workday demands of this student population. Thus, the program is structured for the convenience of the participants and their employers. In fact, the endorsement and sponsorship of the employing organization is one requirement of admission. To lessen interruption of the participants' continuing job responsibilities, the program requires two years, with three residence periods each year. One residence period uses housing in a hotel near to the graduate school, with classes held at the School. The other two residence periods are held at a conference center in the New York area. Apart from the residence periods, classes run continuously, one day a week, from 8:30 a.m. to 4:30 p.m., on alternate Fridays and Saturdays.

In addition to the support of the participant's employer, admission criteria include a minimum of 10 years' work experience in the corporate business world; a satisfactory undergraduate record; and solid scores on the Graduate Management Admission Test (GMAT). About 35 participants are selected each Fall. Classes are small and are taught by carefully selected faculty, that is, those most likely to be effective in working with people experienced in the realities of daily business life. The program is rigorous, gives attention to both national and international business, and uses courses selected from the regular MBA curriculum. Methods of presentation include lectures, discussions, case studies, and computer simulations. A policy studies project is the program's capstone experience.

The MBA program in Westchester County was established at Manhattanville College in the late seventies. It grew out of an interest at GBA in developing a suburban market, coupled with inquiries addressed to Dean Dill by Barbara Debs, president of Manhattanville. Dean Dill, who had spent five years with IBM in the area, felt strongly that an MBA program at Manhattanville would attract high-quality students in the Westchester region. President John Sawhill, who became president of NYU in 1975, believed the university should develop other satellite programs, to serve the suburban areas surrounding New York City as well as to build enrollments and tuition revenues. His initiative was not pursued widely by other NYU divisions, perhaps because he left for federal service in Washington, D.C., after being at NYU only a few years. But GBA did proceed, resulting in the MBA program at Manhattanville. The program is part-time, designed to be completed in 33 months. It provides intensive exposure to a general management curriculum. Students must complete the program in six years. Classes are held weekday evenings and are taught by GBA full-time faculty. Dean Dill is convinced that the program has survived and been successful because of the quality of students. Although faculty were originally a bit reluctant to travel to Westchester to teach, they were won over by the ambition and ability of the students, and became enthusiastic.

MBA Matriculants and Graduates in 1993

A summary profile of 1993 MBA matriculants provides a contemporary look at the group's major characteristics. That class numbered 813 people, of whom 365 were full-time and 448 part-time. Its undergraduate grade point average was 3.185, with an average GMAT score of 591. Almost 35 percent of the group was female, 24 percent foreign, and 15.1 percent minority. The average age of the full-time matriculants was 27, while that of the part-timers was 26. The full-time group had full-time work experience averaging 4.2 years. The part-timers averaged 4.8 years of full-time work experience. Almost 32 percent of the group had undergraduate majors in the Social Sciences, while almost 35 percent majored in Business Administration and 18.2 percent and 6.9 percent, respectively, majored in Math and Science and in the Humanities.

With respect to placement of graduates of the MBA class of 1993, a survey of 630 yielded a response from 501. They reported being employed at an average salary of $56,162. That average reflected a salary range of $32,000–$100,000, and compared with a 1992 average salary of $54,697.

The International Business Major

A major observation of this history is the triumph of the PhD degree as the critically needed credential of the full-time faculty. A further dimension of the importance of the doctorate is its associated value structure and mind-set, which inclines faculty to emphasize research over teaching and, of no less significance, to focus on their specialized field rather than the interdisciplinary implications and needs of the MBA program and degree. In governance terms, the faculty became organized into departments, and the reward structure in terms of rank and compensation was determined there rather than in the broader reference frame of the School as a whole.

At the Stern School, and at its premerger entities of GBA and Commerce/BPA, there was a notable and important exception to the general rule. It was the International Business major and later the International Business department, with the former predating the creation of the latter. Originally, Professor John Fayerweather, of the Management department and later Professor Robert Hawkins of the Finance department, developed the program. One remarkable aspect of their work was that it was interdisciplinary; that is, it drew its faculty from the several departments. A new Department of International Business (IB) was not created until years after the major was introduced. Instead, faculty in such departments as Management, Finance, Marketing, and Accounting, having particular research and teaching interest in IB staffed and implemented the program. Their rank, tenure, and compensation decisions continued to be made in their respective departments. While Professors Fayerweather and Hawkins wanted a voice in those decisions, as well as in hiring of faculty having an IB focus, they did not want them removed from the governance oversight of their respective functional departments. An important consequence was the maintenance of respect for the IB program, since each functional department could not assume an attitude of professional superiority as against the IB faculty, that is, their colleagues working with the IB program.

Dean William Dill is convinced that the early avoidance of a separate departmental apparatus was a major factor contributing to the great reputation and success of Stern's IB program.[12] Professors Fayerweather and Hawkins used well the flexibility of the informal staffing arrangement to build an outstanding IB faculty. In so doing, they were greatly strengthened by their success in finding outside funding to support conferences and research involving both non-NYU and NYU people. In later years, a Department of International Business was created, but it continues to function on an interdisciplinary basis.

International Management Program

The IMP program, described briefly in Chapter 5, is now examined in greater detail. Among the first such programs in the United States, it reflects the cosmopolitan character of New York University. Located in one of the world's greatest metropolitan centers, the Stern School's graduate division has about one-third of its student body drawn from over 60 foreign countries, and almost 35 percent of the faculty come from foreign countries. Further, Stern's International Business department is consistently ranked among the best in the United States (the 1992 *U.S. News and World Report* survey ranked it second).

Begun in 1974–1975, the IMP at NYU is probably the largest such program in existence, now embracing 24 programs at 20 of the world's best business schools. Originally, it involved N Y U, l'Ecole des Hautes Etudes Commerciales in Paris, and the London Business School, with students from each spending one semester at each of the other two schools. Since modified, the program today allows for a one-semester or a two-semester experience. Between 1980 and 1990, a total of 615 foreign students came to N Y U, while a total of 541 N Y U students studied abroad. The two leading foreign schools involved in the exchanges continue to be the original ones in Paris and London.

The central purposes of the program are: (1) education for management in an increasingly interdependent international marketplace, increasingly occupied by global enterprises; (2) cross-cultural exposures made most meaningful by study and living abroad; and (3) first-hand observation and contact with foreign business. But there were significant educational, financial, and physical aspects of the program which had to be resolved for it to be successful.

The educational aspect involved qualitative parity in the course work done in the participating institutions. This required examination of faculty resources, as well as laboratory and library facilities. It required also a look at the relationship between prospective participating schools and the business communities in their countries. Fortunately, the development of high-quality management programs in Europe by the mid-seventies made the program feasible. Its extension to the Middle East, Asia, and South America waited on comparable development in those areas.

A major problem, especially in the early years of the program's extension beyond Paris and London, involved bilingual fluency among participating students. That problem is partly reflected in the greater difficulty of finding American students to send abroad as against foreign students to come to the United States. A further difficulty which inhibited the extension of the program to certain foreign countries was the large disparity in the physical accommodations at foreign institutions, compared with those available in New York. This problem was especially difficult in mainland China and led to the discontinuance of that exchange program. Another problem was financial, involving the monetary disparity in the tuition, residential, and other living costs between particular countries. The resolution involved students paying the costs in their home institution and getting a one-to-one equivalence exchange with a student in the foreign school. Of course, it is implicit that there will be a balanced trade between schools over time, and a balance of trade record is kept by the participating schools. Unfortunately, the balance is off the mark in some cases, so that there is a continuing need to monitor the financial side of the exchanges. In any case, these obstacles have so far been surmountable, and the program appears to be a great success.

Master of Science Programs

Two MS programs were begun in the decade of the seventies: the first is the MS in Accounting program (1972–1973); and the second is the MS in Statistics and Operations Research program, originally the MS in Quantitative Analysis (1974–1975). There is also a variant of the latter program that specializes in Actuarial Science. Of the two programs, the MS in Accounting is the more significant in terms of students enrolled and firms participating (i.e., employing and sponsoring students).

The MS in Accounting program was designed for nonbusiness holders of baccalaureate degrees, especially in Liberal Arts and Engineering. The program is intensive, spanning 15 months beginning in June of one year and ending in October of the following year. The 15-month span embraces two summers and two academic semesters. The first summer is spent in full-time intensive study. The two academic semesters which follow (September through May) involve full-time work in a participating accounting firm, with part-time evening study. The second summer is again a period of full-time intensive study. A period of full-time work with an accounting firm satisfies the New York State "experience" requirements for the CPA certification, as well as the requirements for other states. Participating accounting firms, including America's most prestigious companies, visit the campuses of Ivy League schools in the Northeast to recruit and sponsor candidates for the program, who then apply for admission. The candidates meeting GBA standards are accepted into the program. For the duration of the program, the students are compensated by the participating firms as full-time staff members. But those who cannot find sponsoring firms must transfer their acceptance to the school's MBA program. Dean Dill recalls that the MS in Accounting program, a success in itself, also impacted favorably on GBA and its MBA program, thereby confirming Professor Michael Schiff's correctness in strongly advocating adoption of the program. Dean Dill says:

By targeting recruits from the best liberal arts colleges, with GMAT scores averaging close to 100 points above the then-current MBA average, and by challenging them and satisfying them once they came, he [i.e., Professor Schiff] established a network for good word-of-mouth advertising back to those campuses for graduate business study in general.[13]

The MS program in Statistics and Operations Research (originally Quantitative Analysis) was designed to train people to apply statistical and OR techniques to a substantial range of problems in business and government. Students are required to complete 15 full semester courses, of which up to three can be waived for equivalent work. Typically, the student takes five courses per semester, making three semesters the normal duration of the course for full-time students. Generally, students with undergraduate majors in Mathematics, Science, or Business Administration are most likely to find the program attractive. Of interest is the fact that the program can involve courses taken at N Y U's Courant Institute of Mathematical Sciences.

Both MS programs and their variants reflect faculty and administration perceptions of market demands worthy of educational response and service. Of course, these perceptions are not always accurate, and may change in time. The point is that the Academy is concerned about and responsive to the market.

Do not overlook the important point that MS programs are *specialist* in concept and design. Recall the observation by the Ad Hoc Review Committee for the MBA Program chaired by Professor Gerald Glasser, that one of the major strengths of N Y U's graduate school is its ability to mount a rich variety of specialized programs. Thus, we see in the MS programs, as we do in the Certificate programs next discussed, an effort to employ supply capability to meet perceived market demand niches.

Certificate Programs

The Advanced Professional Certificate program (APC), briefly mentioned in Chapter 5, was introduced in 1972–1973 and quickly found an audience. Paralleled by the Professional Program in Business (PPB) at the undergraduate school, it was set at a higher educational level, requiring possession of a master's degree or its equivalent in Business, Law, or other professional fields. Designed to meet the *specialized* needs of experienced managers, it recognized that such people frequently want further study: first, to move into a new field; or, second, to learn about new developments in their existing field. Again, the program seeks to use the graduate school's rich resources to meet perceived market demands. A wide range of modules quickly developed in every major functional area, with flexibility provided to allow the modules to vary with the specialized objectives of individual students. Typically, the APC plan consists of a group of five or six related courses which provide in-depth training in a specific area. The modules can usually be completed in one calendar year of part-time study. Students could originally opt to be graded on a pass/fail basis or on a standard grading basis. But the former option was quickly abandoned. In the latter case a minimum grade point average of 2.5 had to be maintained. Some transferability of course credit was provided for students who had taken and completed courses at the graduate school as so-called "special" or "visiting professional" students. As in all graduate school programs, the program must be completed within time limits.

A second program, the Certificate in the Audit and Control of Computer Systems, was introduced in the early eighties. This was designed for college graduates having responsibility for the audit and control of computer systems. Again we see a program designed to meet a specialized need. Computer systems are today omnipresent, and the flow of computer-generated information is enormous. But the advantages of the computer in speedily producing and manipulating data are offset somewhat by the danger of inadequate controls to prevent and detect errors, accidents, and frauds. There are also issues of privacy and unauthorized access to data banks, an activity that assumed the status of a sport among so-called "hackers." Concern has grown about the quality of computer-generated information, and the provisions of the Foreign Corrupt Practices Act have sharpened the sensitivity of top executives and boards of directors to the risks noted.

The Certificate in the Audit and Control of Computer Systems is constructed to meet the needs of specialists working in this field, or who plan to work in it. Two types of students were in the minds of those who designed the program; people with accounting backgrounds and those with information systems backgrounds. Prerequisites for participation in the program are the baccalaureate degree and relevant work experience, plus GMAT and prior academic records equivalent to those required for admission to the MBA program.

Careers in Business Program

In the mid-seventies it became obvious that newly graduated PhDs in the Arts and Sciences, especially the Humanities and Social Sciences other than Economics, were having great difficulty finding employment. A terrible societal waste and underutilization of a valuable resource was perceived. In this context the National Endowment for the Humanities financed a project to discover whether such PhDs could be retrained for careers in business. The conclusion of the study was affirmative, and New York State selected N Y U's GBA to implement the program, which became known as Careers in Business.

Professor Ernest Kurnow, director of GBA's doctoral program, became director of the new program, which was initiated in 1978.[14] For this intensive seven-week summer certificate program, student selection was on the basis of prior PhD work, achievements outside the respective fields of study, and motivation to make a career change. The program typically invited 120–130 applicants for interviews, from which number about 90 were accepted to obtain a matriculant group of 60. Equally divided between men and women, the group usually had a median age of 33 and an age range of 25–46, and came from about 30 institutions and 20 disciplines. Most came from English and History, with Romance Languages providing the next-largest group.

The program was full-time over seven weeks. During the first five weeks intensive courses were offered in Accounting, Economics, Finance, Management, Marketing, Statistics, and Career Decision Making. Informal luncheon sessions with business executives were part of the program, as were workshops in resume writing, communications skills for the job search, networking, interviewing, and business library use. Aimed at providing the students with basic concepts and skills in key functional areas of business, the program emphasized the practical application of those concepts and skills. In Professor Kurnow's words: "In content, courses cover by and large the same material as do the corresponding M B A courses. The unusual ability of CIB students to acquire new knowledge makes such coverage possible in relatively few class hours." The sixth week of the program involved analyzing actual business cases, while the seventh week was devoted to on-campus job interviews.

Professor Kurnow, in a statement prepared in August 1993, wrote:

By 1986 the demands for programs like CIB had practically disappeared. Only NYU and Virginia offered programs that year and both had great difficulty finding students. These programs had apparently accomplished their purpose by then. The reasons for the dwindling demand follow:

(1) The number of students enrolled in Ph.D. programs in the humanities and social sciences had decreased significantly because of the absence of jobs in academe. Princeton, for example, stopped admitting Ph.D. students to its Romance language programs because it could not guarantee jobs to graduates.

(2) Liberal arts colleges during the 80s were restructuring their programs and requiring courses in the humanities and social sciences for all undergraduates. This increased the demand for teachers and there was a broader market for the shrinking number of Ph.D. graduates.

(3) Programs like ours helped businesses lose their fear of Ph.D. graduates. After a while, Ph.D.s were hired by business firms even without the benefit of a CIB program. You no longer needed specific business training to apply for and get a job if you had a Ph.D. In fact, we would advise applicants who were not accepted in our program to try for a job on their own. Many were successful.

Table 6.1 shows the employment record of Careers in Business graduates, by industry, in the 9–year period 1978–1986. Numbering 480, the graduates represented a successful university effort to redeploy a valuable societal asset. However, as Professor Kurnow observes, market conditions changed and the program, having served its purpose, was discontinued. But it reflects again the interaction between academia and market forces.

Urban Business Assistance Corporation (UBAC)

UBAC, founded in 1969, is a student-founded, student-run nonprofit corporate entity, receiving financial support from business and government sponsors, as well as from the Stern School (office space and support services). It is an unusually effective bridge between the business school and small minority-owned businesses in the metropolitan area. Since its founding it has served more than 2,400 client firms, and more than 6,500 business people have attended UBAC's small business education program.

Started by five GBA students, UBAC sought from the beginning to provide management consulting services for small minority and

Employment of Careers in Business Graduates by Industry,
1978–1986

Industry	Total	Percent of Total
Banking	79	16.5
Consulting	65	13.6
Manufacturing	51	10.5
Advertising	44	9.2
Nonprofit Administration	44	9.2
Publishing	39	8.2
Finance	34	7.0
Insurance	21	4.4
Government Administration	15	3.2
Retailing	12	2.4
Communication	7	1.4
Utilities	7	1.4
Public Relations	5	1.0
Real Estate	5	1.0
Accounting	3	0.5
Academia	49	10.2
Total	480	100.0

SOURCE: Professor Ernest Kurnow's records.

women-owned businesses. Its consulting services are provided by carefully selected graduate students, who have the support of faculty, and a board of trustees that includes bankers, lawyers, and business people. UBAC benefits from a small paid staff that handles its affairs in a business-like way, so much so that it does not run deficits and has accumulated a Reserve Fund Balance of $83,828 as of year-end 1992. With a 1992 expenditure of $103,370, it generated revenues from donor grants of $78,889, educational services of $18,666, consulting services of $7,930, and some Fund Balance interest. Donors in 1992 numbered 30 companies, foundations, and individuals. Among the corporate sponsors were Automatic Data Processing, Avon Products, Borden, CBS, Chase Manhattan Bank, Consolidated Edison, IBM, Macy's, McGraw-Hill, Merrill Lynch, J. P. Morgan, New York Telephone, Pfizer, Sony, Toyota, and U.S. Trust Company. Its principal expenditures were for consulting ($41,912), management and general ($29,933), and education ($27,964). It is a powerful testimonial to the competence and integrity of its student staff and consultants that it operates successfully.

Concentrating on *consulting* and *educational* programs, UBAC offers these consulting services: (1) Accounting and Bookkeeping; (2) Financial

Management; (3) Government Contracting; (4) Management, Organization, and Planning; (5) Management, Administration and Personnel; (6)
Marketing Analysis and Planning; and (7) Information Systems and
Computerization. These services are applied to the development of business plans, marketing strategies, organizational analyses, loan proposals,
accounting systems, and feasibility studies. Educational programs include classes and workshops such as: Small Business Management, Writing a Business Plan, Loan Strategies, Business Accounting, Sales Techniques, Marketing, and Computers. From the standpoint of the
participating GBA students, who receive modest compensation as well
as the satisfaction of providing a significant service, they gain invaluable
experience in real world situations. They handle practical problems that
yield to intelligent analysis and productive solutions.

Note needs to be taken of Dean Dill's comments about UBAC.
He wrote:

> It was about a year old when I arrived, one of at least a dozen efforts
> nationwide by graduate schools and graduate students to provide con-
> sulting advice to minority businesses. It is probably the only one that has
> survived. I would encourage a specific bow to two people who have
> helped generations of deans and students keep it working: Allen Thomas,
> a lawyer with Paul Weiss Rifkind, who served in early years as UBAC
> board chairman and who invested incredible time and energy into every-
> thing from overall structure and fund-raising to counseling current offi-
> cers through day-to-day challenges; and Rick Caro, then a staffer and
> MBA student at NYU, now after 25 years still a great backer and
> booster.[15]

Academy and Market: Interaction and Conflict

The story of change spanning three decades told in this chapter is rich in
illustrations of the interaction of educational and market forces, as well
as the not infrequent conflict between them. Thus we see Dean Taggart,
anxious to build GBA's academic reputation, turning significantly away
from the School's traditional sole emphasis on evening study to the
building of a full-time day program. We witness him also turning the
School away from significant market demand for industry-specific, vocationally oriented, continuing education programs. Deliberately, he
moved to direct such programs to the School of Continuing Education,
or other university divisions willing to service them. A little later under

Dean Dill's administration in the seventies, GBA developed a number of new programs (Master of Science and Certificate). All were designed to satisfy perceptions of market demand, but demand thought to be consistent with the School's perception of itself in terms of proper educational purpose and quality. Other reflections of interaction between the Academy and the market involved interinstitutional comparisons of teaching loads and compensation. We shall refer to these matters in a later chapter.

Other Developments

The graduate school's prestige was enhanced in the sixties and thereafter by the Salomon Brothers Lecture Series, which was funded by that firm. The lecture series brought a number of famous personalities to GBA, and they attracted attention among prominent people, especially in the New York City financial, business, and political communities. Perhaps the most prominent of the Salomon Brothers lecturers was former President Lyndon B. Johnson. The Herman Kroos Lecture Series, named for one of GBA's great teachers, was also prestigious, but it survived only for a relatively short span of time. Finally, the C. Walter Nicols Award was presented annually to an outstanding American business leader. The luster of the award was directly related to the extraordinary quality of the awardees, which being exceptional, enhanced the school.

SEVEN

The Stern School: Union at the Square

The Stern Gift

There are defining moments in the lives of individuals and organizations, moments that are decisive in determining the future course of events. One such moment came in 1988 when Leonard N. Stern, chief executive of The Hartz Group Inc., and a trustee of New York University, agreed to donate $30 million to the university. His decision responded to a plan for the future development of NYU's business schools that had been created under the leadership of Dean Richard West.

Dick West, dean for nine years (1984–1993), had a major impact on the Stern School. While Leonard Stern's gift was the most dramatic evidence of his impact, other important manifestations are found in changes in academic programs, construction of the new Management Education Center (MEC) at Washington Square, the move of the graduate school to that location, and its unification there with the undergraduate school. It is a fortunate truth that Dean West's experience prior to his arrival at NYU equipped him to have a major and constructive impact. He had served previously as dean of the B-School at the University of Oregon and of the Amos Tuck School of Business at Dartmouth. Apart from his administrative experience, he was a highly respected scholar and professor of Finance.

Stern is an alumnus of both Commerce and GBA, and had already made substantial gifts to the university. But the $30 million commitment was a blockbuster, the largest single gift yet made to any American business school. On top of the material aspect of the gift was an overlay of publicity that generated enormous excitement. With one dramatic action, Leonard Stern catapulted his alma mater to a level of public prominence it had not previously commanded. His gift was the subject of a major story in The *New York Times Sunday Magazine,* as well as in innumerable other influential journals. It positioned the School for the twenty-first Century.

There was synergy in the gift, for N Y U's business schools were already prominent and among the top 20 in the country. The graduate school was generally seen externally as somewhere between 10 and 20 in the ratings, while the undergraduate school was rated as fifth or sixth in the country. The higher rating of the undergraduate college was due to the fact that a number of the top graduate schools do not have under-graduate programs. Perhaps reflecting an inherent bias, the faculty of N Y U's schools rated their school higher than external evaluators did. The Stern gift shook up the perceptions of outsiders, thereby exerting a significant influence on their view. In recognition of the importance of his gift, the university renamed N Y U's School of Business as the Leonard N. Stern School of Business.

Seen in the broadest terms, the Stern gift positioned N Y U's B-school to move forward with confidence into its second century. Commenting on his gift, Leonard N. Stern wrote:

> The founders of N Y U set out clearly their reasons for establishing this great university in 1831: To offer the children of the city's burgeoning immigrant population an education that would enable them to become productive, prosperous citizens in a growing United States.
>
> In early 1926, my late father, Max Stern, recently arrived in New York from his native Germany, founded Hartz Mountain Pet Supply Company. Indeed, Hartz' first offices were only a few blocks from the University's Washington Square Campus.
>
> As an alumnus of this University, it gives me great pleasure to help yet another generation acquire skills that will allow them to reap America's opportunities and contribute to the growth and prosperity of our nation for the well-being of generations to follow.[1]

The Management Education Center

Leonard N. Stern's magnificent gift activated the school's long-range plan, focused on four major goals: (1) the construction of a state-of-the-art management educational facility, at Washington Square, to bring together the graduate and undergraduate schools at the location which is the heart of the university; (2) a modest reduction in the size of the Stern School, to enhance the overall student/faculty ratio and to advance further the quality of its programs and students; (3) an adjustment in full-time and part-time MBA enrollments, with the aim of achieving a better balance (i.e., a somewhat larger proportion of full-time students); and (4) the achievement of a firmer and more secure financial base for the Stern School, characterized by a substantially larger endowment that would reduce the School's historic dependence on tuition revenue.

Dean West, at the time of the dedication of the new Management Education Center, which tied together a new 11-story building, Tisch Hall, and a substantially remodeled part of Shimkin Hall (the old home of the School of Commerce) wrote:

> With more and better classrooms and the very latest in computing and communications technology—not to mention superb location at the heart of NYU's dynamic Washington Square Campus—the center is, without question a state-of-the-art facility. As such, it provides the Stern School with the "academic vessel" it needs to offer management education of uncompromised quality—education designed to produce graduates equipped to excel in an increasingly competitive global market place.[2]

Dean Diamond, in his remarks on the occasion of the dedication, observed that the union of the Stern School's faculty at the Square would have major benefits in improved operational efficiencies, as well as in vastly increased opportunity for faculty and student interaction. Further, the interaction between the graduate and undergraduate divisions of the Stern School, and among the graduate division and other NYU schools, would be greatly encouraged and improved.[3]

Among the advantages attendant on the creation of the Management Education Center was its proximity to the Bobst Library. The physical juxtaposition of that facility and the MEC made possible moving the business library to a convenient location adjacent to the Stern School. Downtown, at Trinity Place, the library had been moved to rented quarters a few blocks from Nichols and Merrill Halls. Other advantages accrued from the now convenient proximity of the Coles Sports and Recreation Center, and the many dormitory and residential facilities which the university had built in the area of Washington Square. All in all, an educational and physical critical mass was achieved.

Curricular Changes

Curricular review and change have become a hallmark of the Stern School. It was not always so. At Commerce, once the BS curriculum was in place in 1926, it was not changed materially for 30 years, until the mid-fifties. Since then it has undergone a number of changes, at least one per decade and sometimes two. The record was similar at GBA. Except for the elimination of the MCS and DCS degree programs in the thirties, the MBA and PhD curricula remained stable from the early thirties to the sixties. Since then the record is one of frequent review, reexamination, and change.

I am fascinated by one particular aspect of this dynamic process of review and change. It involves the fairly frequent reversal of direction that occurred, with tomorrow's innovation a return to an older pattern. Examples are easy to find. One involves the return to the 1:1 contact hour-credit hour relationship in the MBA program in 1993. Another involves the return to the three contact hour-three credit hour course module in the BS program in 1994. But the overall degree structure built on a general core, a major area of concentration, and electives (often with the possibility of a minor concentration) persisted. At the undergraduate level the general professional core is almost always in line with and parallel to the MBA core. Often there is the possibility of a double major. There is also the undergirding provided by the general studies core in the Liberal Arts and Sciences. Here some fluctuation occurs in the proportion of work in the baccalaureate devoted to the Arts and Sciences as against the professional courses. The ideal of a 50–50 division continues to have important influence, and is reflected in the accreditation standards of the American Assembly of Collegiate Schools of Business (AACSB). But the standard is not rigid, and has been interpreted as permitting some business school courses to be counted in the "general education component" (i.e., Arts and Sciences portion) of the baccalaureate program. Examples of such courses are Statistics and Computer Based Systems. Consequently, business school courses can use 60 percent of the curriculum, leaving 40 percent for courses offered by the Arts and Sciences faculty.

The MBA Program. The MBA program is the financial backbone of the graduate division, in terms of tuition revenues, staffing needs, physical

plant required, and supporting services. Its nature is therefore an inescapable obligation and concern of the faculty. The most recent review of
it began at the end of the eighties, and its current curricular structure
was implemented in 1993–1994. *The single most significant change was a
shift from the two contact hour-three credit hour course module to a three contact
hour-three credit hour module.* That shift restored the traditional 1:1 contact
hour-credit hour relationship, and involved large changes in courses
offered, teaching loads, and staffing profiles.

The program requires the completion of 60 credits of course work.
Of that total, 36 credits are in required core courses, 12 credits in a
major area, and a further 12 credits in nonmajor and elective courses.
While the overwhelming majority of the courses are of the 3-credit
variety, some variations involve half courses of $1^{1}/_{2}$ points each and
one $4^{1}/_{2}$ point required core course in Data Analysis and Modeling for
Managers. Much care was exercised in determining that Data Analysis
and Modeling for Managers warrants $4^{1}/_{2}$ credits, rather than 3 or 6.
This comment is not made facetiously or with tongue-in-cheek. Faculty
in the nonquantitative functional areas had to agree that, while a basic 3-
credit course would serve for each of their areas,[4] it would not meet the
quantitative needs of the students and the program. Table 7.1 summa-
rizes the program. Students can use all nonmajor and elective course
credits to achieve a second major (co-major). Students in the major
leading to certification for a career as a CPA are required to take all
the major and nonmajor elective course credits in required accounting-
related courses.

Other features of the MBA program are: (1) the clear effort to
broaden the perspective of the content and teaching of the core courses,
evident in the course titles and their emphasis on globalization and
overall decision making; (2) the emphasis on the acquisition of a strong
quantitative skill base by students; (3) the emphasis on developing communications skills, a reversion to an emphasis which had characterized
the earliest years of the N Y U business schools; and (4) an explicit concern
with ethics. The program can certainly be regarded as generalist in
nature, with the major constituting only 20 percent of the 60 credits
required (i.e., 12 out of 60).

Not evident from a surface look at the program is an effort to foster a
greater interdisciplinary approach by the faculty, especially in the required core courses. This effort reflects a strong tendency of faculty in
the functional departments to structure their courses in compartmental-

TABLE 7.1
The MBA Program, Effective 1993–1994

1. *Required Core:*	
a. Microeconomics for Global Business Decision Making	3
b. Understanding the World Macroeconomy	3
c. Financial Accounting: A User Perspective	3
d. Managerial Accounting	1.5
e. Data Analysis and Modeling for Managers	4.5
f. Managing Organizational Behavior	3
g. Marketing Concepts and Strategies	3
h. Managing Information Technology and Systems	3
i. Foundations of Finance	3
j. Operations Management	3
k. Management Communication I	1.5
l. Markets, Ethics, and Law	1.5
m. Business Strategy and Policy	3
	36
2. *Major:*	
4 courses	12
3. *Nonmajor and Electives:*	
4 courses	12
4. Total	60

ized boundaries. As of this writing, the effort is still exploratory. It involves arrangements to stimulate interdepartmental meetings and discussions among faculty, intended to activate consideration of required core course content across the boundaries of the respective disciplines. The underlying point is as simple as it is compelling; the accounting, finance, management, and marketing decisions of a business executive are not discrete and without bearing upon each other. The academic program that pretends to prepare future executives for such decision making is a sham, if not a fraud, if it does not reflect that reality. The sad truth is that the professional and research interests of the faculty typically run in narrow rather than broad channels, so this effort across departmental lines faces strong inbred cultural biases. Nonetheless, the effort is worthwhile, even necessary, and I hope it will succeed.

The BS Program. The implementation of the new MBA program was associated with a thorough review and reworking of the baccalaureate program. That review was complicated by the existence of the four-course module and structure that dated back to the late sixties, and involved the curricular interrelationship between work in the Arts and Sciences and in the Stern School. Generally, and in spite of these problems, the restructuring that finally emerged followed the essential directions set in the MBA program. In particular, the same class scheduling module was adopted (i.e., there should be two class sessions per week, each one hour and 20 minutes in duration). Also, the program continued to allow double majors, new to the MBA program but not to the baccalaureate, and moved to enhance work in ethics, management communications, and globalization.

The major features of the program are: (1) 64 credits required in liberal Arts and Sciences; (2) 52 credits required in the professional core and professional electives; and (3) 12 credits in free electives. If all free elective credits are used to take professional courses, then the proportion of such courses to the total is 50 percent, making it equal to the Arts and Sciences component. If all free elective credits are used to take Arts and Sciences courses, then 59 percent of the program is in that area and some 41 percent in professional courses. But 10 credits counted among the Arts and Sciences are in Statistics and Information Systems, which are taught in the Stern School and could be considered professional.

If Statistics and Information Systems are counted as professional courses and all 12 points of the free electives are taken in professional courses, than only 42 percent (54 credits) of the program would be in Arts and Sciences. Yet, AACSB continues to insist that at least half the baccalaureate curriculum be in the "general education" component (usually interpreted to mean the Arts and Sciences). But AACSB considers certain "professional" core courses to qualify as "general education," e.g., Economics and Statistics. Wharton and the Stern School would add Computer Based Systems (or course equivalents). The philosophical issue is not complex. It centers on the conviction that an education appropriate to life in a modern society must include an understanding of the basic information-handling capability of computers, plus the data comprehension capacity associated with an elementary knowledge of statistics. In short, these subjects are viewed as basic knowledge for everyone, and so a fitting addition to "general education." Put differently, *the Arts and Sciences no longer have an exclusive, proprietary hold on the basic knowledge that every educated person should have.* While this may be shocking to the Faculty of Arts and Sciences, it is a reality of modern life that can be ignored only to the detriment of future generations.

The overall credit requirements do not reveal the complexity of the present program. This complexity reflects the need to maintain some conformity with the Arts and Sciences 4-credit module while concurrently adjusting the professional courses to the new 3 credit module of the MBA program.

The solution arrived at was to make five of the seven required professional core courses worth 4 credits each, while the other two would be worth 2 and 3 credits respectively (Managerial Accounting and Business Policy). The five 4-point professional core courses are: Financial Accounting, Financial Management, Management and Organizational Analysis, Introduction to Marketing, and Operations Management. The 10 credits of Statistics and Information Systems are placed in the General Education Component of the program, with the Arts and Sciences, although some, as noted above, would consider them part of the professional core. The 10 credits involve three courses, two worth 4 points each and one worth 2 points. All other courses in the Stern baccalaureate program are worth 3 credits each. Finally, the programs of study in Accounting, Actuarial Science, and Statistics are more prescriptive than others.

An intriguing device was used to mesh the four credit hour-four contact hour core courses with the three contact hour-three credit hour scheduling and teaching load module of the MBA program. Instead of meeting twice a week, for one hour and 20 minutes per session, these course meet three times a week. Two of the sessions are of one hour and 20 minutes, and are taught by Stern faculty. *The third session is of 50 minutes duration, is tutorial, and is served by teaching assistants (or an arrangement meeting tutorial objectives).* This arrangement eased the problem of setting teaching loads and assignments across the graduate–undergraduate programs. What it means in terms of educational quality depends on the competence of the teaching assistants, and the direction given to them. Reflecting this concern, the program calls for enrollment in the tutorial sessions to be limited to 30 students, while enrollments in the twice a week one hour and 20 minute sessions are set at 60 on average.

The Committee that proposed the program to the faculty was very sensitive to the quality issue and pointed out that the use of teaching assistants in the tutorial sessions would require the setting up of an administrative mechanism for recruiting, training, and scheduling assistants. They thought that the experience gained from the use of teaching assistants in the MBA program would be very helpful in implementing the Undergraduate program. They believed that the experience of being teaching assistants would significantly strengthen the learning experience of MBA and PhD students. It was noted also that the arrangement would keep the staffing and budgetary implications of the new curriculum at acceptable levels. Both concerns, the educational and the financial, weighed heavily. In any case, it should be clear that both considerations were involved in the final arrangements. It should be clear also that the creation of some three credit courses might necessitate the development of additional courses to satisfy the 128-credit program. But enlargement in the numbers of courses offered could result in some increase in the number of faculty. In view of this fact, an earlier version of the new baccalaureate program proposed by the undergraduate division's Academic Affairs Committee on December 2, 1992, pointed out that an increase in average class size and/or use of adjunct faculty, along with additional teaching assistants, would moderate the budgetary impact. Obviously, educational decisions are not free of financial or market considerations.

Table 7.2 provides a sample illustration of the new BS program, which was adopted by the faculty in April 1993 to be implemented on a pilot basis in 1994–1995, and in full in 1995–1996.

Teaching Loads

The new MBA program restored the 1:1 relationship between contact hours and credit hours. Thus, where three courses previously involved nine credit hours and six contact hours, three courses now involved nine contact hours for nine credit hours. If the number of courses required in the School's teaching load remained unchanged, then a de facto increase in teaching load of 50 percent would occur. It should occasion no surprise that the faculty was not receptive to this outcome of the curriculum reform. Consequently, the teaching load was reduced from six graduate or undergraduate equivalent courses per year to three courses per year (nine contact hours per year, or four and one-half contact hours per semester, per week). This change reduced the contact hour teaching load by 25 percent. Further, the policy statement on teaching loads and released time allowed further reductions for certain nonteaching duties. Plainly, this action had expensive financial implications, especially when coupled with the cost increasing aspects of the new BS and MBA programs. Significantly, in the 1993–1994 academic year, the use of adjuncts and graduate assistants (i.e., PhD students) in undergraduate courses amounted to some 40 percent of the total staffing. This staffing

TABLE 7.2
Stern School, Undergraduate Curriculum,
1995–1996

Freshman Year	
Computer Based Systems	4 points
Economics (2 courses)	8 points
Calculus	4 points
Writing (2 courses)	8 points
Social or Natural Science	4 points
History/Literature/Art/Language	4 points
8 Courses	**32 points**
Sophomore Year	
Financial Accounting	4 points
Managerial Accounting	2 points
Statistics	4 points
Regression/Forecasting	2 points
Ethics	4 points
Oral Communication	4 points
Social or Natural Science	4 points
History/Literature/Art/Language	4 points
Liberal Arts Elective	4 points
Free Elective	3 points
10 courses	**35 points**
Junior Year	
Finance	4 points
Management	4 points
Marketing	4 points
·Operations Management	4 points
Liberal Arts Electives	4 points
Stern Electives (4 courses)	12 points
9 courses	**32 points**
Senior Year	
Business Policy	3 points
Stern Electives (5 courses)	15 points
Free Electives (3–4 courses)	11 points
9–10 Courses	**29 Points**

profile is hopefully a reversible slippage from the one achieved in the late sixties. At the graduate level, in 1993–1994, 26 out of 86 course sections were taught by adjuncts (i.e., 30 percent), and the new MBA and BS programs were yet to be fully implemented.

Dean George Daly understood these implications, and moved quickly to address them. In one of his earliest memos to the Faculty Council, he announced the appointment of a new Professional Program Review Committee to review other degree programs (MS, Executive MBA, and PhD). The essential thing is that these programs, especially the doctoral programs, are expensive in their demands on faculty and other resources, and so need to be examined in the context of the School's total and limited resources.

Dean Daly said in his memo:

> Recent changes in our educational programs and faculty teaching load policies have important implications for the demands placed on Stern's teaching resources. The current budgetary situation at the School and University suggest that we are unlikely to expand our faculty in the foreseeable future. Given these realities, I believe that it is important that we establish curricular and programmatic priorities that are consistent with our faculty resources.
>
> These areas that have yet to be explored consist of our MS, Executive MBA and Ph.D. programs. Recent market developments, as well as the resource constraints and demands that confront us, suggest that these areas be explored as well and policies established regarding the role of such programs in Stern's future.[5]

If one accepts our earlier observation that the MBA program is the backbone of the Stern School's graduate division, then Dean Daly's memo implies a real possibility of curtailing or dropping some of the School's doctoral, MS, and Executive MBA programs. Recalling the nature of the academic mind-set and pecking order, it is more than likely that any review of the doctoral programs will be painful. There are implications also for the undergraduate program. The inherent hazard is that the "solution" that emerges will excessively favor research over teaching. The further hazard is that the undergraduate program will be exploited for the advantage of the graduate programs.

Some additional details on the School's teaching load policy will provide an even clearer insight into the nature of the problem. These details were spelled out in a memo dated March 8, 1993, from Associate Dean Richard P. Brief to the department chairmen. Dean Brief noted that the policy would probably be interim, observing that "the question of teaching loads and release time will be revisited next year." The major features of the policy are: (1) three courses per year for the full-time tenure track faculty; and (2) four courses per year for visiting and clinical faculty. But release time is available for chairmen, the director of the PhD program, undergraduate program directors, endowed chairholders, research professors, and faculty supported by grants, fellowships, or endowed funds. Directors of Centers and Institutes might get release time at the discretion of the dean, and department chairmen had some discretion also in providing release time. Interestingly, chairmen and undergraduate directors could get extra compensation for teaching a very limited number of extra courses. Special note must be taken of the *prohibition* on full-time faculty teaching more than two courses in a single semester. Obviously, the underlying concern is that some faculty might teach three courses in a single semester, and then seek to take off the following semester. Such a development would be highly disruptive, and could compromise the rationale underlying sabbatical leave policy. Similarly, it is specified that if only one semester is taught (e.g., when a faculty member is on sabbatical or other leave), then at least one and one-half courses must be taught in that semester. If two courses are taught, then the excess one-half course can be banked and applied to the following year's teaching load.

Faculty Compensation

There is a stereotype abroad in the land that depicts teachers as under-paid, overworked, unappreciated people, who, in addition, often work under hazardous conditions that warrant some form of combat pay. That picture is probably accurate for some inner-city secondary schools in the public school system. It is not accurate for the professoriate in America's premier Academies of higher learning, especially in those faculties enjoying tight markets (Law, Medicine, and Business are exam-ples). What one sees when one looks knowledgeably is a very attractive life-style, well, if not richly, rewarded. Ample leisure time is afforded, for the academic year is a nine-month year. Travel abroad is therefore not an unusual phenomenon, and is accepted as an appropriate, even necessary, experience for learned people, to teach or attend conferences, engage in research, or simply for pleasure. Any additional teaching, say during the summer, is at additional pay of one-ninth or two-ninths of base, depending on whether one or two months are involved. And we have noted earlier that the basic teaching load at Stern is now three courses per year, representing four and one-half contact hours per week if averaged over the academic year. While research output is demanded, and class preparation plus other duties consume time, the total academic demands on a professor's time provide great flexibility and discretionary time. There is also the reality of the freedom of expression associated with tenure, and the privilege of being part of an essentially self-governing group. Only highly privileged, elite social groups have been able to enjoy such life-styles in past history, and such groups were regarded as the aristocracy. While no professor would likely regard him- or herself in that light, the life-style depicted is real, not fictitious.

Table 7.3 puts more flesh on the skeleton of academic life at the apex of the professoriate. It shows *base salaries* for a nine-month academic year at the Stern School in 1992–1993, as well as comparative data for 12 top American B-schools. What must be kept in mind while examining the numbers in Table 7.3 is that they show *base salaries for 9 months*. Many faculty obtain research grant money and/or engage in consulting, which supplement their salaries. The base salary data *do not include salary supplements* (e.g., pension contributions, social security contributions, medical coverage, etc.). These supplements have been calculated as being some 27.5 percent of base salaries. Further, any summer teaching above the basic three course load involves additional compensation. When the resulting total compensation amounts are considered, along with current working conditions, a picture altogether different from that of the embattled inner-city secondary school teacher emerges.

It is not my intention to paint a pejorative picture of the inner-city teacher, and, through use of such a strawman, to paint an excessively glowing and optimistic one of the professoriate in our prestigious Academies. In short, life in the Academy could be better, but, in the meantime, it is far from bad, at least in the top B-schools. Professors of classics and other subjects in the humanities might gnash their teeth when they see the figures of Table 7.3, but their colleagues in the Faculty of Business undoubtedly make their comparisons with the outside markets of the business world and fail to perceive any particular advantage in their position, except perhaps in the area of discretionary time available. We should note that the Stern School is closely in line with the 12 school mean averages for associate and assistant Professors. In those ranks, its minimums are better, probably reflecting emphasis on the recruiting side. We are somewhat behind in the full professor rank, but that condition could be helped greatly by the addition of more endowed chairs. No doubt, that will continue to be a fund-raising focus of the school.

TABLE 7.3
Faculty Salaries, Stern School and 12–School Average, by Rank, 1992–1993
(dollars)

School/ Salary Measure	Rank			
	Professor	Associate Professor	Assistant Professor	Instructor
Stern School:				
Maximum	144,000	92,000	83,500	41,000
Minimum	60,500	60,000	56,000	30,300
Median	101,500	76,000	66,500	30,300
Mean	102,201	76,449	68,176	33,533
12-School Average:				
Maximum	210,200	123,500	90,000	na
Minimum	42,210	43,900	43,000	na
Median	106,000	77,268	66,750	na
Mean	107,618	76,938	68,790	na

SOURCE: Dean's Office, Stern School.
Median—median of medians reported
Mean—mean of means reported, weighted by school, not by number of faculty in each rank
na—not available

Endowment, Tuition, and Other Funding

When I came to the School of Commerce in 1947, endowment and nontuition sources of revenue were practically non-existent. That situation prevailed also in 1965, when I became acting dean. The situation in 1992–1993 is markedly different, if one gives only a quick glance at the numbers. Thus, the Stern School's endowment in 1992–1993 amounted to $49.9 million, of which slightly over $10 million represented undergraduate scholarship endowment. The $49.9 million figure includes also the endowments of Institutes, Centers, and named chairs. It does not include the $30 million Stern gift, for half of that went toward the construction of the new Management Education Center, with the other half accruing to the overall benefit of the university. Also, funds raised for the construction of Tisch, Nichols, and Merrill Halls went into the building of those structures and did not get added to the Stern School's endowment.

There was an internal debate in this last connection, especially as it affected Tisch Hall. Some $7.5–$8.0 million was raised in a so-called Tisch Hall Building Fund. But the building's construction was covered by the Tisch brothers naming gift and the proceeds of a bond issue. The Tisch Hall Building Fund was invested and yielded income. When the

TABLE 7.4
Stern School, Estimated Revenues, 1993–1994

Income Category	Dollar Amount (000)	Percent
Gross Tuition Revenue	87,399	—
(Unfunded & Financial Aid)	(7,538)	—
Net Tuition Revenue	79,861	90.3
Unrestricted Annual Giving	1,300	1.5
Restricted Gifts	1,500	1.7
Endowment Income	4,114	4.6
Fees, Royalties & Subscriptions	1,567	1.8
Miscellaneous	77	.1
Total	88,419	100.0

SOURCE: Dean's Office, Stern School.

university charged the School of Commerce (BPA) for the costs of its space in Tisch Hall (including bond redemption and interest), I argued that the School was entitled to be credited with the income from the Building Fund. Despite the passion with which I argued my point I did not win. Essentially, the outcome means that some fund-raising that is presumably for the benefit of individual schools actually goes for the overall benefit of the university. To that degree, the schools that are most successful fund-raisers are taxed for the benefit of less successful units.

Table 7.4 shows the 1993–1994 estimated revenue picture of the Stern School. The main point revealed is that the School is still overwhelmingly dependent on tuition for its revenue (90.3 percent). Despite the considerable growth in endowment over the past three decades, to $49.9 million, endowment income represents only 4.6 percent of total income. Unrestricted annual giving and restricted gifts represent another 3.2 percent, with fees, royalties, and subscriptions (nonendowment income of centers and institutes) providing a further 1.8 percent.

A look at the expenditure side of the picture is mandatory, to get a proper perception of the School's budgetary picture. Such a look reveals a far healthier situation than prevailed in 1946, when the School was almost 100 percent dependent on tuition, *and when the university was profoundly dependent on the School.* Overall expenditures in 1993–1994 were estimated at $83.9 million, including university indirect costs of $12.2 million, an indexed tax to the university of $2.145 million, debt service for the Management Education Center of $4.0 million, and mothballing costs of $1.04 million associated with the unsold Nichols and Merrill Halls. With that financial load on top of normal operating (direct) cost, the Stern School still produced a further surplus of $4.487 million, on top of the $2.145 million tax to the university. But here there is a profound change from the earlier experience of NYU's business school. The $4.487 million of pure surplus is treated as retained income for the School, with almost $1.0 million (.968) going into endowment accounts. This treatment reflects an enormous shift in the university's perception of the Stern School, and augurs well for the future.

A further point must be made. The surplus of the Stern School is no longer a dominant, overhanging element in the university's total budgetary picture. The $6.6 million of tax plus retained income is small potatoes in an aggregate university budget of some $1.6 billion. It is worlds away from the $1.0 million surplus of the School of Commerce in 1947, when the University's total budget (including the medical center) was some $11 million. In that past age, financial trouble in the university placed enormous pressure on the "cash cow," that is, Commerce. That is no longer the case. The profound change in the situation is healthier for everyone.

EIGHT

Institutes and Centers

The traditional units perceived as the building blocks of a university's organizational structure are schools and their faculties (e.g., Arts and Sciences, Medicine, Law, Business, Education, etc.). These units, in turn, consist of departments that focus on some functional aspect of each school's sphere of knowledge and research. But this perception is incomplete, for universities and their schools embrace a considerable group of additional units, variously designated as Institutes or Centers. Institutes or Centers are usually narrower in purpose and scope than schools, although in occasional instances this distinction is not self-evident. In such a case the name is not a clear indicator of purpose and scope, and the true substance of the entity needs a closer look.

The Stern School has embraced a number of Institutes and Centers, some no longer in existence. Our experience indicates that several factors are important in determining the success or failure of these organizational units, among them: (1) a clear definition of purpose and mission; (2) funding adequate to the accomplishment of that purpose and mission; (3) support among the faculty, specifically a willingness to participate meaningfully in effecting the unit's goals; and (4) real external support in some business and/or government sector for the unit and its goals. I believe these conditions are necessary to success, so that the absence of one or more of them endangers the enterprise. Other conditions are undoubtedly significant, for example, the energy and competence of a director, but that deficiency can be more easily corrected and overcome than a deficiency in one or more of the four critical factors noted.

Institute or Center Purposes

Institute and Center goals are variegated and can be fairly numerous. Some units are more ambitious than others. They will have a wider spectrum of purposes that they seek to achieve. Others will be more limited in scope and will be satisfied if they achieve one or two objectives. Viewed broadly, Institutes and Centers may seek to do these sorts of things: (1) engage in research and publication of its results; (2) arrange conferences; (3) organize and operate management training programs; (4) support fellowships for graduate students; (5) support an endowed professorship, typically for the unit's director; (6) engage in fund-raising to further the work of the unit; (7) educate future teachers to advance the mission of the Institute or Center; and (8) act as a recruitment agency in behalf of an industry or some other external entity.

The foregoing activities do not address the critical and central matter of mission or purpose; that is, to what *end* are these things being done. It is vital that the *end* be clearly defined. A multitude of activities unaccompanied by a clear definition of central purpose is likely to fail to generate the internal and external support necessary to success. Typically, statements of purpose involve focusing on performing the activities noted in behalf of an *industry, government sector, or cause*. The first two are more self-evident than the last; for example, an Institute for Retail Management or a Center for Urban Planning. An example of the last-named purpose would be an Institute for Entrepreneurship, or one for the Study of Quality and Productivity.

Institutes and Centers are easier to create than they are to kill, even though their creation is not simple either. The reason is quickly evident; once created, they bring into place people who have a vested interest in their perpetuation, as well as their expansion. In this regard, at least two dangers face university presidents and deans: first, there are almost always individuals among the faculty and/or external to it who will promote a new Institute or Center; and, second, if *some* funding is available, then the temptation to go ahead can be very powerful. But the funding may be inadequate, and therein lies the danger, for the immediate prestige of being able to announce a gift that seems significant on its face is most enticing. All of which brings us to the issue of funding.

Funding

I turned down at least two Institute proposals because I believed the funding offered was inadequate to the grand purposes put forward. In both cases, later proposals were successful, but the temptation to proceed with the original ones was great, and overcome only by a careful analysis of means and ends.

The first case involved an effort to create an Institute for Accounting Research. The study and advancement of what was then called the "higher accountancy" was a major purpose underlying the creation of the School of Commerce, Accounts, and Finance in 1900. The first dean was Charles Waldo Haskins, an accountant. Throughout the history of the school, the Department of Accounting had enjoyed the largest proportion of majors among the student body. Dean John T. Madden, who served in that office for 23 years, had been chairman of the department. A very large, loyal, and prosperous proportion of the school's alumni were CPAs. And, in 1970–1971 and the years following, the accounting profession was facing major issues of theory and practice. Finally, in 1970 the School of Commerce received endowment funding for a chair in Accounting from Vincent C. Ross, a prominent alumnus and former treasurer of the publisher Prentice-Hall. With the Ross Chair providing funds to support a professorial director for an Institute, conditions appeared propitious to seek funding for an Institute for Accounting Research. It seemed natural and appropriate for the School of Commerce, located as it was in New York, the nation's greatest financial center.

I approached a prominent accounting firm headquartered in the city, whose top leadership included a couple of alumni. The "asking" amounted to $1 million, to be paid in a limited time period and to become an endowment fund that would generate a future stream of income. At a meeting between President Hester, Professor Michael Schiff, and me with the Management Committee of the accounting firm, it became clear that the ideas of the Committee were very different from those of the university people. The accountants offered to contribute approximately $60,000 per year for an undefined future period, in exchange for a School Institute bearing the firm's name and committed to take over a number of existing in-house programs (training, firm specific studies, etc.) that would consume all, and possibly more than all, of the annual contribution. Plainly, no match existed between the firm's purposes and those of the school. I opined that, if I failed to make these mismatches clear, then President Hester should fire me for not carrying out my responsibility to all parties present. With that statement, the meeting adjourned. The proposal was set aside.

Subsequently, however, I approached Vincent Ross and asked him to fund an Institute bearing his name, to be headed by the professor occupying the Ross Chair. Mr. Ross warmed to the proposal, and agreed after a period of discussion as to purpose and accommodations for the Institute in Tisch Hall. The Vincent Ross Institute for Accounting Research was born. We will review later its subsequent work.

The second case involved a nonalumnus with a strong belief that entrepreneurship was of key importance to the future well-being of America. To further this belief, he wanted to finance a Center or Institute in one of America's top business schools. He had been turned down by one school, presumably because there was a mismatch between the prospective donor's practical business orientation and approach and the theoretical approach of the faculty who would be involved at the school. Unfortunately, the early discussions between the prospective donor and me were conducted through an intermediary, who, it turned out, had his own agenda. His agenda included pressure in behalf of a particular faculty member to be guaranteed the position of director. In addition, the intermediary had a grand scheme of Institute activities that I estimated would cost at least several hundreds of thousands of dollars per year to perform. In exchange, the intermediary held out a sum of some $1 million, to be paid out in undefined amounts over a period of years. I did not find it difficult to turn down this proposal, although my decision involved a meeting with the chairman of the university's board of trustees. That meeting was the result of the intermediary's attempt to portray me as an impractical academic unable to understand the grandness of the proposal.

That was not the end of the matter. Another intermediary became active, as did the prospective donor. After a few years, a meeting of the minds did take place, and the Center for Entrepreneurial Studies came into existence at GBA. We will have more to say about this Center later in this chapter.

What is an adequate level of funding (i.e., endowment) for an Institute or Center? It depends upon: (1) the scope of activities envisaged;

(2) whether or not an endowed chair for the director is included; (3) the outlook for rate of return on the endowment (interest rates, etc.); and (4) inflation.

We looked earlier at the *scope of activities*. The degree to which each prospective activity is to be developed is also a matter of concern. Thus, a substantial research program, coupled with publication of the results and production and distribution of a newsletter, involves a considerable expenditure. A number of activities, however, can generate income, including *sponsored research*. But, it needs to be understood at the outset that activities like research, conferences, management training, and such are expected to be associated with fees and/or grants that will make them wholly or substantially self-supporting. This consideration is important because it means that the *interest and purpose* of outside parties will have to be considered, and may be ruling, with respect to the revenues generated. It is simply insufficient to have only a theoretical interest among some faculty in this case. Put differently, a market test needs to be considered.

This writer believes the funding for an Institute or Center should include provisions for an *endowed chair*. One reason is that Institutes or Centers require directors to develop and implement the mission, and his or her cost is as real as the cost of the spectrum of activities to be performed. Another reason is that the success of the unit requires acceptance and support among the faculty. Academic sympathy is more easily gained when the director is a respected professorial chairholder.

Volatility in the *rates of return* during the past quarter century is an important determinant of the amount needed in the corpus of an endowment. Corpus and rate of return determine if there will be revenue adequate to implement the purposes of the Institute or Center. The relationship is inverse, that is, higher rates of return make possible somewhat smaller endowments. Actually, the matter is not that simple, because the outlook for *inflation* is a factor in the calculation. High rates of return tend to be associated with sharply rising price levels. Consequently, the director of an Institute or Center, in such an environment, needs to have an ever-larger income stream as the future unfolds. To obtain this margin of financial safety, the original funding of an Institute or Center should allow explicitly for the eventuality by anticipating the impact of future developments. One way to do this is to set aside a portion of each year's revenue stream, to be added to the corpus of the endowment. While prudence makes such action reasonable, the eagerness to accept and publicize a sizable gift, as well as to create an Institute or Center, may blind university and school officials to future financial problems.

What do the foregoing observations mean in money terms? In the early seventies, when rates of return were high (double digit), $500,000 for an endowed chair and $1.5 million for Institute endowment seemed reasonable. Using a 10 percent rate of return, one envisaged annual revenue of $200,000, a quarter of which ($50,000) would be added to the endowment corpus. Over a 20-year period, the corpus would increase by $1 million (to $3 million). That corpus would yield $210,000 per year at a 7 percent rate of return. It would not be enough to offset the full effect of double-digit inflation during the entire period, but it would be significant in almost any event, and surely so if the rate of inflation moderated.

Looking at the matter in 1994, this writer believes that funding for a new Institute or Center would require $4 to $5 million, of which $1.5 million would provide for an endowed chair. At a 6 percent rate of return, possibly somewhat too high, the revenue stream would be $240,000–$300,000. A well-developed institute, with a clear purpose and substantial range of activities, would certainly need that sort of revenue base to go about its mission with a sense of confidence.

Warning: Be wary of donors bearing inadequate gifts. But the warning is not a prohibition. The creative and innovative potential of a particular Institute may be so promising in academic and financial terms, that a university or school official decides to accept the risk of sparse initial funding. It is a matter of judgment, and the admonition set down here is intended to advance the cause of informed judgment.

An as-yet-unsaid observation must be made. The illustrative endowment, rate of return, and income stream numbers used above indicate that funding for Institutes or Centers is a sensitive and touchy business. Prospective donors at the $4 million plus level are not as numerous as bees around a hive. Quite the contrary! Consequently, a tension is always present between accepting a multimillion-dollar gift and looking as hard as one should at its adequacy. It is a corollary that the job of an Institute or Center director, like that of dean, embraces a need to engage in fund-raising and to be alert to the financial aspects of an Institute or Center. Failure to recognize that reality is bound to lead to frustration and disappointment.

Potential Problems

The creation of a new Institute or Center generates excitement and anticipation. If the new unit is established on the sound bases of a clear mission and proper funding, then success depends on the director and the match between the Institute's mission and the external and internal interests it seeks to serve.

However, some potential problems exist. In addition to the possibility of future financial burdens growing out of inadequate initial funding, consider these possible pitfalls: (1) encouragement of faculty interest in some narrowly specialized area, which can distract attention from the central mission of the school; and (2) as a corollary, incitement of some degree of divisiveness and possibly jealousy among faculty, as some benefit financially from an Institute's funding while others feel left out. These are not sufficient reasons to eschew the establishment of Institutes. But they are worth awareness and attention, so that their potential for mischief is avoided, or at least minimized.

With the preamble provided, we turn now to a review of the several Institutes and Centers of the Stern School, both past and present.

The Institute of Retail Management (School of Retailing)

The Institute of Retail Management was discontinued in the early eighties. But it had a long and significant history, most of it as the independent, degree-granting (Master of Science) School of Retailing. Its history is pregnant with meaning, for it highlights a number of the points made earlier. Primarily, its story emphasizes the importance of a match between external and internal university support. As a corollary, it emphasizes the consequences of an eventual breakdown of that match, a breakdown significantly reflecting the gradual development of a distaste for narrow, industry-specific programs in the top American B-Schools, including our own at NYU.

The School of Retailing, founded originally in 1919 as the Training School for Teachers of Retail Selling, was renamed in 1921 and empowered to award the degree of Master of Science in Retailing. It had a specific purpose; namely, to prepare people directly for careers in retailing and as secondary school teachers of students interested in such careers.

At the outset it worked closely with the School of Commerce, Accounts, and Finance and the Washington Square College of Arts and Sciences. The Commerce-Retailing program was a four-year *evening* program leading to the degree of Bachelor of Commercial Science from Commerce, but with the retailing courses taught by the School of Retailing. The Washington Square College-Retailing program was a five-year *day* program, with the first three years in the College and the last two years in Retailing. After four years, the student received the College's Bachelor of Science degree, and after the fifth year the Master of Science in Retailing degree. In both the Commerce BCS and the College BS degree programs the degree requirements of those schools had to be satisfied. In addition, the School of Retailing offered a two year graduate program to students with a degree from an approved college or university. The program involved a cooperative educational arrangement with a number of leading stores in New York City. Students would spend the morning in the classroom and the afternoon in the stores. Since compensation was paid for the time students spent in the stores, the enrollment in the program was limited to the number of positions provided by the cooperating business enterprises. No doubt, both the academic and business partners perceived mutual advantages in the arrangement. On the academic side, the practical experience gained by the students was considered valuable. On the business side, the recruitment of well-trained, capable people for subsequent full-time employment was also valued.

The School's first dean was Norris Arthur Brisco, possessor of a Doctor of Philosophy degree. Interestingly, its original faculty of 15 included eight holders of the doctorate, a substantially higher proportion than characterized the first years of the School of Commerce. This representation of doctorates probably reflected the fact that the School of Retailing was a graduate entity, with research among its major purposes.

The teaching, research, and recruitment goals of the School were reflected in the composition of an Advisory Council, which appears to have wielded significant influence. It numbered 12 members, of whom 6 represented contributing members (i.e., sponsoring businesses, one of whom had to be a representative of a retail selling organization other than a department store); 3 represented New York University, 2 the Department of Education of New York, and 1 the Department of Education of Newark, New Jersey. That the 6 contributing members' representatives were the Executive Committee of the Council indicates to me that they wielded important influence. In general, the composition of the group shows a match between external and internal interests vital to the School's subsequent success in achieving its goals.

That success was substantial over the next 40 years, as the School satisfied the research, recruitment, and training needs of the major department stores and other retailing businesses in the metropolitan New York region. In fact, by World War II the School had expanded its cooperative arrangements within the university to include the School of Education. More, it also offered students interested in retailing the opportunity of earning doctoral degrees in the Graduate School of Business Administration. In all degree programs other than the MS in Retailing, the School of Retailing functioned as a department of the School actually awarding the degree, that is, the baccalaureates in WSC, Commerce, and Education, and the doctorates in GBA and Education.

The expansion of the School of Retailing involved also an enlargement of its Advisory Council, which by 1944–1945 included 27 representatives, one each from 27 cooperating stores. However, the Executive Committee still consisted of 6 representatives from the cooperating stores, plus 3 from NYU and 2 from New York's Board of Education. The satisfaction of the parties with the School is reflected in these extracts from its 1944–1945 bulletin:

> Through the generosity of the cooperating merchants, a unique system of training has been made possible. The cooperation, not only of the chief executives in the stores but of the executive staffs, has assisted to a remarkable degree in the development of a system of training for store executives that approaches the ideal. Graduate students are in the classroom in the morning and in actual service in the stores during the afternoon. While in the stores, they are under the supervision of store executives. These executives are ever willing to assist them in grasping details and in linking practice with underlying principles. . . .
>
> The close cooperation between the stores and the School of Retailing is aided by the services of an experienced coordinator. The duties of the coordinator are to make the proper contacts for the students in the stores and to keep in close touch with them and with executives in order to make adjustments with a minimum of friction.[1]

By 1948–1949 Dean Brisco had been succeeded by Charles M. Edwards, Jr., as dean. The standing of the School in the eyes of its business supporters was so great that the Executive Committee of the Merchants' Advisory Council turned over to the university "a fund of more than half a million dollars that had been accumulated since the founding of the school."[2] The Advisory Council expanded to 30 members, with a "major executive from each of the school's cooperative stores."

But things changed by the beginning of the sixties. The N Y U Self-Study Report of 1956 looked askance at the narrow specialization and vocational character of the school, and called for it to be discontinued as a degree-granting entity, becoming instead an Institute in the Schools of Business. That action was taken in 1963, as an integral part of President Hester's program to implement the 1956 report. Dean Edwards and his associate dean, Elmer O. Schaller, continued to carry those titles and to have a small office staff to perform such functions as the Institute could implement. Essentially, these were: (1) career counseling, with an implied recruitment aspect, among secondary school and college students through annual career conferences; (2) a limited number of seminars; (3) scholarship awards; and (4) perhaps most importantly, publication of the *Journal of Retailing.* The *Journal* disseminated the results of research relevant to the field of retailing.

The conversion of the School into an Institute broke the match between external and internal constituencies. The Schools of Business, both GBA and Commerce, were moving away from an industry-specific, vocational orientation. Yet, at that point in their history they were ordered to embrace and welcome the School (now Institute) of Retailing. The small faculty of the former School were lost in the sea of Commerce-GBA faculty. Some faculty were transferred to the School of Education, which had a department devoted to educating secondary school teachers of commercial subjects. Compensation of some faculty continued to come from the ample funds available to the Institute.

In fact, the funding of the Institute explained its continued existence for almost another 20 years. Thus, in the Institute's 1969–1970 annual report, its funding was estimated to have a value of slightly more than $2.5 million. The major components of the funding consisted of 48,700 shares of W. T. Grant Common Stock, valued at $1.8 million, and some 4,000 units of N Y U's investment fund, valued at almost $650,000. Given this level of funding, the Schools of Business made an effort to find a match of objectives between the Institute and themselves. Thus, a handsome office suite was made available on the second floor of Tisch Hall when it opened in 1972. Honesty demands us to note that the office suite was not a gift, not evidence of open-handed generosity. The Institute bought the space with $200,000 of its funding. Perhaps more important was the consistent effort of the School of Business to find a director who would be able to bridge the evolving academic orientation of the faculty and the traditional mission of the Institute to serve a specific sector of the economy. Dean Edwards retired in 1970, being followed as acting institute director by Associate Dean Elmer Schaller. But Dean Schaller retired in a few years, to be followed by people who could not accomplish the goal. Finally, a decision was made to commit a portion of the Institute's endowment over a period of several years, with the purpose of increasing the *annual* funds available for research and other activities specific to the retailing industry. It was hoped that the additional monies would attract some faculty to the mission of the Institute. To further this end, Professor Jacob Jacoby was brought from Purdue University to become the Institute's director. Professor Jacoby had a national reputation for significant research in the field of marketing, and it seemed that he would be able to achieve a match between Institute and School purposes. That hope was stillborn. After several years of effort, Professor Jacoby, Dean May, and I agreed to terminate the Institute, and to take its remaining endowment of somewhat over $1 million and apply it to the funding of a new chair to be known as the Merchant Council's Chair in the Department of Marketing. The surviving members of the old Merchants' Advisory Council agreed, and the Institute ceased to exist.

The lesson to be learned is that significant funding will not bring success for an Institute or Center when its purpose does not conform with the purposes of the host school and the faculty of that school.

Center for Science and Technology Policy (CSTP)

The story of the CSTP is instructive. It was transferred into GBA from the Graduate School of Public Administration (GPA) in 1981, after being set up in GPA in 1978 and having failed to achieve a viable relationship there. In the case of this center, the factor that appears to have ruled the transfer from GPA to GBA was the enthusiasm of one person, the vice-dean of GBA.

The director of the Center appeared to be well connected in governmental and corporate scientific quarters, and seemed also to have credibility, fund-raising ability, and managerial competence. At least that is how he appeared to the vice-dean.[3] The vice-dean perceived these additional advantages of a transfer of the CSTP to GBA: (1) it would bring a major source of funding for policy-oriented research on science and technology policy, economic growth, and international competitiveness; (2) the CSTP's research assistants were largely from GBA, and that relationship would be enhanced by a transfer from GPA; (3) the CSTP had a good support staff; (4) in GBA, the Center would be a potential attraction for high-quality junior faculty with an interest in the field; (5) the Center could serve as a focal point for raising GBA's emphasis on management in the technological environment of the future, and as a means for introducing executive programs and courses in those fields; and (6) the Center would encourage research and program interest in the study of energy and materials.

The vice-dean perceived some possible dangers: (1) a financial risk; (2) a diffusion of faculty interest and activity; (3) space problems (i.e., adequacy of physical plant); and (4) possible problems in allocation of overhead and other costs. Despite these potential problems, the vice-dean was enthusiastic and pushed persistently in favor of moving CSTP from GPA to GBA. The proposal was put before the Faculty Council. The chairman of the Council expressed concern that the transfer of CSTP into GBA did not meet the criteria set down by the Council for the establishment of new Centers or Institutes. In particular, the criteria having to do with a match of purposes between Center and School, funding, space requirements, and so on did not seem to be adequately met.[4] Yet, a proposal to effect the transfer was put before the Faculty Council at its meeting on May 21, 1985, to be considered at the June 11 meeting. As the Council's chairman would be out of the country in June, he left the following memo as an expression of his views:

> Since I will be out of the country on 11 June, here are some comments on the move of the Center to GBA.
>
> In my view, the proposal does not meet the points stated in our criteria for institutes and centers, set down several weeks ago.
>
> 1. The research focus of the Center is fuzzy, and where it is reasonably well articulated the topics seem to be technical and far removed from faculty expertise.
> 2. Faculty links (real and prospective) are superficial at best—people talk a good game, but when forced to specify precisely how the relationship is likely to evolve, the conversation often quickly evaporates.

3. The spillovers for our teaching programs are equally unclear, and any initiatives along these lines would necessarily have to come from the faculty if they are to succeed.

4. Aggressive fund-raising by the Center is likely to cross lines with other funding priorities for GBA, no matter how hard we try to avoid this.

5. I am not convinced that the financial projections, in terms of real dollars, are at all realistic.

In short, I can think of some initiatives along these lines that would represent a worse "fit" for GBA than this one—but not many. I've said my piece, for what it's worth.[5]

The rest of the story is quickly told. The vice-dean's enthusiasm was not fulfilled by ensuing events. The reality was that the Council chairman's reservations proved correct. No true match of purposes existed between Center and School. Financing never fulfilled promises, resulting in deficits and chronic financial strain. On July 2, 1986, Dean Richard West wrote to the director of the Institute that the Center had unfortunately not "become an economically viable enterprise nor has it garnered sufficient academic interest from our regular faculty." Consequently, the CSTP's relationship with GBA was terminated, effective September 1, 1986.

But it took five years to terminate a Center that was brought into GBA against substantial opposition. Further, the opposition was clear, focused, and based on policies adopted by the Faculty Council. The lesson here, in addition to the lessons drawn from the experience of the Institute of Retail Management, is: *be wary of narrowly based enthusiasm.* Remember the need for a match of purposes and for proper financing.

The Salomon Brothers Center for the Study of Financial Institutions

Now it's time for some pleasant news, as we turn from instances of disappointed expectations and failed initiatives to those blessed by success. The Salomon Brothers Center for the Study of Financial Institutions is a leader among the Stern School's successful Institutes and Centers. Actually, that statement may be too restrained. The Salomon Brothers Center can make the claim that it is the foremost independent research organization for the study of problems and issues related to

American and global financial structures. Its success clearly reflects the close match between the Center's purposes and those of its host school. Finance has long been a major area of strength in the Stern School. Its faculty have been in the forefront of important research output, and its curriculum and alumni have reflected the strength betokened by that productivity.

Equally important is the fact that the Salomon Brothers Center has attracted strong financial support. It began with a $3 million gift in 1971, of which $1 million was for space in Merrill Hall and $2 million for endowment (to be paid in annual installments over 10 years). Further funding was received, for example, endowment gifts from Dr. Henry Kaufman to establish the Sidney Homer Directorship and the Charles Simon Chair. Also, the Center receives operating funds from banks, securities firms, insurance companies, investment houses, and industrial companies in the United States and abroad. These contributors are called Center Associates.

Candor compels recognition of a delicate difficulty which sometimes comes up in sponsored research projects. Occasionally the sponsor, who may be a business competitor of Salomon Brothers, balks at a research project supported by them which is prominently identified with another firm. The Center, while sometimes disappointed by such a reaction, has not suffered in its long-term development. The point to be made is that naming gifts by active business entities need to be adequate to the purposes envisaged. Support of a new Center or Institute can be frustrated if other and rival entities hold back because of the name.

Returning to purpose, the Salomon Center focuses on: (1) supporting analyses of the dynamic, perhaps revolutionary, changes occurring in financial institutions and markets; and (2) serving as an organizing and stimulating center for critical discussion of public policy issues surrounding the fast-paced evolution of financial systems. To these ends, the Center (1) conducts academic research studies; (2) sponsors conferences that bring together academics, practitioners, regulators, and legislators; (3) publishes and disseminates, through working papers, monographs, and books, the results of the research and conferences; (4) presents leading-edge executive seminars in a "Frontiers of Finance" series; and (5) publishes, in cooperation with Basil Blackwell, of Oxford (England), two journals (*Financial Markets, Instruments, and Institutions* and the *Journal of International Financial Management and Accounting*).

The match between the Center's purposes and those of the Stern

School is enhanced and further illustrated by its "seed grants" and "Center Fellowships." The former uses a portion of the Center's funds that is reserved for grants to faculty for pioneering research in the financial and economic sectors and for generating external funding. The latter applies Center funds to stimulate basic financial research at the Stern School by providing substantial, untied monies for the School's most productive middle-rank scholar/teachers and for visiting faculty members. The mutual strengthening of Center and School purposes through the close interaction described is enormously important to both, and reinforces the point made over and over again in this chapter about the critical nature of the match in contributing to the success of any Institute or Center.

The writer would be remiss if he failed to note the major contribution of Professor Arnold Sametz to the Center's success. Professor Sametz was director of the Center from 1975 to his retirement some 16 years later. The first director was Professor Kalman Cohen, 1972–1974, followed by a brief, interim directorship under Professor William Silber, 1974–1975. Professor Sametz's successor is Professor Ingo Walter, an internationally recognized scholar in international business and finance, and long a leading member of the Stern School's faculty. One can say with confidence that the Center's distinguished past performance is only a prologue to future achievements.

The Vincent C. Ross Institute of Accounting Research

Like the Salomon Brothers Center, but to a somewhat lesser degree, the Vincent C. Ross Institute stands as an example of a successful Institute. Again, a sound match of Institute and School purposes, plus significant funding, are major factors making for success. Also, the Institute has been fortunate in having a series of prestigious directors who enjoyed faculty respect, most importantly so in the departments of Accounting and Finance. Starting with the first director, Professor Michael Schiff, they include Professors George Sorter, Hector Anton, Frederick Choi, and Joshua Ronen.

Established with endowment gifts of $1.5 million in 1971 and a predecessor gift in 1970 of $500,000 to fund a chair, by Vincent C. Ross, the Institute occupies handsome quarters on the third floor of Tisch Hall. That space embraces facilities for research staff, a conference room, a library, and a director's office. The Institute's purpose is to bring together professional accountants, financial executives, government officials, and academicians to exchange ideas on research and to stimulate the advancement of accounting principles and practices. To these ends, the Institute fosters these activities: (1) large-scale research studies funded by professional organizations and government, with emphasis on improving and extending financial reporting; (2) conducting conferences, seminars, and round-table discussions of key research issues, such as emerging problems in internal controls and other financial management areas; (3) publication and dissemination of the results through working papers and monographs; (4) publication of the quarterly *Journal of Accounting, Auditing, and Finance;* and (5) serving as a research facility for PhD candidates and faculty.

The Center for Japan-U.S. Business and Economic Studies

Newer than the Salomon Center, but close in scale of activities and achievements, the Japan-U.S. Center is a vigorous element in the Stern School. The match resides in this case in: (1) the Center's purpose of promoting greater cooperative efforts between the United States and Japan through research, education, publications, and conferences; and (2) the outstanding quality of the Stern School's faculty in International Business and Finance.

Substantial funding was guaranteed by equal contributions to the Center's endowment by American and Japanese companies and organizations. Of special significance in funding are: (1) a major gift from the Long-Term Credit Bank of Japan to establish a visiting professorship (occupied by Professor Paul A. Samuelson, America's first recipient of the Nobel Prize in Economics); (2) an endowment from the NEC corporation for a Faculty Fellow Program; (3) the Sanyo Keukyujo Foundation endowment for the study of U.S.-Japan economic relations; (4) the Sanova Bank Ltd. endowment for the study of international financial markets; (5) the C. V. Starr Foundation endowment and challenge grant; and (6) the Takeshi Iizuka and TKC corporation endowment for research in accounting, auditing, and data processing. The Center also enjoys the endorsement and support of the Keidanren (Japan's Federation of Economic Organizations) and the Japan Foundation. Finally, funds are forthcoming from sponsored research grants and a large and distinguished group of Corporate Associates.

Like the Salomon Center and the Ross Institute, the Japan-U.S. Center (1) conducts academic studies that employ theoretical and empirical techniques to evaluate major issues, in this case relating to Japan and the United States; (2) sponsors seminars, public lectures, and conferences that bring together academic, business, and government leaders to discuss major issues concerning economic policies and foreign trade and investment as they relate to Japan and the United States; (3) publishes and disseminates the results of the foregoing activities through working papers, occasional papers, transcripts, and books; and (4) supports the development of courses in the Stern School, to provide graduate students and executives with an understanding of Japanese and U.S. business practices and economic environments.

No doubt the success of the Japan-U.S. Center was enormously advanced by the appointment of Dr. Ryuzo Sato as director and C. V. Starr Professor of Economics. The clarity of his view of the Center's purpose was evident in this message, which introduced a Center brochure:

> Japan and the United States stand at a crossroads. . . . Japan's emergence as a major economic power is often perceived as a threat in the United States. Many Americans believe that Japan invades markets too aggressively, prices below costs and engages in somewhat unethical business practices. But Japan's productivity and growth are really opportunities and challenges to the United States, not threats. . . . Japan's rapid economic growth and export orientation have led to problems; the most obvious ones are trade imbalances and friction. . . . These problems . . . are the major focus of the Center. While social and cultural dimensions of both countries are important, the Center focuses on them only as they relate to economic and business issues. In this respect, we are quite different from an Asian studies Center.

Other Institutes and Centers

Three Institutes and Centers remain to be examined. While they are not on the scale of the Salomon Brothers Center, the Ross Institute, or the Japan-U.S. Center, they are significant, because they are viable. The three are: (1) the Center for Entrepreneurial Studies; (2) the L. Glucksman Institute for Research in Securities Markets; and (3) the Center for Research on Information Systems.

The Center for Entrepreneurial Studies was established in 1984, following a gift of $500,000 from the Price Foundation. A second gift of $500,000 was made in 1987 which, with the first, was used to endow the Harold Price Professor of Entrepreneurship. The holder of the professorship, who serves as the director of the Center, is presently Dr. Avijit Ghosh. As part of the funding arrangement the university committed itself to provide the Center with the income from an additional $500,000, out of its general funds. Thus, the income available to the Center was equivalent to that generated by an endowment of $1.5 million.

The Center's purpose is to foster the study of entrepreneurship and new venture creation, which it does through sponsored research projects. But that is not its entire purpose. In addition, it seeks to encourage interest in entrepreneurship among students, through offering elective courses as part of the School's curriculum, and through organizing seminars. It sponsors also an annual entrepreneurship training retreat, during which 18 students can test themselves and their ideas relating to creating new ventures. These retreats bring together a select group of students, faculty, and successful entrepreneurs for three days. The retreats are intended to enhance the students' business knowledge and skills, while subjecting their ideas to critical analysis.

The *L. Glucksman Institute for Research in Securities Markets* has an endowment of $1 million, given by Lewis Glucksman. Its director is Professor William L. Silber, occupant of the Dean Abraham L. Gitlow Professorship. It implements its purpose, which is made clear in its name, through offering grants to faculty and students that support research on equities, bonds, futures, options, and other financial instruments and on the markets where they are traded. Also, five Glucksman Fellows are designated annually from among first-year full-time MBA students. During their second year of study, these Fellows receive cash stipends and are paired with full-time faculty members on research projects in securities markets. Participating faculty members receive unrestricted grants as well. The program exposes some top MBA students to the rigors of formal academic research in the practical areas of financial economics. Significantly, the Institute coordinates its activities with the Salomon Brothers Center. Plainly, there is a match between the Glucksman Institute and the School.

The Center for Research on Information Systems lacks an endowment, relying on funding by an Affiliates Program that embraces major corporations having an interest in its activities. The activities embrace research studies, seminars, an annual Spring symposium, and publication of working papers and other documents. All these activities relate to information technologies and their effective management in organizations. The central focus is on management policy and planning for systems, approaches to systems analysis and design, the role of information in organizations, information systems performance, data bases, artificial intelligence, and so on. The Center also organizes an annual career evening to facilitate student efforts to locate part-time or full-time employment. The Center's match with the School is through the Computer Applications and Information Systems department. Its director is Professor Jon A. Turner.

External Evaluation and Accreditation

Background

An interesting and significant feature of twentieth-century American higher education is the development of external agencies and organizations that evaluate and accredit universities and colleges.[1] In the field of collegiate education for business, the external guardian of quality is the American Assembly of Collegiate Schools of Business (AACSB).

AACSB is part of a large structure of evaluative and accrediting bodies. The United States Office of Education sits atop the structure. Beneath it is the Commission on Recognition of Post-Secondary Accreditation, which came into existence in 1994 and replaced the Council on Post-Secondary Accreditation. The Council was preceded by another entity, known as the National Commission on Accrediting. These bodies recognize the accrediting authority of two broad groups of subordinate accrediting agencies: (1) *Regional, that is, geographic, accrediting bodies,* like the Middle Atlantic States Association; and (2) *specialized, that is, professional, accrediting agencies,* like AACSB and other professionally oriented entities (e.g. the American Bar Association, the National Association of Schools of Music, etc.). These two groups of agencies overlap and cut across each other. A consequence has been multiple accreditation visits to universities. They have been a chronic source of annoyance to university presidents who are themselves organized and joined together in the American Council on Education. Also, the specialized accrediting agencies concerned with business were formerly joined in a now defunct body that was known as the Council on Professional Education for Business.

Flux characterized the American accreditation scene in 1994. To the long-standing unhappiness of university and college presidents over the proliferation of specialized accrediting bodies was added growing criticism in Congress and elsewhere of variations in the accreditation standards of the major regional accrediting bodies, as well as explicit concern over the introduction into the accreditation standards of some bodies of efforts to promote cultural diversity, gay rights, and affirmative action policies.[2] The disaffection stimulated the convening of a conference in Tucson, Arizona, under the aegis of the American Council on Education. The conference sought to address four questions: (1) should the six regional associations that evaluate entire institutions and the many specialized accrediting agencies be merged into a single, national accrediting body? (2) if not merged, should the regional associations adopt a common set of minimum standards for evaluating, and what should they be? (3) if a common set of minimum standards is adopted, should there be variations to allow for different types of institutions (e.g., two-year colleges as against research universities)? and (4) should the accrediting bodies continue to certify the eligibility of colleges for receiving federal aid? The conference agreed: (a) to seek a new set of common criteria for evaluation; and (b) to eventually cease certifying the eligibility of colleges for federal aid.[3] The six regional associations at the conference also agreed on a policy change possessing major possible long-term importance; namely, to issue public reports on the evaluation of individual institutions. The policy and practice has been merely to report to the public whether a school was accredited, unaccredited, or on probation. But the reasons for a school's classification were not given. With that brief general background, we turn now to the AACSB.

The AACSB was organized in 1916, at a meeting of 21 representatives of 17 universities with schools or programs in business. The meeting was held in Chicago, having been initiated by E. F. Gay, the founding dean of the Harvard Business School, L. C. Marshall, dean of the University of Chicago's College of Commerce and Administration, and A. E. Swanson, acting dean of Northwestern University's School of Commerce. The 17 attending institutions were Columbia, Cornell, Dartmouth, Harvard, New York University, Northwestern, Ohio State, Tulane, California, Chicago, Illinois, Nebraska, Pennsylvania (U of P), Pittsburgh, Texas, Wisconsin, and Yale. Professor Major B. Foster was NYU's representative. L. D. H. Weld, of Yale's Sheffield Scientific School, missed the initial meeting.

Following adoption of a constitution on June 17, 1916, 16 institutions were invited to become members of the new Association of Collegiate Schools of Business. The name was changed to the American Association in 1925, and to the American Assembly in 1968. Cornell University was not included among the invitees, perhaps because such program as it had was in the College of Arts and Sciences. Of the 16 invited, 14 accepted. Two, the University of Illinois and Yale University declined, although Illinois became a member in 1924.

Purpose

At the beginning, there was a certain amount of ambiguity in the AACSB. The original constitution of June 17, 1916, stated in Article II that "the object of the Association is the promotion and improvement of higher business education in North America."[4] Inherent in this objective is the establishment, improvement, and promotion of some standards. Yet Article VIII said that "no act of the Association shall be held to control the policy or action of any member institution."[5] The reality that evolved was that minimum standards relating to curriculum, faculty, facilities, and such were developed and applied in determining institutional accreditation and reaccreditation. And denial or loss of accreditation became a powerful implement in enforcing and promoting acceptable standards, albeit the association concurrently maintained that it sought to avoid rigidity and to allow a substantial degree of freedom for innovation and individual institutional initiatives.

One thing is certain. The AACSB's efforts to promote and improve higher education for business were expansive in nature, leading it to multiple but reinforcing purposes. These purposes, broadly viewed, can be categorized as: (1) quality control; (2) research and information exchange; (3) support for the business school against adverse pressures from within or outside the university; and (4) monitoring the market.

Quality Control

Promotion and improvement of standards, identified here as quality control, are the original and basic purposes of AACSB. Those purposes have meant, in practice and in the most immediate sense, the establishment of standards, first undergraduate and later graduate, and then their enforcement through the process of accreditation and reaccreditation.

Organizationally and operationally, this process involved the creation of committees and visitation procedures. It involved additionally the expansion of AACSB's purposes into the three broad areas noted above, that is, research and information exchange, support for the B-School, and monitoring the market. In short, quality control has been an *expansive purpose*. It demanded organizational and operational growth and, inevitably, *accumulation of enforcement power* through the granting or denial of accreditation. Of course, such power would not have developed if accreditation had not been so deeply desired by educational institutions as a symbol of quality. But it was desired, and so the power that rested on that desire came to be a reality. Quality control was expansive also as *its purview became more extensive,* growing from undergraduate to graduate, and most recently, doctoral, programs. In the seventies it grew also into explicit establishment and maintenance of accreditation standards in the field of Accounting.

The inherent implications of the Association's pursuit of quality quickly revealed themselves in the early exhortations of a 1920 Report of the Committee on Degrees.[6] The report, while eschewing adoption of a policy, showed a clear preference for a full four-year baccalaureate program and for a minimum two-year master's program for students who lacked satisfactory undergraduate work in business. The report also worried about the scarcity of properly qualified faculty to teach business, and encouraged the development of doctoral programs, preferably PhD, to enlarge the supply of qualified researchers and teachers. Finally, quality differences were implicitly recognized between day and evening programs. Thus, equivalent credit and recognition was to be given to evening programs only when their "character and content" (that is, quality) were equal to the day programs.

The year 1925 was highly significant. It marked the adoption of new standards for admission to AACSB. The following requirements were adopted: (1) the faculty of the business school had to include at least three full-time full professors, giving nearly all their time to teaching courses in the B-School, and the majority of the faculty had to give the greater part of their time to the school; (2) the full-time full professors had to have the doctor's degree, or equivalent training and experience (as judged by the Association's Executive Committee); (3) faculty salaries, again as judged by the Executive Committee, had to be adequate to sustain high-grade work; (4) at least 40 percent of the 120 credit hours required for a bachelor's degree had to be taken in commercial and economic subjects;

and (5) at least 40 percent of the baccalaureate credit hours had to be taken in subjects other than commerce and economics. Points 3 and 4 implicitly mandated a four-year baccalaureate (120 credit hours) and an even split between professional and general education courses.

It was in 1925 that John T. Madden became dean of N Y U's School of Commerce. It was also the year in which Commerce's existing three-year, 96-credit Bachelor of Commercial Science degree was marked for oblivion. The concurrence is too great to be coincidental. I had always given credit to Dean Madden for initiating the change. No doubt he still deserves credit, but it is now clear that AACSB must have been a powerful external stimulus. So we see how the history of Commerce reflects the evolving role and influence of AACSB.

The year 1928 was marked by a manifestation of concern over whether all member schools were complying with the standards required of schools seeking admission to the association. But expressions of concern did not close the matter. The annual meeting noted that the Executive Committee should conduct an investigation and recommend appropriate action regarding schools that had fallen below the admissions standards. We see here a willingness to exercise enforcement power that overrides the promise of Article VIII of the original 1916 constitution, that "no act of the Association shall be held to control the policy or action of any member institution." Does a threat to withdraw accreditation control policy or action? Only if an institution is deeply concerned over such withdrawal. I did not see one that was not so concerned in 20 years as dean. In the crunch, all institutions appear deeply concerned. Even the most prestigious AACSB members, who occasionally chafe under standards that they feel are necessary for lesser institutions but not for them, show concern.

The 1928 action was followed in 1931[7] with more explicit warnings. The annual meeting adopted a resolution authorizing the Executive Committee to: (1) correspond with member schools to determine conformance with standards; (2) inspect any institution thought to be deficient; and (3) warn any deficient institution that failure to conform within a two-year period would be followed by the institution's being dropped from membership.

Seven years passed before the next major action on standards. In 1938[8] a new statement was adopted. It mandated that: (1) *admission requirements* in the business school be at least of "such quantity and quality of work as is deemed standard by the highest accrediting agencies and leading universities"; and (2) *instructional loads* be reasonable, that is, instructors teaching freshmen-sophomore work not exceed 15 semester credit hours a week, nor 12 semester credit hours in junior-senior work (but reductions should be made to allow for multiple course preparations). The statement also denied membership to any school subject to "undue political influence." In a separate action, it was decided to strengthen enforcement of AACSB standards by placing supervision of them under a committee having more continuity of personnel than existed before.

An interesting and significant exchange took place between Dean C. C. Fichtner of the University of Arkansas and Dean J. A. Fitzgerald of the University of Texas at the Association's annual meeting in 1940.[9] The exchange concerned enforcement of standards. Dean Fichtner observed that the Association had held applicant schools generally to rather high standards, but he felt it had not been as demanding with member schools. In that connection, he said: "This Association has never dropped a school from membership." He commented that the Law School Association was far more demanding, dropping and otherwise disciplining schools. To which Dean Fitzgerald replied that AACSB had put member schools on probation but never publicized the matter.

The World War II years witnessed little action in AACSB, as attention was concentrated on other matters. However, in 1941–1942 the universities of Georgia and Arkansas were involved in charges of undue political influence and faced possible loss of membership. We shall return to this at a later point.

A major move forward in the AACSB standards occurred in 1947.[10] The Committee on Standards had evaluated a number of applicant schools. The Executive Committee, confronted by the need to explain inadequacies to schools found wanting, found the existing standards vague. Responding to that need, the Committee on Standards suggested these more precise standards for faculty: (1) at least 50 percent of the entire teaching staff have the terminal degree in the appropriate field of specialization, that is, the highest degree awarded in the field; (2) staff members should possess at least a baccalaureate in economics or business, or a combination of the two, plus a higher degree in the field of specialization; (3) the *maximum* teaching load should be 12 hours a week, including all teaching both on and off campus; (3) graduate assistants or outside lecturers could be used as part-time instructors, but all third and fourth year courses should be taught by full-time staff; and (4) faculty could teach nonprofessional courses, but such courses should be only a minor part of the teaching load and should be stated. However, recognizing substantial variety in *curriculum* requirements among member schools, the Committee on Standards did not believe it could act in that area. But it did suggest that there was a fairly well-defined group of "core" courses, which it thought should be required, plus an opportunity for students to major in each of the core group fields, at least to the extent of two courses. Also, the Committee felt that the amount of specialization should be limited. In 1949[11] the meaning of terminal degree was defined further as being: (1) the doctorate in Business or Economics in all fields; (2) in Accounting the MBA plus the CPA; (3) the LLB in Law; and (4) Advanced Engineering degrees for teachers in Industrial Management.

Our review of the development of AACSB Standards must be interrupted at this point, to allow consideration of a major controversy over the role of AACSB and other specialized organizations. We noted at the beginning of this chapter that there was overlap between specialized and regional accrediting agencies. This overlap and the multiple accreditation surveys they required troubled university presidents. The annoyance of the presidents surfaced openly in 1939, when a report of the American Council on Education complained that there were too many accrediting agencies, and they often interfered in the internal workings of the universities.[12] During World War II and the immediate postwar years the issue seems to have lain dormant. But in the decade of the fifties it erupted with a vengeance. Thus, the university presidents organized the National Commission on Accrediting (NCA) in 1949 to eliminate the problems connected with multiple accrediting agencies, while preserving their contribution to higher education.[13] In 1952, the NCA worked out an arrangement with the regional accrediting agencies. In November of that year the AACSB and six other specialized accrediting agencies were advised to stop accrediting activities and to work with the regional associations. Fortunately or unfortunately, depending on one's point of view, the regional associations were not all well developed and able to assume the responsibility thus thrust upon them. Also, uniformity of standards was lacking among the regional associations. Other difficulties involved the imposition of a hiatus on accreditation in collegiate education for business, and the problem faced by a university when one or more of its professional schools proved to be inadequate (presumably endangering thereby overall accreditation).

Probably as a consequence of the problems noted, the NCA lifted its ban on AACSB accrediting prior to AACSB's 1953 annual meeting, but only for the rest of that year. However, in November 1953 the NCA extended its lifting of the ban, but required the specialized accrediting agencies to submit annual reports describing progress in their fields in January of 1954, 1955, and 1956. In the meantime, AACSB and other specialized agencies in the business field organized a new group known as the Council for Professional Education in Business. Concurrently, AACSB adopted (in 1953) a statement expressing its "willingness and readiness" to work with the Middle States Association of Colleges and Secondary Schools, as well as with other regional accrediting associations. The accreditation conflict was resolved finally in 1961, when NCA gave formal recognition to a number of specialized accrediting associations. The AACSB was among them.[14]

Another development in the fifties involved the Ford Foundation. During that decade, the Ford Foundation showed great interest in collegiate education for business. That interest was evident in its Gordon-Howell report, *Higher Education for Business,* published in 1959 with major effect. In fact, the foundation's interest was more extensive. It involved AACSB, which was notified on March 15, 1955, that it would receive $25,000 for a conference to examine ways to increase the supply of well-trained, qualified faculty. AACSB was to consider means of: (1) attracting able students into graduate study for business; (2) improving the study programs provided for them; and (3) improving the material and nonmaterial aspects of teaching careers in B-schools.[15] And in 1957 AACSB received a further grant of $120,000 from the Ford Foundation to support a three-year trial effort involving an Intercollegiate Clearing House for case materials in business administration. The Harvard Business School was to administer the Clearing House, through its Office of Case Distribution, but the Executive Committee of AACSB was to be the advisory board for the Clearing House on general policy matters.[16] It should be noted that between 1954 and 1963 the Ford Foundation spent $24 million to encourage and improve education for business.

Returning to the development of standards, the AACSB adopted standards for the MBA degree in 1958.[17] The standards stated, in general qualitative terms, the requirements for admission of students, curriculum, faculty, facilities, and administration. But the annual meeting in 1959 deferred action on the standards and they were not finally adopted until the annual meeting in May 1961. By March 1962 the Executive

Committee of AACSB began to implement accreditation of graduate (i.e., master's) programs. Sixty-nine schools applied for accreditation of their master's programs and at the January 1963 meeting of the Executive Committee 53 schools were approved. The move of the AACSB into graduate program accreditation reopened the conflict with the National Commission on Accrediting.[18] Thus, the Executive Committee noted in its April 1963 meetings that the NCA was concerned over AACSB's action to accredit master's programs, *without prior consultation with the NCA*. The committee noted also that the NCA, while continuing to list AACSB as an official accrediting agency, would footnote the listing with an explicit statement that it was so recognized and listed only for baccalaureate degree programs. The footnote listing troubled AACSB's Executive Committee, which decided to press for its elimination. However, a further widening between the two organizations appeared. It involved AACSB accrediting policies and activities relative to evening programs and unreported activities. The situation was apparently resolved by AACSB action in April 1964 requiring NCA review of AACSB policy in the area of evening programs and unreported activities, *prior to implementation*.[19] As a result, NCA recognized AACSB as the official accrediting agency for *both* master's and baccalaureate programs in business. Also, in 1964 11 additional schools were accredited at the master's level, making a total of 64.

The first-half century of AACSB's existence ended in 1966 with several further steps concerning educational standards. These steps[20] specified that: (1) membership eligibility in AACSB required a school to be a "distinct and independent degree recommending unit responsible directly to the central administrative authority of an institution of higher learning" with other independent degree recommending units; (2) only the B-school could recommend baccalaureates in business; (3) degree and nondegree offerings had to be separate and distinct, and the B-school's effort had to be devoted to the formal degree program; (4) minimum staffing profiles were spelled out as regards full-time terminal degree qualified faculty at the junior-senior level, as well as at off-campus, evening, extension, branch, or other operations; (5) an institution with a member school could not offer identical degree business programs through an unaccredited unit; and (6) the senior year's work had to be taken in residence at the main unit of the B-school.

In the 28 years since the half-century celebration of AACSB's founding, its standard setting and accreditation activities have continued to expand. The *expansion* involved: (1) the academic and physical requirements set down as minimal; (2) expansion from undergraduate to graduate levels, as well as from main unit basic programs (bachelor's and MBA) to evening, branch, and other activities; (3) extension from business administration to separate accounting standards and accreditation; (4) movement from irregular questionnaires and surveys of member schools to structured, official surveys and visits on a periodic and scheduled basis for reaccreditation, following initial accreditation; and (5) finally, a requirement that *all* programs had to be accredited, that is, if a school had graduate as well as undergraduate programs, lack of accreditation or failure to maintain accreditation in one would cause the loss of accreditation in the other. In the last connection, doctoral programs are now included for examination as a part of the accreditation process. Expansion of academic and physical requirements embraced so-called *preconditions* of accreditation (e.g., the independence of the B-school as a degree-granting unit and the absence of political influence), as well as *definition of faculty credentials* (i.e., terminal degrees), *staffing profiles,* (full-time, part-time), *teaching loads* (number of courses and preparations), *curriculum* (general education component at baccalaureate level, plus business core, degree of specialization permitted, etc.), *physical facilities* (library, computer resources, office space, etc.), and *support staff* (secretaries, etc.). The *academic qualifications of students* matriculating in the business degree programs were also a subject embraced by the standards. Here, AACSB standards required that "admission and retention standards should compare favorably to those of the university or college as a whole."[21] Transfer students were to be accepted and awarded transfer credit only when their prior work was of a quality equivalent to that of the admitting school and subject to validation procedures that permitted satisfactory completion of the upper division work at the admitting school. Graduate student admissions were limited to baccalaureate degree holders from COPA (Council on Post-Secondary Accreditation) accredited institutions, and they had to show "high promise of success in post graduate business study." A lengthy statement about the determination of high promise accompanied the standard.

A major transformation in AACSB's accreditation standards was made effective in 1993. The essence of the transformation involved a refocusing of the standards to the school's educational mission, recognizing that individual missions are diverse, and, consequently, that the application of the standards had to relate to variations in individual school missions. Thus AACSB's 1993 accreditation manual states:

> The accreditation review focuses on a school's clear determination of its mission, development of its faculty, planning of its curricula, and delivery of its instruction. In these activities, each school must achieve and demonstrate an acceptable level of performance consistent with its overall mission *while meeting AACSB standards*. Substantial opportunity remains for schools to differentiate themselves through a variety of activities." (Italics added)[22]

In addition to the sharper focus on mission, the new standards emphasized requirements for demographic diversity in the student body and faculty, as well as curriculum coverage of "ethical and global issues, the influence of political, social, legal and regulatory, environmental and technological issues, and the impact of demographic diversity on organizations."[23] While the new standards reduced somewhat the specificity and detail of earlier accreditation standards, the range and scope of the standards continued to be broad. And the detail with which faculty composition, qualifications, development, and deployment were spelled out continued to be substantial, as did the detail provided with respect to curriculum content and evaluation at baccalaureate, master's, and doctoral levels. We noted that 1993 marked the first time that the AACSB moved into the accreditation of doctoral programs. The standard concerned with doctoral programs required acquisition of advanced specialized knowledge and development of advanced research skills. It required also explicit attention to the role of the specialized area in managerial and organizational contexts. Of special interest for students aiming at teaching careers was the added requirement that they receive experience that would prepare them for teaching in higher education. The last requirement probably reflected growing concern in the Academy over the professoriate's general lack of enthusiasm for teaching, especially at the undergraduate level.

This book has spoken about the dominance of the doctorate as the major requisite of terminal degree qualification, as well as the associated value structure that inclines PhDs to prefer research as against teaching, and, when teaching, to prefer the graduate to the undergraduate level. The AACSB standards reflect the belief that graduate-level teaching is more demanding than undergraduate. The terminal degree qualifications, staffing profiles, and teaching loads are more rigorous at the graduate level. At the same time, by setting minimum acceptable requirements at the undergraduate level, the standards protect quality there and define limits to any arrangement that would use the undergraduate program as a cash cow able to be milked for the benefit of graduate programs.

The standards stating and defining faculty characteristics and deployment continued to be quite detailed and specific in the 1993 version.[24] Thus, the *minimum full-time equivalent faculty* (MFTE) required was defined as the sum of: (1) one full-time equivalent for each *400 undergraduate* student credit hours per term; and (2) one full-time equivalent for each *300 graduate* student credit hours per term. While variation is allowed, in accordance with the school's mission, the following additional minimum numerical guidelines are set down: (1) at least 75 percent of the MFTE (as just defined) should be full-time faculty; (2) at least 60 percent of the student credit hours taught in each discipline should be by full-time faculty, and this requirement should apply also to evening programs and branch operations; and (3) teaching loads should not exceed 12 hours per term, and should be adjusted downward in schools emphasizing "greater intellectual contribution," that is, research, doctoral programs, etc. Finally a lengthy interpretation of the standard requiring the faculty to "have sufficient academic and professional qualifications to accomplish the school's mission" was set down. Generally, academic qualification requires a doctorate in the area of teaching. For faculty teaching Business Law or the Legal Environment of Business, the JD satisfies the requirement. For teachers of Taxation, the LLM in Taxation with the CPA or the JD plus a master's degree in Accounting is satisfactory. Where faculty hold a doctorate in one business field but teach in another, supplemental preparation in the form of professional development is required. The same requirement holds for possessors of doctorates outside of business, but applicable to business. Where a doctorate outside business and not applicable is involved, additional (rather than supplemental) preparation is required, for example, course work and/or personal study. In such cases, the school under review carries the burden of proof that the additional work is adequate. Faculty *without the doctorate* are allowed, but only *in limited* numbers and with substantial specialized course work in the field of primary teaching responsibility. Again, the burden of proof as to adequacy rests upon the school being reviewed. And the numerical guideline requires that "the total number of FTE faculty who are either academically qualified or professionally qualified (or both) must constitute at least 90 percent of the MFTE faculty."[25]

We must now consider accreditation of Accounting programs. Many accountants are unhappy at the lack of status they feel is accorded to their profession, especially as compared with attorneys. Not a few of them feel also that the establishment of Schools of Accounting, subject to accreditation standards set by the profession, would go a long way to remedy the situation. Thus, in September 1973, the American Institute of Certified Public Accountants (AICPA) announced that it strongly endorsed any action that would provide strong professional programs. To that end, it added that it preferred the establishment of schools of professional accounting at qualified and receptive colleges and universities. It was implicit that these schools would be independent of business schools. Consequently, AACSB perceived the AICPA's action as a significant danger.[26]

In July 1974, the AICPA took the further step of establishing a Board on Standards for Programs and Schools of Professional Accounting (BSPSPA). The board consisted of three AICPA members, three members of the American Accounting Association (AAA), three members of AACSB, and three members from the National Association of State Boards of Accountancy (NASBA). The Board was charged to set standards which would, when met, entitle a school to recognition by the accounting profession (i.e., accreditation).

Dr. Cyril C. Ling, in his 1976 report as executive vice president of AACSB, said: "It is my personal view that AACSB must make every effort possible to work out a cooperative relationship with the accounting field to forestall separate accreditation. The continued splintering and proliferation in accreditation does not appear to be in the public interest nor will universities likely tolerate it much longer."[27]

In the years following, a continuing dialogue developed between AACSB and the accounting profession, especially, AICPA and AAA. Carefully and with considerable sensitivity to the feelings of the accountants, the AACSB developed the case against separate schools of accounting with separate standards of accreditation, proposing rather that accounting programs should be within business schools (even if recognized as separate) and subject to cooperatively worked out accreditation standards.[28] The Financial Executives Institute (FEI) and the National Accounting Association became part of the ongoing dialogue. And,

along the way, individual State actions, like New York State's move in
1979 to increase from a minimum of 120 to 150 credit hours the work
required to qualify for the CPA (to be effective September 1, 1985), had
to be countered.[29] Gradually a consensus emerged that AACSB would
accredit accounting programs.[30] Finally, proposed AACSB standards for
accreditation of accounting programs were developed by the Accounting Accreditation Planning Committee, submitted to and approved by
the Accreditation Council at its meeting on June 13, 1980. Three types
of accounting programs were recognized for accreditation: (1) type A—
baccalaureate degrees with a concentration in Accounting; (2) type B—
Master of Business Administration degrees with a concentration in Accounting; and (3) type C—Masters of Accounting degrees.

The 1993 changes in accreditation standards for business administration were accompanied by parallel alterations in the standards for accounting accreditation. Thus, doctoral degrees with a concentration or
major in accounting were added to the baccalaureate and master's programs subject to review. Added also were masters degrees in Accounting (other than the MBA) described as including 150-hour programs
with admission at the undergraduate level, as well as specialized master's
degrees such as those in taxation. The 1980 designation of type A, B,
and C programs was dropped in 1993, and they were no longer separately accredited. Instead, all Accounting degree programs in a school
became subject to simultaneous review and accreditation. Finally, the
standards required for the qualifications of Accounting faculty specified
that "the accounting faculty as a whole *must possess a level of relevant
practical experience in business and accounting* and must demonstrate an
appropriate level of professional interaction consistent with the accounting unit's mission" (italics added).[31] As of April 20, 1993, there were
100 schools with accounting accreditation.[32] And so, with patience and
persistence, all interested parties came to a constructive conclusion of
what could have been a highly divisive and destructive fight.

A final illustration of the cooperation currently characterizing
AACSB and the Accounting profession is the December 1993 agreement
between AACSB and the Federation of Schools of Accounting (FSA).[33]
In that month, AACSB took over administrative operations for FSA.
The FSA is a national organization of leading programs in Accounting
with accounting firms, professional organizations, and supporting industry associates. Before 1990, FSA membership was limited to schools
having or seeking a formal school of accountancy. But, in 1989 and

1990, FSA was reoriented and focused on the development of high-quality postbaccalaureate degree programs. Consequently, FSA membership is now open to academic institutions pursuing its objectives and offering AACSB-accredited graduate degrees in Accounting. Other membership categories are available for AACSB-accredited baccalaureate programs and former FSA members as yet unaccredited by AACSB. According to William K. Laidlaw, AACSB executive vice president, the FSA-AACSB agreement provides for specified administrative services for an initial three-year period, with compensation sufficient to cover AACSB costs.

We cited earlier Dr. Cyril C. Ling's admonition against proliferation of accrediting agencies, and the likely lack of university tolerance for such growth. Dr. Ling's caution was associated with the AICPA move toward accounting accreditation. But there are a number of other groups with interest in programs relating to administration. Among these groups are: The National Association of Schools of Music, the National Association of Schools of Art, the National Association of Schools of Theater, the National Association of Schools of Public Affairs/Public Administration, the Accrediting Commission on Education for Health Services Administration, and the Accreditation Board for Engineering and Technology. In a May 1990 *Addendum to the AACSB Accreditation Council Policy Manual,* the AACSB described its agreements with each of these organizations relative to their respective roles in accrediting activities. In particular, the agreements involved joint degree programs and recognition of work taken in one professional area by the other professional area. The *Addendum* dealt also with granting of academic credit by AACSB schools for formal course work taken in noncollegiate organizations (e.g., labor unions, correspondence schools accredited by the National Home Study Council, business and industry educational programs, as well as similar programs run by professional associations and government agencies). These programs are known collectively as the Program on Noncollegiate Sponsored Instruction (PONSI), and are recognized and evaluated by the American Council on Education and agencies approved by it.

I hope that the foregoing fairly extensive review of the development of the AACSB's activities in setting standards and applying them to accreditation of business administration and accounting programs at all levels is a clear and conclusive demonstration of its importance in exercising a quality control function for America's B-Schools. It has not simply set standards. It has steadily elevated them. However, some people question whether it has adjusted them to the educational needs of a dynamic society. An illustration of the point is provided by the 1966 standard requiring accredited schools to be distinct and independent degree-recommending units of an institution of higher learning *with other independent degree-recommending units.* The literal application of this standard left free-standing business colleges out in the cold. Schools like Babson, Bentley, and Bryant faced a lengthy and difficult struggle before winning accreditation. It is probably true also that a number of deans have felt frustrated over the years by a perception that AACSB has been too literal and quantitative in interpreting and applying the standards. Consequently, the charge has been made that the AACSB standards tended to force conformity at the expense of experimentation and innovation. The safe course was to hew rather closely to the standards. Departures contained an element of risk. The resulting tension was probably a significant factor underlying the large changes in the standards in 1993, with their emphasis on the importance of each school's mission. Time will tell whether experimentation and innovation are now accommodated more easily.

Research and Information Exchange

Information exchange was an immediate aspect of AACSB activities, being inherent in the nature of annual membership meetings. By 1925, however, the process became more structured. In that year a bulletin on *Teaching Personnel and Training* was published.[34] The publication contained a list of the faculty of each school, in addition to details of their academic career, publications, faculty status, and fields of specialization. Perhaps more significant, AACSB's secretary also collected information from the survey on average salaries and teaching loads.

The *average* salary data were provided by rank, as they were in the case of teaching loads. The salary range for full professor was $4,000–$7,000, with ten schools reporting an average of over $5,000, eleven schools reporting $4,000–$5,000, and five schools reporting under $4,000. Average salaries for associate professors ranged from $3,000 to $5,000. Assistant professors ranged from $2,200 to $4,000, and instructors from $1,600 to $2,900. The survey noted that schools in large cities paid more than those outside those areas. Teaching loads for full professors ranged from 8 to 16 hours per week. The most common loads were 12 hours in 7 schools, 10 hours in 4 schools, 9 hours in 5 schools, and 8 hours in 5 schools. Associate and assistant professors, as well as instructors, were required to teach from 8 (3 schools) to 18 hours per week (1 school), with the most frequent load being 12 hours per week. Although the loads varied from school to school, 9 schools required the same teaching loads of all faculty ranks, while 9 other schools required fewer hours of full professors than of other ranks.

A powerful principle operates in connection with the dissemination of such data, and it must be noted. No one, whether an institution or an individual, enjoys being in the below-average portion of an array of data. Consequently, great peer pressure is exerted for the below-average group to achieve at least the average. Psychologically, failure to do so stamps one as being implicitly inferior. *But, as the below-average group improves itself, the average moves up.* This observation rests on a basic principle of elementary arithmetic, and it applies to averages involving all sorts of data (including executive salaries). The result is that upward pressure, where higher quantities are sought, is continuing and inexorable. And faculty, department chairpeople, and deans are the agents and instruments through which the pressure is exerted on central administrators and boards of trustees. In short, a whipsawing process is unleashed, which has a built-in tendency to raise salaries and reduce teaching loads, as the principle and process are applied in the Academy.

The 1925 AACSB meeting voted, also in connection with data gathering, to create a permanent standing committee on business research.[35] And in the 1927 meeting action was taken to institute winter meetings of the association, with the specific purpose of involving faculty in the organization's activities and encouraging the presentation of papers on topics of interest. In 1950 the AACSB and Beta Gamma Sigma each contributed $10,000 for a study of the educational problems of collegiate schools of business.[36] In 1954 AACSB, concerned over the number of questionnaires being circulated to deans of member schools by various individuals and organizations, decided that it would approve only those originated by member deans.[37] Concurrently, an annual salary survey by the Standards Committee in the fall of each year was approved.[38] In the years that followed, surveys and special studies were authorized, and the results distributed. Inevitably, their impact reflected the principle elucidated earlier, and improvement occurred.

Supporting the B-School

Standards, accreditation, and the comparative results of surveys provide strong support for the business school, offering protection against sometimes seemingly rapacious central administrators seeking to use the B-school as a cash cow. Denial of accreditation, or the threat of its loss, can sober any university administrator and restrain his or her enthusiasm for transferring funds to other divisions and programs. I served as a member and sometimes chairman of enough accreditation teams to observe the process in operation at first hand. More often than not, cordial conversations between team members and university officials are sufficient to effect improvements. When they aren't, a critical visitation report, plus a recommendation for corrective actions within some specified time period, will do the trick. If such action is inadequate, loss of accreditation is almost always followed by corrective action. This language should not leave the wrong impression. The AACSB avoids punitiveness in the application of its standards. Its avowed aim is not punishment, but the encouragement of positive steps to improve education for business.

When we move from the economic to the political sphere, the AACSB displays steadfastness in its behavior and actions against those who would exert improper external influence on the B-school. In 1938 the AACSB's standards included a specific prohibition against any school becoming or remaining a member if it was subject to undue political influence. The prohibition was followed in 1941 by actions taken against the administrations of the University of Georgia and the University of Arkansas.[39] On December 28 of that year, the Executive Committee decided to suspend Georgia and to inspect Arkansas. Although both institutions were considered to be subject to political interference, the situation in Arkansas was probably complicated by the fact that Dean Fichtner of the Arkansas College of Business Administration was also president of the AACSB. Dean Fichtner, who was one of the chief figures in the University of Arkansas case, had resigned as dean of the College. Then he submitted his resignation as president to the AACSB's Executive Committee. The offer to resign was not accepted by the Committee. Dean Fichtner continued to serve as president, and the "inspection" of the University of Arkansas, which was postponed until after AACSB's 1942 meeting, was classified as a routine inspection rather than a special inspection for political interference. One could infer from the record that Arkansas was treated more gingerly than Georgia because of Dean Fichtner's position as president of AACSB. In any case the University of Georgia, which was officially dropped on September 1, 1942, was reinstated on April 21, 1943. And following an inspection visit to the University of Arkansas on November 10–12, 1943, no action was taken against the university. That conclusion was reached because of corrective steps taken to eliminate any further exercise of undue political influence, although evidence was found of such influence in 1941 and 1942.

The actions taken in the above two cases, based on the standard against undue political influence, must have had a salutary effect, because I discovered no other cases mentioned in the history of the AACSB's first half-century. And I heard of no other similar AACSB actions in my 20 years as dean between 1965 and 1985. Of course, that is not conclusive evidence that undue political influence was or is completely absent. It may demonstrate only that, if and where it exists, it is most circumspect, cautious, and wary of arousing AACSB suspicions. One thing does seem sure. Any dean of a AACSB-accredited school who is subjected to undue political influence need only "blow the whistle" to bring the weight of AACSB into the picture. Of course, that requires the dean to have the courage to make the matter an issue, and, if necessary, to resign as dean as a protest against the exertion of political influence.[40]

It is implicit that, whether the issue is economic or political, the B-school dean is the key figure in using AACSB as a counterweight to pressure exerted against his or her school. A sophisticated dean can be subtle, or, if necessary, blunt. But, either way, AACSB is the counterweight, and a useful one it is.

Monitoring the Market

Monitoring the market is an aspect of quality control. Accredited schools carry a stamp of approval that yields a certain status and has importance in positioning them in the academic marketplace. Schools without accreditation are likely to be perceived as qualitatively lacking, and, consequently, inferior. This issue of status was a bone of contention between member (accredited) and nonmember (unaccredited) schools prior to 1968. The nonmember schools, at least a number of them, felt that AACSB operated as a sort of privileged club, with an unstated aim of protecting their place in the market from encroachment by schools with different educational approaches. Seen this way, AACSB's standards could be perceived as something other than an exercise in quality control.

A recent lawsuit filed by the Massachusetts School of Law (MSL) against the American Bar Association highlights the point.[41] The School charged the ABA with violating the antitrust laws. MSL, which was founded in 1988, was accredited by Massachusetts education officials in 1990. Its graduates can take the bar exam in that state and seven others, but in 42 states only graduates of ABA-accredited schools can take the bar exam. And ABA refuses to accredit MSL, because its operations do not meet the ABA's standards. MSL is a practice-oriented school, featuring courses taught by practicing lawyers and intensive legal writing instruction. In admissions, it eschews the traditional Law School Admission Test, aiming at a student body from more diverse backgrounds than usual. And its tuition is $9,000 per year, modest compared with ABA-accredited schools. The main thrust of the lawsuit charges that ABA's standards are intended to protect the economic interests of professors, librarians, and test services, rather than the educational needs of students. The suit complains further that ABA's ability to exclude MSL's graduates from the bar exam in 42 states enables it to boost professorial salaries, reduce teaching loads, and prevent competition from innovative programs.

While AACSB does not possess power to bar access to professional certification and licenses to the graduates of unaccredited schools, the status conferred by accreditation was perceived by many as a form of market control. However, the AACSB's action in 1968, when it became an Assembly rather than an Association, appears to have quieted those schools without accreditation. More was involved than simply changing the name. The 1968 action opened up the membership of AACSB to unaccredited schools and to nonacademic organizations. Admission to the clubhouse opened the doors, and removed the aura of exclusivity which had earlier rankled nonmembers. It was a positive step also in helping to expose unaccredited schools to AACSB's deliberations and procedures, thereby enhancing moves toward wider accreditation. We should note, in this connection, that AACSB voted in 1964 to accept into full membership Canadian and Mexican schools that met its standards and desired to join.

The AACSB's openness to unaccredited schools, while commend-able, does not and cannot overcome the market control inherent in its standards and in the status associated with accreditation. That comment is an observation, not a criticism. The benefits that flow from standards, accreditation, research and information exchange, as well as the support thereby engendered for accredited B-Schools, are great. At any rate, that is my conviction.

A Few Words about AACSB's Staff

The development of AACSB's activities, on its present scale, could not have been accomplished minus the creation and augmentation of a substantial staff. Still, AACSB managed to conduct its affairs for 33 years, until 1949, without employing any full-time staff. The work of the organization was done by the member deans who were officers and committeemen, no doubt with the assistance of their own college staffs. But reaccreditation was not well structured. There did not seem to be scheduled, periodic visitations to review continuing compliance with standards. Occasional but repeated complaints arose that, once accred-ited, some schools slipped and were not held to the standards applied to applicants for initial accreditation.

Finally, in 1949, C. E. Gilliland, an assistant to the dean of the business school at Washington University in St. Louis, was hired by AACSB as a full-time executive secretary. Between 1949 and 1967, six people served in that position: C. E. Gilliland 1949–1953; Mark R. Green, 1953–1955; Richard C. Reidenbach, 1955–1958; James M. A. Robinson, 1958–1960; Richard R. Weeks, 1960–1964; and James F. Kane, 1964–1967. In 1967 Dr. Cyril C. Ling became executive secretary. In 1969 a second full-time administrative position was created. Dr. Ling's title was changed to executive vice president in 1970, in which year a third full-time administrative position was created, to be followed by creation of a fourth such position in 1971. Of course, in those few years AACSB's membership was greatly enlarged, by the 1968 change to an Assembly. The organization's elections were opened to all mem-bers, and representatives of nonaccredited schools and nonacademic or-ganizations could be elected to serve on the board of directors. Probably more directly related to the enlargement of staff was the substantially increased structure of the accreditation-reaccreditation process, as well as the expansion of research and information-gathering activities. Also, programs were initiated to help newly inducted deans to better prepare for their jobs. And international ties were developed.

In 1971, an office was opened in Washington, D.C., and Dr. Ling moved there. The new location was justified on the ground that AACSB needed a closer tie to Washington agencies involved with accreditation, education funding, and legislation. But the ongoing work of accreditation continued to be handled by the St. Louis office. The physical split into two locations was problematic and expensive. Many member deans questioned the expense and the priorities which were put forward in support of two locations. The matter came to a head following the September 1975 appointment of William K. Laidlaw, Jr., as managing director, with headquarters in the St. Louis office. At that point AACSB's truncated structure was no longer acceptable, and it was decided to discontinue the Washington office, while maintaining a "presence" there. Concurrently, AACSB's activities were reconsolidated in St. Louis.

Dr. Ling left AACSB in 1976, having completed nine eventful years as the organization's chief full-time official. In that period the number of accredited schools grew to 178, almost $900,000 was raised in grants for various projects, and the budget increased from $88,000 to $550,000. The staff had expanded to 16 people. William K. Laidlaw, Jr., has been executive vice president since 1976, holding that office for 18 years (counting only to 1994), twice the length of time of his immediate predecessor. The two of them together account for more than half the years served by all the executive secretaries/vice presidents (27 out of a total of 45). And Laidlaw alone has served as long as the first six executive secretaries did collectively (18 years and continuing). As of 1994 AACSB's staff consisted of 6 full-time administrators and 23 staff.

I would be remiss if I failed to comment on one aspect of the growth of a large, full-time staff at AACSB. That aspect is the gradual accumulation of power by the staff. Such accumulation is inherent in the nature of accrediting organizations, and probably also in other associations of professional groups. The power grows out of the permanency of the staff, as against the turnover in the deans who comprise the Assembly's membership. The fact that the tenure in office of business school deans has declined in recent decades, and now averages about three-four years, is a contributing factor. Even long-service deans, who rise from the ranks to national office and committee memberships and chairs, do not continue in those offices for many years. The danger is the development of a bureaucracy, with bureaucratic patterns of thought and behavior. Excessive literal mindedness and narrowness can get exerted by the staff and influence Assembly committees in their accreditation deliberations and decisions. While that is a genuine danger, and has sometimes allegedly appeared, I believe it has been contained reasonably well.

In sum, AACSB had become a dynamic, flourishing organization richly fulfilling the original objective of its founders, that is, to promote and improve higher education for business and management. Along the way, it embraced the specific obligation of setting standards and engaging in accreditation for Accounting as well as Business programs.

Student Life

Student Perceptions of the University's Mission

In student minds the central purpose of the university is teaching. The faculty are the teachers, and the critical point of contact is the classroom. The student's aim is to complete successfully a program of study, following which a degree is obtained. That degree certifies to the world that the student has acquired a body of knowledge, and a set of skills and insights that enlarge his or her competence to think, to analyze, and to do. This perception is largely true, but not entirely so, for students have from the beginning to the present sought more from the traditional four years of undergraduate study. They have sought a vigorous social life, as well as recreational uses of their time. More recently, and periodically through the history of universities, they have also perceived the Academy as the appropriate locus of radical, even revolutionary, political action. All the while, at the graduate level, students have been more sharply focused on preparation for careers in a profession.

The *Commerce Violet* of 1910 captured the point of the preceding paragraph:

> In the beginning the School was a school—and only a school. Each night . . . students would come together and study. They were there to grind, and not for a good time. . . . As early as 1903, some of the leading spirits came to realize that earthly happiness is not to be scorned. So they proposed a School Banquet as a means of cultivating closer friendships.[1]

The *Violet* goes on to describe the growth, one could say the proliferation, of a wide range of social, fraternal, academic, sports, and other clubs and activities. These embraced class banquets, fraternities, a Glee

Club, a Debating Society, a Junior Prom, school publications like the *Violet,* theater parties, a Student Organization (i.e., a student governance body), smokers (not so common now), a Senior Hop, and some foreign student clubs (e.g. the Japanese Club and a Deutscher Verein). As always, a relatively small minority of active students sparked these activities. But their enthusiasm and energy produced a spectrum of nonclassroom related organizations and activities that attracted the participation of much larger numbers, and thereby enriched greatly the total learning experience of the college years.

Certain student organizations warrant special mention. Among them are Alpha Kappa Psi and Delta Sigma Pi, the first formed in 1904 and the second in 1908. Both were professionally oriented, established specifically as business school fraternities, and thereby distinguished from purely social fraternities. To illustrate, the founders of Alpha Kappa Psi set down its purpose as being: "To create a fitting memory of Charles Waldo Haskins, founder of the school, and to lift the degree of Bachelor of Commercial Science to a place of commercial importance."[2] These two organizations grew mightily over the years, and today have chapters at business schools across the nation. For example, in 1993 Alpha Kappa Psi had 249 chapters on college and university campuses, and 82 alumni chapters.[3] The Alpha chapter is at N Y U's Stern School, as is that of Delta Sigma Pi.

The Commerce chapter of Beta Gamma Sigma, the B-school's academic honorary that parallels Phi Beta Kappa in the Arts and Sciences, was established in 1933. A chapter was created at the graduate school in 1971. The roster of scholastically gifted students who have won membership over the years is lengthy and distinguished by their subsequent achievements. Students who excelled in particular fields of study were recipients of a variety of awards and prizes established over the years, usually by grateful alumni having a special interest in the respective fields. Students who were outstanding in their participation in student government and other nonclassroom activities were honored by election to the School's Hall of Fame, as well as Sphinx (the Day Senior Honorary) and Arch and Square (the Evening Senior Honorary).

The degree to which the School of Commerce generated a wide spectrum of activities may seem surprising in a school without significant residential facilities (a commuter school), and with a very large evening student body. One's surprise is quickly overcome, however, when we remember that by the late thirties the School enrolled 10,000 students. If only 5 percent were active in student organizations, then we find 500 people so engaged. That is a large number, and they could stimulate student government, clubs of all kinds, fraternities, sororities, student newspapers, the yearbook, and much more. The same point applies to GBA.

We would be remiss if we failed to note the following comment in the *Commerce Violet* of 1908:

> It is with mingled feelings that the editors present to you . . . the first Commerce Violet. . . . It is with no malice that the publication of this volume has been undertaken. Circumstances compelled it. *The Heights Violet Board have eliminated all professional schools from their book and one of two alternatives was presented: no representation, or else a book distinctly our own.* The question was put to the Student Body, and it is with pleasure that we record a unanimous decision to publish our own Violet. (Italics added)[4]

Once again, we discover evidence of the split personality that marked New York University when it had the beautiful campus at University Heights, with its Stanford White buildings of classic design, and the one-time commercial buildings at Washington Square (at least before the major construction programs that began there in the 1950s). No matter. The downtown "campus" developed its own rich range of student activities.

The Fiftieth Anniversary edition of the *Commerce Violet* reveals how rich was the range of student activities. In addition to Alpha Kappa Psi and Delta Sigma Pi, the fraternities established to promote collegiate education for business, and Beta Gamma Sigma, the national scholastic honorary for business students, as well as Sphinx and Arch and Square, there were nine Greek letter male social fraternities, five sororities for women, over half a dozen departmental Greek letter honoraries (e.g., Beta Alpha Psi in Accounting), an Inter-Faith Greek letter junior society (Alpha Phi Sigma, to build a bridge between Christian and Jewish students), a variety of departmental student clubs, a Pre-Law club, and another nonsectarian society (Kappa Iota Gamma). Religiously oriented student clubs included the Newman Club, the Jewish Culture Foundation (successor to the Menorah Society, which was founded in 1914), and the Christian Association. Broader student organizations embraced those involved in governance, for example, day and evening Student Councils, Inter-Club councils, and Student Service Organizations. The cultural side had Sock and Buskin, a theater group, the Glee Club, the Debating Society, and *Varieties,* a student magazine modeled after the *New Yorker.* Finally, there were three important student publications; the *Commerce Bulletin,* a student newspaper; the *Commerce Violet,* the Yearbook, and the *Commerce Log,* a student guide to activities, clubs, and other information of interest. All in all, a rich panoply of clubs, societies, and other organizations.

The Troubled Sixties

Things changed dramatically in the sixties. Students showed much less interest in social affairs and college yearbooks, turning instead to political activism. The shift was most marked among students in the Humanities, the Social Sciences, Law, Social Work, and Education. Students in the Physical Sciences, Engineering, and Business did not seem to share the activist enthusiasm of the others to the same degree, although all were sensitive to issues raised by the Vietnam War and the legacy of racism in America.

One is reminded of Dickens's *Tale of Two Cities,* with its famous opening line: "It was the best of times, it was the worst of times." So it was in the 1960s. Society was everywhere under attack, with university students in the vanguard. The destructiveness of those attacks was not seen by many, but their consequences continue to bedevil the educational system. Student cries for curricular relevance more often than not became a cover for tearing down intellectually rigorous courses. Demands to do away with grading systems became a blanket under which students could hide lack of effort and poor performance. Academic quality deteriorated. The destruction of parietal rules in dormitories, pressed in the name of freedom and liberty, brought with it an enormous increase in risks to students. Security mechanisms were destroyed. With student residence halls open to easy access by practically anyone, they became havens for deviants, drug users, and generally undisciplined members of the student body and their friends. License triumphed, parading always under flags of freedom and relevance to issues more important than one's studies. "Rapping," sit-ins, and confrontations with the established authority became the order of the day. As usually happens, the majority was overwhelmed by the hyperactivity of the radicals at the extreme end of the social spectrum. None of this implies the absence of real problems in the social and educational order. But, in this case, the "cure" was worse than the disease.

Eileen's story provides a tragic illustration. She matriculated at the School of Commerce in Fall 1965, being admitted as a University Scholar on the basis of a very fine high school academic record. Eileen was an unusually bright and articulate young lady. An Irish beauty, fair of complexion, luxuriant red hair framing attractive features and blue eyes, and a figure to match. She was a stunning girl.

Almost immediately, given her mental ability and physical attractiveness, she commanded the attention and admiration of many fellow students. She became active in student affairs and was elected an officer of the student government. Her energy was great. In addition to academic and student activities, she earned money as a model, enjoying no small success. Eileen's academic performance lived up to her high school record, and she was among those outstanding students whose names appeared on the dean's list of honor students. So her school career unfolded, through the end of the junior year.

In Spring 1968 Eileen was elected president of the Student Council. Everyone expected her senior year to live up to the promise of what had gone before, to be followed by graduation and continued success thereafter. But, at that time, Eileen was caught up in the maelstrom of events which reflected more profound happenings in American society. The Reverend Dr. Martin Luther King was assassinated in early 1968. As part of the revulsion that act engendered in millions of Americans, the higher education community felt a great responsibility to advance the movement of American blacks into the larger society. Many American universities instituted special scholarship programs, and intensified recruitment of young black students. Black students already matriculated at universities were caught up in the ferment of the time, and organized themselves into separate student societies. A common demand made by these students was for the creation of Black Studies programs, and the establishment of Institutes of Afro-American Affairs. The names varied, but the main thrust of the Institutes was to coalesce black students as a group, and to build in the larger student body and university an awareness of the history and role of blacks in American society, as well as their problems in the contemporary world. More generally, they sought to further, through whatever means might seem appropriate, the position of blacks in society at large and in the universities.

N Y U was a microcosm of the scene. So, in mid-1968, the university announced the Martin Luther King Scholarship Program, funded by the university with $1 million, and aimed at recruiting black students. Concurrently, black students organized a Black Students' Association and pressed the university to establish an Institute of Afro-American Affairs. The university agreed, establishing the Martin Luther King, Jr. Afro-American Student Center and an Afro-American Institute. The latter is an academic support program, originally headed by Professor Roscoe Brown, and intended to encourage black studies, build awareness of black problems, and increase support among faculty, staff, alumni, and the larger public. Professor Brown, later president of Bronx Community College, is a black man with substantial scholarly credentials. He commanded the respect of faculty and students, and smoothed the development of black studies programs.

But there was a problem in finding a director for the Martin Luther King, Jr. Student Center. The black students seemed to desire a black activist as director. To that end, they located a man who they thought met their criteria. He was the Reverend Hatchett. The title reflected a religious training and background. Hatchett had a degree in divinity and had done graduate work in philosophy at both Columbia and N Y U. Also, he had a record as an activist, which, while well known to the students, was not known to the university administration.

The university's Chancellor, who was executive vice president for academic affairs, decided to accede to the student demand and appointed the Reverend Hatchett as director of the King Center. Following its usual practice, the university issued a press release. Leonard Buder, a writer on educational matters at the *New York Times,* recognized the Reverend Hatchett's name, and looked him up in the *Times* library. His search quickly disclosed an unhappy history. The Reverend Hatchett had been employed by the New York City public school system, but, shortly after being appointed, became the center of a major controversy. He was an inflammatory figure, and following his employment by the Board of Education, tried to organize black teachers. His aim was not just the advancement of blacks in the public school system, desirable and justifiable in itself, but rather to change what he publicly denounced as ethnic imbalance in the City's public school system. In particular, he charged the system was dominated, both in classroom and administration, by Jews. Hatchett criticized them, as well as some black school administrators and teachers, for treating black students as though they were incapable of learning. That was his allegation, and it placed particular blame on Jewish teachers and administrators. In a brief period, he polarized the City school system. He made speeches and issued statements which generated conflict. He was discharged for taking students to a memorial service for Malcolm X which had been prohibited. After being fired by the public school system, he came to the attention of the Black Students' Association at N Y U, and was put forward as director of the King Student Center.

Having discovered these facts, Mr. Buder wrote a story which appeared on the front page of the *New York Times*. It caused a sensation. The university administration was embarrassed. Thousands of N Y U's Jewish alumni were outraged. These events occurred in early August 1968, prior to the beginning of the Fall semester in late September. Buder's story led to hastily called meetings of the university's top administrators, in particular deans and vice presidents. They were summoned to meet with the Chancellor, who explained the situation and asked their opinion. Almost unanimously, they recommended that the Reverend Hatchett be discharged immediately, before the Fall semester began. They suggested Hatchett be held harmless financially, with his salary for the contract year to be paid. The Chancellor was loathe to take that advice.

The president, who was abroad, returned. Upon his return, meetings were held with a small group of institutional leaders in whom the president placed great confidence. In addition, he contacted Arthur Goldberg, a prominent Jewish attorney who had a distinguished career. Originally an attorney for the AFL-CIO, Goldberg became Secretary of Labor, and then Associate Justice of the United States Supreme Court. He left the court at President Lyndon Johnson's request to become U.S. Ambassador to the United Nations. By late Summer 1968 he had resigned that position, returned to the practice of law, and was a serious candidate for the governorship of the State of New York.

N Y U's president asked Arthur Goldberg to meet the Reverend Hatchett, discuss the situation, and then advise the president. Goldberg agreed and met Hatchett. Having done so, Goldberg advised the president that it would be all right to keep Hatchett.

With Goldberg's opinion in hand, the president decided not to discharge Hatchett. The Fall 1968 semester opened at N Y U with the Reverend Hatchett in place as director of the King Student Center. He moved immediately to use the Institute and the Black Students' Association as a base for organizing meetings and protests aimed at the university community, and also at the larger polity of the country. Fall 1968 was a time when such activities found fertile soil. Senator Robert Kennedy had been assassinated, immediately following a stunning victory in the California primary. The Democratic Party's convention had met in Chicago to nominate its candidate for the presidency. That convention was marred by terrible controversy. The streets of Chicago erupted in riots. The Reverend Hatchett was busy making speeches and issuing public statements characterized by outrageous attacks on all established components of the American government.

The university president recognized that Hatchett had become much more than an embarrassment. But the president took no action until just before the presidential election. Hatchett made a speech and issued statements which so demeaned the presidential candidates and the political process that the university president summarily discharged Hatchett.

The black students were outraged, and called a student strike. The most radical elements among the white students, sensing an opportunity to seize the issue and steer the strike in directions of their own choosing, jumped in. While appearing to offer support, they sought to gain control of the strike. They were rebuffed by the black students, who were not fooled. But the black students could not marshal sufficient student support to shut down the university and make the strike successful.

Unable to achieve their goal, the black students decided on a hit-and-run strategy. They would move, in a group of perhaps 20–25 people, into a particular academic building, seek to obstruct entrances and exits, interfere with the operation of the elevators, and try thereby to disrupt normal classroom activity. When challenged or thinking they had achieved as much as they could at one locale, they would move to another building and repeat the tactic. Students in sympathy with the strike sought the support of the several student councils in NYU's colleges and schools. Generally, Student Council members were more responsive to activist causes than the student body at large. In certain colleges, notably the College of Arts and Sciences, the student council seemed to favor support.

The majority of the School of Commerce's Student Council was opposed to the strike. They reflected the general sentiment of the business school students, who were overwhelmingly against activities which disrupted their attendance at class and their academic progress. They were career oriented, wanted to get on with their education, graduate, and get jobs. They were interested in the larger events of society, but they did not see any practical gain from the activities of the activist students.

But Eileen, the Student Council president, and several fellow members of the Commerce Council, favored the strike. They manipulated a vote in the Council to indicate support. But they did not have the support of their student body. That became clear when a group of black students invaded the Commerce building lobby and barred entry to the elevators. They were opposed by a group of white students, and for some tense moments it looked as though there would be a battle.

Notified of the confrontation, I hurried to the lobby with several colleagues. I had a bull horn, and managed to break up the confrontation. Some white students were outraged at what took place. One asked, "What can we do to fight these activities?"

I suggested, "Call a meeting. Everybody at the university is calling meetings. There are more meetings than classes."

"Could we meet in Lassman Hall, the large student lounge?"

"Yes, it is there for students. If you wish, you can have the meeting there."

So a rump group of students was organized, and announced a meeting of the Commerce student body, to take place in Lassman Hall. That action was taken without any reference to the elected Student Council government. Within an hour of their activity becoming public, I received a phone call from Eileen. She objected to the students meeting in Lassman Hall. When I asked what her objection was, she said bluntly, "You have no right to allow the hall to be used for any meeting without my approval."

"You are under a very serious misapprehension. You are president of the Student Council, but I am dean of the School. I, not you, have authority over the use of School facilities. I approved the meeting, and my approval is ruling. But you can come in and see me if you wish."

She did. When we met I suggested that rather than trying to stop the student group from meeting, Eileen and her Student Council colleagues should join the rump student group, and convert the meeting into a joint one. Then she could preside as Student Council president. She accepted that suggestion. Hundreds of students showed up at the meeting. Eileen and her small coterie of supporters in the Student Council were shouted down when they tried to explain their support of the black student strike. The meeting ended with the Commerce students forbidding the Student Council from supporting the strike. The meeting was a disaster for Eileen, just how much so being revealed only in the next few months.

Eileen came to me shortly after the student meeting. She asked if she could attend a faculty meeting, hoping to enlist support in that quarter. I counseled her not to do so, knowing there were faculty who were very angry over student disruptions. These faculty did not make their opinions public, but expressed them strongly in private discussion. If Eileen appeared before the faculty, I was convinced those faculty members would use the occasion to vent their spleen against the general course of events. They would direct their concentrated anger against her. But she was adamant.

As I look back I suppose I allowed her to go ahead because I was angry at her, and did not feel inclined to protect her from her own ignorance and inexperience. She appeared at the next faculty meeting. Everything that I feared would happen, did. She was verbally savaged by several members of the faculty, who pressed question on question and interrogated her in a way which was traumatic. I cut it off finally, dismissing her from the meeting.

What followed was unexpected, and I learned about it only after the event. Eileen was so upset psychologically by the rejection of her fellow students and her treatment at the faculty meeting that she stopped attending classes, and did not take her examinations at the end of the Fall 1968 semester. Only after the second semester began did I become cognizant of what was happening. Her parents appeared in my office one day and said she had disappeared. They were honest, decent, hardworking people of very modest means. To that moment they had been enormously proud of their daughter, with good reason as earlier indicated. They couldn't understand the terrible turn of events in her life.

I called the university security office. Student friends were contacted and a search was started. Eileen was found living with a boyfriend. She had begun to use drugs, and had dropped out of the normal academic scene. Her parents took her home and sought medical help. I do not know firsthand what followed, but I heard Eileen was given electric shock therapy, with horrible results. I had not known it before, but I learned as a consequence of this case that electric shock therapy can have the adverse effect of destroying memory and impairing mental ability. That was the terrible after-effect of Eileen's treatment.

She dropped out of school and disappeared from the scene. I wondered about her fate many times. A couple of years later someone reported seeing Eileen and her mother shopping in a neighborhood store. I was told that she was then metamorphosed from her earlier beauty, brightness and promise, behaving as though she was simpleminded.

It was a tragedy, a terrible blighting of so much promise. When I think of the late 1960s, I think of Eileen. I do not know how many other bright young people had their lives ruined by the excesses of that time. But I do know that I shall never look back on those days with any sense of nostalgia or pleasure.

One of the other aspects of the troubles of the sixties was the growth of an intense insistence on individual and group rights, especially along ethnic, racial, and sexual lines. This insistence was reflected in student life by a proliferation of clubs organized ethnically, racially, and sexually, that is, Hispanic, Afro-American, and Gay and Lesbian. Religiously oriented clubs and organizations had existed for many years, and continued with their activities, but possibly on a more intense level of self-awareness. Fraternities, sororities, and similar organizations suffered a decline, and their number and membership were considerably reduced. At least that was the situation at N Y U, including Commerce. The extent of the decline was somewhat less marked at the Graduate School of Business Administration, perhaps because it did not suffer the same proportionate decline in enrollments as did Commerce. Remember an earlier point: huge enrollments are likely to be associated with an active student life, because even a small minority of active students will amount to a substantial number in absolute numeric terms. This point was most clearly revealed at Commerce, where the collapse in the evening student population literally killed the previously active and separate evening student government, newspaper, and other organizations.

Affirmative Action and Quotas

Among the more important results of the civil rights disturbances of the sixties was the emergence of a range of affirmative action programs. They have had a deep impact on the public and private sectors of the American polity. The underlying idea justifying these programs is that certain minority groups, deeply disadvantaged by generations of discrimination based mainly on race and sex, need positive, productive programs to enable younger generations to overcome societally inherited barriers and enter the mainstream of American society.

A host of programs were instituted, some under the pressure of governmental regulation and newly enacted laws, and some by individuals and institutions seeking to correct past wrongs. The academic world was no exception to the trend of the times. In fact, it became a major focus of attention. Education was seen as the key to the future progress of minorities, by preparing them to enter the professions and the more highly skilled areas of economic life.

Most people do not argue against the ideal, for it seems so obviously just and equitable. Yet, affirmative action programs quickly became a source of great controversy and deep division. Groups, long-time allies in fighting discrimination, suddenly found themselves opposed. The catalyst which precipitated this sad transformation was pressure to convert affirmative action programs into quota systems. Advocates of affirmative action argued with great conviction that minorities ought to be represented across the spectrum of economic and political activity in the same, or approximately the same, percentages as they were found in the general population. In highly simplified form, if blacks in the general population, or more particularly in a particular labor market area, comprised X percent of the population, then that percentage should become the goal for the number of that group to be found among physicians, attorneys, accountants, political office holders, business managers, and so on.

Other minorities, who had already overcome discrimination and were now represented in the professions and other highly desirable spheres of activity in proportions greater than their percentage of the population, became deeply concerned, indeed frightened, that the imposition of highly specific numerical goals, that is, quotas, could be achieved only at their expense. These groups argued that affirmative action in a free society must not mean specific numerical goals. They were painfully aware that quotas had been used historically by majority groups to limit minority access to opportunity. Everyone should have equal access to educational, economic, political, or other opportunities. What happened, given such opportunity, would then depend entirely on competence and performance. Against this background I relate an incident which, to me, throws into high relief the many-faceted nature of affirmative action.

The incident occurred in the late 1970s, while I was still dean of the College of Business and Public Administration. It involved a graduating senior. The student had applied to several law schools, and, in accordance with established procedure, came to the dean's office for recommendations. The student was a young black man, of fine presence, handsome, well dressed, and articulate. He saw the assistant dean who was responsible for advising law school applicants, and for helping them with their applications. The assistant dean also prepared letters of recommendation from the dean's office.

I heard first of the meeting of the student with the assistant dean when the former appeared in my office, quite upset, indeed very angry. The student maintained that the assistant dean was a racist, and was trying to abort his application to the law schools of his choice. I knew my assistant dean, having promoted him several times in recognition of his ability and genuine interest in students. The assistant dean came originally from a job at the Board of Education of the City of New York, and took a position as an administrative assistant at a $5,000–$6,000 reduction in annual salary. He did that because he wished to enroll in the PhD program of the Graduate School of Public Administration, obtain a doctorate, and then continue into an academic career. He had followed his plan successfully. At the time of the incident described he had completed his doctorate, and had been promoted to the position noted. He did not have a racist bone in his body. Believing as I did, I was surprised when the black student made his complaint. I asked,

"What makes you think the assistant dean is racist?"

"When I spoke with him, he asked me to which schools I made applications. I told him I applied to Harvard, Yale, Columbia, Chicago, Stanford, and N Y U Law Schools."

That is a most imposing roster of law schools, in fact six of the most prestigious schools in the country. The student added that the assistant dean had then reviewed his academic credentials, paying particular attention to his grade point average in college and his Law School Aptitude Test score, more commonly known in the academic world as the LSAT score. Given that information, the assistant dean suggested that it would be wise to apply to two or three additional law schools, as "back-up" schools, schools of lesser prestige. That suggestion outraged the black student, and was construed by him as a reflection of the assistant dean's desire to steer him away from the best schools, those of his choice.

Feeling outraged, he challenged the assistant dean's suggestion, and pressed him for the reasons underlying his suggestions. The assistant dean pointed to the student's grade point average and LSAT score. The GPA was, as I best recall, around a 3.2, equivalent to 87 percent. The LSAT score was around 520, out of a possible 800. Both scores are respectable and reflect good student performance, at the B grade level. They do not reflect incompetence of a student. But the minimum acceptable credentials at the law schools chosen were substantially above them. The six law schools selected typically required a minimum GPA of 3.6 and LSAT score of 700 at that time. Apprised of these facts, the student told the assistant dean that he considered them totally irrelevant.

The assistant dean asked, "Why do you think that?"

"Haven't you ever heard of affirmative action?"

"Yes, of course."

"Well then, why do you try to discourage me, when the preference involved in affirmative action should clearly overcome the differences in the scores to which you point?"

"I agree that affirmative action will offset a significantly lower GPA and LSAT score, but the variation from the minimum in your case seems very large, and that is why I suggest you have two or three safe schools. I am not implying in any way, that you should not also submit your applications to the schools of your choice."

This response did not satisfy the black student. He came to my office and lodged a complaint against the assistant dean. When I reviewed the case, and found the facts to be as described, I told the student I did not accept his charge of racism and attempted discrimination by the assistant dean. I added,

"I think the assistant dean was trying, in good faith, to provide color blind advice. In so doing, and out of a desire to be helpful, he may have made his point more strongly than he should. If you do not wish to apply to any schools other than the most prestigious ones, I have no objection. It is your choice, and you are entitled to it. I will be happy to give you my recommendation, in accordance with your record and qualifications." I did.

But the black student remained unsatisfied. Reflecting his sense of having been unfairly treated, he organized a Black Business Students Association, which proved successful. It afforded an opportunity for black students to be in a social grouping where they could discuss their particular problems, and engage in dialogue with college officials as a group, as well as individuals.

The upshot of the story is that the student was admitted to one of the prestigious law schools, which he attended and from which he graduated several years later. I have no information subsequent to his graduation, and assume that he is pursuing a successful career. I certainly hope that is the case. What is striking, over and above everything recounted, is that the young man who is the subject of this story was not a product of a ghetto. He was a young man of color, who had been born into and raised by a middle-class or upper-middle-class family of black professional people. There were attorneys in his family, and, although I am not certain of this, I was told that one of his relatives was a judge.

Those aspects of the case raise rather interesting questions with respect to affirmative action. Remember the original idea. Affirmative action is to help people who have been discriminated against, and who need an "edge," a bit of reverse discrimination, in order to enter the American mainstream. Yet, we have here a young man who is in no way a product of the ghetto, who grew up in socioeconomic circumstances not unlike those of white middle-class children and who is convinced that he is entitled, by virtue of color, to favoritism in pursuing his academic and career goals. If one believes and argues that a dark skin in the United States inherently and by itself is a profound barrier, no matter what the family circumstances of the individual are, then perhaps our young student is correct. But, if one realizes that this student's admission into a highly prestigious law school, which limited the number of students it admitted, had to be and was at the expense of some other student who had an LSAT score of 700 and a GPA of at least 3.6, then it seems serious issues of equity are involved.

A more serious side exists in the attitude described in the story just told. It is being recognized by growing numbers of people, both black and white, because of increasing awareness of its long-term implications and consequences. The major one is the development of a perception that any consequential achievement by a black person is the result of preferential treatment rather than of competence. One illustration involves Duke University.[5] In 1988 it announced an affirmative action policy of increasing its black faculty by one in each of its 56 departments within five years. In 1993, a net of only eight had been added. In the consequent outcry by activists, a central issue became the available supply nationwide of black faculty *who met Duke's academic standards* in each of its departments. Critics contended that Duke's departments had failed to meet the goal because of racism. Defenders claimed an inadequate supply of suitably qualified candidates. *Some outstanding black professors refused offers from Duke, fearing that their appointments would be viewed as based on preferential treatment rather than on competence.* This outgrowth of affirmative action is a Catch-22 situation.

Another case described in the *Wall Street Journal* involved the *Harvard Law Review*.[6] Law school review editorial staffs are comprised of students. Traditionally, they come from the academic elite, and are selected on the basis of their scholastic records. At Harvard Law School, it was apparently felt that this method of selection deprived the *Review* of an adequate number of black student staffers. Now some editors are selected solely on the basis of their writing skill, while others are chosen to fill affirmative action slots. In this case, a black assistant professor facing a tenure decision submitted an article. The article was assigned to two black student editors for review by the co-chairman of the articles office, without going through the normal process for assigning articles for review. The article was immediately accepted for publication. Ms. Emily Schulman, the elected student president of the *Review* and a third-year student with an untarnished liberal record, apparently thought the procedure was questionable and voiced some doubts. The result was an outcry which, while unintended as to its consequences, cast doubt on the quality of the assistant professor's article. That is as tragic as it is serious for Harvard, for the black assistant professor, for all universities, and for America.

Student Discipline

Perhaps the most striking aspect of student life that reflects culture change in America is discovered in student discipline. Until the late sixties the typical statement of university policy regarding student discipline was brief, usually amounting to a short paragraph in the School's bulletin. As an example, the bulletin of the School of Commerce for 1940–1941 said:

> While attendance at the School of Commerce, Accounts, and Finance is a privilege and not a right, the atmosphere of the school is one of reasonable conformity to reasonable requirements. Students are expected to conduct themselves, at all times and in all places, in such a manner as to reflect no

discredit upon the good name of the school. Any student deemed undesirable may be refused registration or requested to withdraw from the school at any time by action of the administration or the committee on discipline.[7]

That's it! All of it! No lengthy attempts to spell out unallowable behavior. No technical, legalistic efforts to define due process procedures. Instead, the simple statement that attendance is a privilege, not a right, and that students must conform to reasonable (undefined) requirements and conduct themselves so as not to bring the school into disrepute. Further, the School's administration or faculty Discipline Committee may deem any student undesirable and refuse him or her registration, or "request" (a euphemism for require or demand) withdrawal.

In dramatic contrast, the 1993–1994 *Student's Guide to* N Y U[8] contains 10 large pages of small print detailing university policies and procedures respecting: (1) rules for the maintenance of public order (i.e., conduct and enforcement); (2) policy on student conduct (i.e., preamble, statement of principles, basic rules of conduct, academic freedom, invitations, demonstrations, protests, use of university facilities, disciplinary proceedings); (3) student disciplinary procedures (almost two large pages of small print dealing with jurisdictional issues, procedures, and sanctions); (4) student grievance procedures; (5) guidelines for the use of university facilities; (6) policy on photocopying; (7) affirmative action/ equal opportunity; (8) Family Educational Rights and Privacy Act; (9) statement on AIDS; (10) statement on sexual harassment; (11) policy on use of alcohol; (12) policy on substance abuse; and (13) policy on religious holidays. The Stern School has an additional *Student Code of Conduct,* an 8½ x 11 inch document covering a list of duties, a definition of plagiarism, rules concerning examinations and resource facilities, and sanctions.

Plainly, the pre-sixties' policy placed enormous discretion and power in the hands of a faculty committee and/or school administration, while the current situation represents a highly legalistic detailing of policies, procedures, and possible punishments. For a period of years in the fifties and early sixties, I was a member and chairman of the Commerce Faculty Committee on Student Discipline. It was a serious business. Cheating, plagiarism, stealing, violence, substance abuse, violations of law and order generally were all treated severely when discovered. To capture the climate of the time, consider cheating on final exams. The School required the presence of proctors to monitor them. Books and other materials were not permitted in the exam room. There were peepholes in classroom doors, so that school monitors could patrol the halls and observe the diligence with which proctors attended to their duty. It was not George Orwell's Big Brother society, but neither was it an exercise in faith or a reliance on some honor system. After every semester the chairman of the Faculty Discipline Committee reported to the entire faculty on the Committee's hearings and decisions. Those reports reflected active enforcement of current concepts of proper conduct, and almost always involved some 20–25 cases (when the School's enrollment numbered over 5,000). In calendar year 1947, there were 44 disciplinary actions.[9] Let us consider some cases.

The first case, an appeal to the entire faculty from a decision of the Discipline Committee to expel a student without any privilege of subsequent reenrollment, occurred in October 1947. It was the first faculty meeting of the 1947–1948 year. The case concerned two students, both war veterans. They had been wagering on the outcome of gin rummy games, which they played in the student lounge in the School of Education building. *Card playing was allowed in the lounge, but not betting.* They had engaged in their activity over a period of time without encountering any significant problems, which led the Faculty Discipline Committee to comment: "It appeared to the Committee that the supervision of the game room in the Student's Building is not of the type which the authorities believe it to be, or at least what they would like it to be, and that this provides a convenient refuge for indulgences such as those engaged in by Messrs. K and E."[10]

A few weeks before the end of the Spring 1947 semester, the two student veterans played a lengthy series of gin rummy games that resulted in one losing $100 to the other. The loser is described in the proceedings as a disabled war veteran. The winner and subject of the expulsion decision was a graduating senior with an unblemished record, both academically and otherwise. In fact he had won membership in Beta Gamma Sigma, the school's scholastic honorary society. The loser had paid $10 of his loss at the conclusion of the game, and had promised to pay the remainder as he was able. But he seemed to be reneging on his promise, because the winner observed him paying off other wagering debts before honoring his obligation to the winner. Infuriated, the winner accosted the loser in a hallway of the Commerce building and "assaulted" him. The loser pressed an assault charge which brought the two unhappy students before a civil magistrate. The latter, after hearing the case and reviewing the facts, reduced the charges to "disorderly conduct" against both students and dismissed them with a warning and suspended sentence. Note! The magistrate held *both* students equally culpable and punished them equally.

But, this was not the outcome of the deliberations of the Commerce Faculty Discipline Committee. The Committee proceeded against only one participant, the winner of the gin rummy games, and expelled him without any possibility of readmission.

What manner of record did this expelled veteran have? He had entered the School in January 1940, and attended with a clean record until July 1942, when he enlisted in the U.S. Army Air Corps. He served until December 1945, when he was discharged with the rank of Captain. During his period of service, he was commissioned as an officer, rising to the rank just noted. As a navigator, he flew 30 combat missions in the European Theater, being awarded the Air Medal with four oakleaf clusters and the Distinguished Flying Cross, plus other decorations and commendations. In January 1946 he returned to Commerce and his studies in Accountancy. By May 7, 1947, the date of his expulsion, he had completed all his studies, become a member of Beta Gamma Sigma, and was at the point of graduation. Also, he had been working part-time for an accounting firm while attending school, and had been promised a full-time job following graduation.

After being expelled, he appealed the decision of the Faculty Committee to the entire faculty. He submitted letters from his prospective employer and from an attorney who was an N Y U alumnus, plus other evidence of his unblemished record until the gin rummy fracas. Finally, he appeared in person before the faculty and appealed to them directly, pleading with them not to destroy his career because of one blunder, but rather to accept his admission of a serious error and allow him to resume his career plan.

Following the review of all the material and the appeal, Dean Madden polled the members of the Faculty Discipline Committee as to whether they wished to change their earlier decision. None did. A faculty member then moved to uphold the Committee's decision, and the motion was seconded. Discussion ensued, followed by a vote of the faculty. More than 75 percent of the statutory faculty voted for the motion. There was only one vote in the negative. And so the decorated Captain and Beta Gamma Sigma member was dealt with. As there is no record of any punishment of the other party to the affair, one must wonder whether there were elements or aspects of the case that are not in the record. One must wonder also what became of the expelled student. This writer cannot help hoping that somehow he recovered, and went on to a satisfying life.

We come now to recent cases. One incident occurred in the Spring 1993 semester. A guard in the Tisch Hall building, housing the undergraduate division of the Stern School, apprehended a student leaving the building with a university computer monitor. Charged with attempting to steal the item, the student claimed he was only borrowing it, and had every intention of returning it. Of course such "borrowing," if permitted, would leave inadequate equipment in the university's academic computing centers for the general use of the student body. Brought before the Faculty Discipline Committee, the student repeated his claim of borrowing, not stealing. The Committee placed the student on disciplinary probation. Note that all disciplinary actions taken by the Committee, including disciplinary probation, become *permanent notations on a student's transcript,* with significant implications for future graduate school application.

In 1991–1992 the Faculty Discipline Committee reported six cases and in 1992–1993 it reported four cases. In addition to the case involving "borrowing" a PC, the other cases involved cheating on a final exam (four cases), surrogate students taking exams for other students (two cases), copying homework assignments (two cases), and attempting theft of library material (one case). In one surrogate case the offending student was expelled, while in the other the punishment was suspension from school for two years. The four cheating cases were punished variously by suspension for two years, suspension for one semester, and disciplinary probation (two cases). The homework assignment cases involved a disciplinary probation and a letter of reprimand. The attempted theft of library material required the student to write a letter of apology to the library. We already know that the computer "borrowing" case involved a disciplinary probation.

One must conclude that the variations in punishments reflect Committee perceptions of the facts in each case and probably the prior history of the several students involved, as well as the genuineness of their contriteness when appearing before the committee. One may conclude also that today's Faculty Discipline Committee might have dealt differently with the expelled Air Force Captain than the 1947 Committee did. It is clear that in the Stern School cheating and other infractions of student rules of conduct continue to be serious business, although there is a less rigorous monitoring environment. Still, this writer, being in his mid-seventies, has the strong impression that the overall cultural climate is more permissive than it was almost 50 years ago. In some ways, that is probably a change for the better. In other ways, it is not.

Grade Inflation

Whether wrongly or rightly, a significant symbol of academic success is a student's grade point average. It is the critical key to graduation with honors (summa, magna, or just plain cum laude). It opens the portal to the prestigious academic societies, like Phi Beta Kappa and Beta Gamma Sigma. It is a major element in the decisions of graduate school admissions officials. It is regarded as equally important by corporate recruiters. It is true also that high grades swell parent pride, and enlarge the ego and self-satisfaction with which parents regard their offspring. While it is no guarantee of future success, only a blind person can fail to see its importance. And students are neither so blind nor so stupid as to fail to see or understand this reality. It is consequently no mystery why students, in the midst of the chaos so prevalent on America's campuses in the late sixties and early seventies, attacked the strictness of grading structures with enthusiasm equal to that attendant on their attacks on rigorous curriculum requirements.

Rationalizations came readily to the minds of students and faculty pressing for grading "reform." Among the most innocent and positive sounding of them was the argument that reducing or eliminating the fear of failure would encourage students to: (1) experiment more widely across subject areas; and (2) take tough courses that would stimulate and stretch their intellects. The claimed benefits turned out to be illusory. As the grade of F was eliminated in a number of universities, and became almost unheard of in many others which presumably retained it, the grade of D became an endangered species, and Cs were discovered on fewer and fewer student transcripts. Pass-fail options became popular. B became the most common or average grade, while large numbers of students became aggrieved and behaved as though unfairly treated whenever a professor was so bold as to assign a B. Indeed, students were aggressive, even litigious, in challenging grades they found distasteful. And the professoriate generally surrendered to student pressure, wanting to escape the hassle and sometimes harassing pressure of those students.

Rationalizations justifying the surrender of the professoriate were not difficult for sophisticated minds. At our most prestigious academies, the selectivity of the admissions process was cited in support of awarding very high ratios of As and Bs. The idea that the standard of performance should be raised, so that a "normal" distribution of grades (i.e., an idealized bell-shaped curve of 10 percent A, 20 percent B, 40 percent C, 20 percent D, and 10 percent F) would be approximated, was not heard and did not command support. At our less prestigious institutions, the argument was made that higher education in America was being democratized, that is, opened up broadly to the mass of the population. It was implicit in this argument that preexisting and more elite intellectual standards should be relaxed, so that the increased flow of students from the less privileged socioeconomic segments of society would not be subjected to the trauma of academic failure.

The result across the spectrum of American higher education in the seventies, eighties, and well into the nineties was a massive inflation of grades. The virus spread vertically, infecting the lower educational levels as well. Disciplined study and rigorous intellectual effort were undermined as many students and their professors slackened their efforts to study and teach at peak levels of performance. An educational and societal scandal was being implemented, and mediocrity everywhere rose in praise at the triumph of the shoddy over the superior. It took almost 30 years for a signal of reversal to be heard, a signal that was trumpeted most loudly at Stanford, one of America's most prestigious universities and one which had enthusiastically embraced grading "reform." [11]

A *New York Times* lead editorial put the matter well and succinctly:

An event of seismic proportions in the world of education occurred last week when Stanford University's faculty voted overwhelmingly to tighten a promiscuous grading system under which hardly anyone flunked out and nearly everyone received A's and B's almost as a matter of entitlement. The failing grade will be restored and teachers will be encouraged to award C's and D's when deserved. Those two letters had virtually disappeared from the dazzling but misleading transcripts that a generation of students at Stanford (and plenty of other places) had used to impress parents, employers and graduate school deans.

The hope is that Stanford's decision to jettison a system that failed equally to reward excellence and punish indifference will be emulated throughout the educational system—not only in elite colleges where rampant grade inflation has destroyed the idea of merit but also in secondary and elementary schools. The sad truth is that Stanford's permissive practices were merely the final expression of a sensibility that seeks foremost to eliminate the fear of failure, holds that feeling good is more important than doing well and assumes that somehow students can be injected with self-esteem rather than earning it by honest toil.

The credibility of the nation's great universities has been damaged by this duplicity but the biggest injustice has been suffered by the students. They have received a false sense of their own worth and have not been given the chance to learn from their mistakes because they have been operating in a mistake-proof system.

At Stanford, for example, an astonishing 93 percent of all letter grades are A's and B's, a huge increase over 20 years ago. Harvard Magazine reported last year that 43 percent of all Harvard grades were A's, twice as many as in the mid-1960's and that the average Harvard graduate carried a B-plus average. The situation at Princeton and Yale is about the same.[12]

It is pleasant to report that, while significant grade inflation did occur at N Y U, it never reached the extreme experienced at Stanford, Brown, or Oberlin. See Figure 10.1 Also, while some grade inflation occurred generally at N Y U, it was probably not equally severe in all schools of the university. Perhaps it is an expression of personal bias, but I believe it was not as rampant at the graduate level as at the undergraduate level, and I believe, further, that it was not as severe in the sciences and business school as it was elsewhere.

My assessment of the degree of grade inflation that occurred in the undergraduate B-school rests partly on memory and partly on available data. My memory of the late forties and fifties informs me that C was the most common grade, and that the distribution of As and Bs, on the one side, and Cs, Ds, and Fs; on the other, was bell-shaped and quite symmetrical. In other words, it approximated fairly closely the idealized distribution noted earlier. My memory informs me also that a significant level of administrative attention was periodically paid to grades, with an eye on differences among departments and individual instructors. That attention exerted a not-so-subtle pressure on faculty and departments to maintain grading standards, and to avoid a reputation for being "easy."

Grading Policies around the Nation

Brown University	Teachers cannot give an F or D. Students can receive academic warnings: these are recorded on transcript.	Students can withdraw from a course without penalty any time before the last day of classes.	Students cannot retake a course for a better grade, but can repeat courses if they did not receive credit. Repeats are not noted on transcripts.	Students can take any course on a pass/fail basis. If they fail, the grade does not appear and there is no record of having taken the course.
University of California at Berkeley	A through F. An F grade appears on the transcript.	Students can withdraw without penalty through the seventh week. After that, students will fail if they do not finish the class.	Students can retake a course for a better grade. The old grade appears but is not counted in the average.	A student can change to pass/fail before the end of the eighth week.
New York University	A through F. An F grade appears on the transcript.	Students can withdraw in the first three weeks of classes. After that a W will appear on the transcript.	Students can repeat courses, but repeats are noted on the transcript. How these grades are recorded varies by college.	Students can take one course a semester on a pass/fail basis, as long as the course is not in their major.
Oberlin College	No grades below a C minus.	Students can drop a class through the second week. After that an NE (no entry) is recorded on an internal transcript. External transcript will not show the course.	Students cannot retake a course for a better grade but can retake a course to study with another professor or if they received an NE.	Students have up to three weeks to decide whether to take courses for a credit/no credit option.

FIGURE 10.1 *(cont.)*
Grading Policies around the Nation

Yale University	Students earn the full range of grades, A through F.	Students can drop a class without penalty up to the eighth week of the term. After the eighth week, a W appears on the transcript.	Students can retake a class but can get credit for it only once. Both grades appear on the transcript.	Students can take any course on a credit/D/fail basis. Option is limited to two courses a semester.

SOURCE: *The New York Times*, June 4, 1994, 6.

It is implicit that such grading policies and practices reflected a realization that entry to Commerce, in those years, was relatively easy, coupled with a determination that graduation be earned only through competent academic performance.

The situation today is very different. First, there is an explicit grading policy, spelled out most recently in a memorandum to the faculty from Associate Dean John Guilfoil.[13] That policy specifies limits on the percent of a class that may receive grades of A, B, or, collectively C, D, and F.

Grade	Percent of Class
A	No more than 20%
B	No more than 40%
C, D, and F	No more than 40%

The policy is not rigid, but provides guidelines which presumably set outer limits. The reality is more flexible than the policy guidelines suggest. Table 10.1 provides grade distribution data for the 106 course sections taught in the Fall 1993 semester. Thus 74 sections awarded As to more than 20 percent of the students in each section. Only 32 sections stayed within the guideline. Twenty-four sections awarded As to more than 30 percent of the students in each section. Almost half the sections, 50, awarded As to 20–29 percent of the students in each section. The conclusion is inescapable: A is not an unusual or exceptional grade, even though it is not most common. The companion conclusion is equally inescapable: B is the most commonly awarded grade. Seventy-four sections exceeded the 40 percent guideline. It is an odd coincidence that the number of sections exceeding the guideline, or remaining within it, were identical in the cases of both A and B grades. For grades C, D, and

TABLE 10.1
Stern School, Undergraduate Grade Distribution,
Fall 1993

Percent of Grades	Number of Sections
A:	
40 and over	3
35–39	7
30–34	14
25–29	20
20–24	30
15–19	23
10–14	7
Under 10	2
B:	
40 and over	74
35–39	19
30–34	8
25–29	3
20–24	2
15–19	0
10–14	0
Under 10	0
Other: (C,D,P,F,I,N,W)★	
40 and Over	16
35–39	23
30–34	18
25–29	15
20–24	12
15–19	9
10–14	5
Under 10	8

★P-Pass, F-Fail, I-Incomplete, N-No Grade, W-Withdrawn.

F, as well as the other grades indicated in Table 10.1, the upward grading tendency manifested in As and Bs is reversed. Here, as the arithmetic of the situation dictates, only 16 sections exceed the 40 percent guideline, while 90 sections stayed within it. Yet, 84 sections awarded grades of C, D, F, etc. to 20 percent or more of the students in each section. Thus, the lower grades were not an endangered species. And they were surely not nonexistent as Figure 10.1 indicates they were at Stanford, Brown, and Oberlin (although Stanford changed the policy in 1994). In fact, six sections gave C, D, F, etc. grades to 50 percent or more of each section, and one section gave an astonishing 73 percent of its students such grades. At the other extreme, one section gave 77 percent of its students As, while two sections issued no grades below B.

The School's guidelines reflect a upwardly skewed grading profile, allowing 60 percent of the grades to be As and Bs (20 percent A and 40 percent B). The skew is rationalized, as indicated earlier, on the basis that the student body is academically elite, being subject to a screening based on high school GPAs and SAT scores. It is difficult to extend that rationalization to embrace the actual grade distribution of Table 10.1. One is compelled to admit a significant degree of grade inflation. But the admission is not a clarion call for a sudden, sharp reversal of practice, even though I believe a reversal is appropriate. It is rather a call for faculty awareness and gradually applied tightening of practice. Rapid, radical reversal presents dangers to those faculty, departments, and schools deciding to be the pioneers of change. The most significant danger is lost enrollments—and jobs. That reality must be recognized. Yet change is called for and should come, and it is up to the more prestigious schools—like Stern—to lead the way.

Life in the Residence Halls

N Y U's transformation over the past 40-plus years has involved a massive effort to acquire and build student residence halls in Washington Square and its environs. That effort has been largely successful, especially at the undergraduate level, and today the university is a residential community of faculty and students. That outcome was greatly desired, and is a huge achievement. The concept of an urban residential community of scholars, both faculty and students, is grand, and was at the core of President Hester's large design for N Y U. It is supposed to advance learning, through enhanced contact and interaction of scholars and students.

Traditionally and even today, undergraduate residence halls have faculty and/or graduate students living on the premises, to provide a sense of structure and order, as well as a resource for students with problems. But it is true that from the earliest years of university dormitory life there were high jinks, pranks, and other evidence of a youthful desire for fun. Occasionally, student ideas of fun would get out of hand, and riotous behavior result. It was this sort of behavior that usually underlay the ancient hostility alleged to exist between town and gown.

What has happened recently in urban universities like N Y U is not a manifestation of the old urge for fun. It is rather a reflection of a more profound development, in which the university's traditional relationship with its residential students, which used to rest on the principle of *in loco parentis,* no longer stands on that foundation. *In loco parentis,* in place of the parent, meant that the university exercised a form of parental authority. It acted in place of the parent in the right to discipline a fractious student away from the structure and strictures of "normal" family life. Of course "normal" family life formerly implied a nuclear unit consisting of a mother, father, and children, living together and bound by ties of blood and civil behavior into a cohesive social entity. That is not so true today, and may well be one root of the problems that confront us. In any case, because of litigation and the emergence of "rights" not perceived in an earlier era, universities no longer stand *in loco parentis.* And the rules governing student conduct in residence halls are the subject of lengthy policy statements and cumbersome, legalistic procedures.

In short, the climate of dormitory life has changed. In former days despite student high jinks and occasional riotous outburst, students could feel safe in the residence halls, study, and contemplate there. In the late sixties and the seventies those expectations were undermined. In the name of freedom, parietal rules were undone, and the least responsible students were able to alter the residence hall environment unfavorably. Substance abuse, rape, and other manifestations of disruptive and criminal behavior occurred. The situation became sufficiently bad that parents and students avoided university dormitories in substantial numbers. The result was a return to greater structure and order, but not to the degree that once characterized student residence halls. It is my impression that, despite improvement, students who spend their freshman and sophomore years in the dormitories make major efforts to find alternative housing arrangements in their upperclass years. It is certainly possible that they are seeking greater freedom, trying to escape such residence hall rules as now exist. But that is not the usual motivation they claim. Instead they allege an atmosphere of noise and unruliness that jeopardizes study, rest, and sometimes even safety. Their allegations may be self-serving and simply a rationalization for doing what they want. They may also be an uncomfortable indication of significant problems.

Recreation

The ancient Greeks believed minds were healthiest in healthy bodies, and so they extolled the virtues of physical exercise and sports. That belief was reflected in American universities through long-accepted curricular requirements of a minimum amount of physical education (often in the freshman year). At N Y U's University Heights campus in the Bronx, the all-male University College of Arts and Sciences required physical education *or* enrollment in ROTC (the Reserve Officers Training Corps program). Most students at the Heights opted for ROTC, and there was an active contingent from Washington Square (with heavy participation by Commerce students). But most students at the Square did not find it convenient to travel to the Heights to avail themselves of the sports and other facilities that existed there. Instead, student life at the Square was characterized by a paucity of participatory physical activities for most of this century.

But the picture at the Square changed completely with the dawn of the eighties. Stimulated by a naming gift from Dr. Jerome S. Coles, an alumnus and trustee, the university built the Coles Sports and Recreation Center on the west side of Mercer Street, between Bleecker and Houston Streets. A diverse, multi-activity facility, the Coles Center includes a competition-size lap swimming pool and diving pool, basketball courts, squash courts, aerobic, weight, and other special-purpose exercise rooms, and roof tennis courts and a running track. Open from morning into the evening hours, it became almost immediately one of the most heavily used university buildings. Thousands of students sweated their way there to sustained good health alongside university faculty and administrators, as well as alumni and some local nonuniversity people. In the naked, democratic environment of the locker room there arose a greater sense of community than had previously been possible. The Coles Center had an enormous impact on life at the Square, completing the academic infrastructure earlier put into place by the creation of the Loeb Student Center, the Bobst Library, Tisch Hall, and other new academic structures and new residential halls.

The Coles Sports Center also revived N Y U's participation in intermural sports, in addition to making possible a revival of intramural sports. Before World War II the university had been prominent on the national sports scene, especially in football and basketball. But football was dropped in the fifties, to be followed by basketball in the late sixties. N Y U's rivalry with the Fordham University Rams—a Thanksgiving Day football feature at one of the great city stadiums—gave way to silence and rustling leaves. The roar of Violet stalwarts no longer rang through the rafters of Madison Square Garden as N Y U's hoopsters sank baskets.

The Coles Sports Center did not revive *big-time* college athletics at NYU. What it did do was to enable the university to pick up meaningful athletic programs and intermural competitions with other schools where academics rule over sports, not the other way around, and where sports activities aim at health, clean fun, and good spirit rather than big money. To this end, NYU joined with several other universities into a "league" of like-minded institutions. The "league" included the universities of Rochester, Chicago, Case Western Reserve, Emory, Brandeis, Carnegie-Mellon, and NYU.

The upshot is that student life at the Square today is a much richer and more rounded experience than at any time in the twentieth century.

The early nineties witnessed a nice addition to the facilities provided by the Coles Sports Center. Specifically, Leonard N. Stern and Arthur Imperatore contributed to NYU adjacent parcels of land owned by them in Hoboken, on the western shore of the Hudson River near the Lincoln Tunnel. The university plans to develop there facilities for outdoor sports. It will thereby enlarge significantly the scope of its activities in that sphere.

Piece by piece NYU is gradually collecting all the elements that comprise a full collegiate experience, intellectual, social, and physical. Its success in this effort is exceptional, and was won in the face of substantial obstacles. In the sports and recreation area, a major internal obstacle was the insistence among a significant portion of the faculty and others that there were higher university priorities, usually academic and usually related to compensation. Without denigrating the importance of such other priorities, I am grateful that a larger and longer-run view prevailed. Interestingly, the retrospective perception of almost the entire university community now agrees on the soundness of the decision to embrace adequate sport and recreation facilities in the university's grand scheme for development.

Sports

The NYU records of sports are largely unorganized, being divided between the Department of Athletics Office in the Coles Center and the university archives in the Bobst Library. Such organization of the records as does exist is largely by the archives. A somewhat cursory examination was made of those records for random years during the forties and fifties. Specifically, the membership of varsity squads, by school and by sport (baseball, basketball, and fencing) was examined. The football records were omitted because they are stored with other material in the Coles Center, and not readily accessible. The baseball and basketball data indicate that the School of Education dominated in terms of student participation, with Commerce running a relatively strong second. That outcome was a little surprising to me. I expected Commerce to reveal a stronger showing. Some reflection reduces my degree of surprise, however, when I realize that the Physical Education department is in the School of Education. And participation by University College and Engineering students, which was weak, was probably partly explained by the popularity of ROTC at the Heights campus as an alternative to physical education. Still, in basketball, there were some years in the fifties when the participation of Commerce students was heavy.

Fencing revealed a sharply different picture of student participation. In that sport, Washington Square College students dominated, with Commerce the runner-up school. One wonders why the participation pattern in fencing was so different. Could it be that there was some sort of "class" influence at work, that fencing was perceived as more of a gentleman's sport, and so more attractive to students in the Arts and Sciences? In the absence of facts, speculation rules, and that guess is probably as good as any.

My early impression that Commerce students were heavily involved in NYU sports is probably based on a limited experience that occurred in the early fifties. It involved a freshman class in Economics! I was a young assistant professor, and prided myself on my assumed ability to explain the content of the course material to the students. Weekly 10-minute quizzes were given, as well as two full-period exams and a final. Having graded the first of the two full-period exams, I was startled to discover that one-third of the class had failed. More startling was the fact that the entire group of failures was concentrated in the last three rows of the class. Much as I tried, I could not find a reasonable explanation. I speculated that my voice was not carrying to the rear three rows, but I could not accept that explanation since the problem was unique to only one class. I wondered if there was some sort of cheating conspiracy, but there was no supporting evidence in the content of the exams or in my observation of student conduct during the exams. My mystification increased when the results of the second full-period exam duplicated those of the first. But the mystery was solved shortly thereafter, when I received a memo from N Y U's football coach informing me that the entire freshman football squad was in that class. Moreover, having registered as a group. they occupied the seats in the last three rows. The coach asked me about tutoring possibilities for the football players, with compensation for such services. I replied that I could not accept the task, and suggested that he seek help from teaching assistants in one of the university's Economics departments (there were two large departments, one in Arts and Sciences and one in Commerce). He must have had some success, because all the players did not fail. But the large majority did.

The incident is significant because it embodies the tension between sports and academics. It is implicit that the primary purpose of the players is the sport, with the academic side second. While that is not necessarily true of all players, at least in the privacy of their own minds and motives, it is built into the financial necessities of big-time college sports. And N Y U was, at that time, still involved in big-time football and basketball. But, as mentioned earlier, the university abandoned football in the early fifties, as it did basketball in the late sixties. One reason was the undeniable tension between the academic and sports sides of the matter. Thus, Dan Quilty, one of N Y U's star athletes of World War II vintage and later director of Athletics, told me that in the era of big-time athletics at N Y U, there was a Board of Athletic Control that placed promising athletes in undergraduate schools and programs that might best suit their academic aptitudes and goals. The usual choices for such placement were the Schools of Education and Commerce.[14] Dan Quilty thereby confirmed my prior impression that the School of Commerce was closely linked to N Y U's athletic programs. He observed, in this connection, that in the thirties and forties the linkage was especially strong in football and basketball, and that Education and Commerce played a dominant role as the schools in which N Y U's athletes were matriculated. But the linkage was broken when N Y U dropped big-time sports. The Board of Athletic Control also died.

Dan pointed out, however, that the academics-sports tension was not the only reason why N Y U abandoned football and basketball. Another reason, one with major financial significance, was that professional football and basketball teams became the dominant sports attractions for the New York City public. This had been the reality in baseball for many years, with the Yankees, the Dodgers, and the Giants the darlings of baseball enthusiasts in the Big Apple. But, in football and basketball local universities were major draws in Madison Square Garden and the great stadiums. With the Knicks and the New Jersey Nets in basketball, and the Giants and Jets in football, college teams in those sports lost their luster and lure as big-time draws. The consequent loss of sports revenues profoundly changed the financial considerations in sports for NYU.

Whatever the reason, NYU withdrew and sports since then have been for recreation, health, and fun, not for national standing and large sports-generated revenues. With the construction of the Coles Sports Center, however, basketball has been revived at NYU. But it is not big-time. It is rather a healthy competitively spirited activity in a league comprised of very strong academic institutions, where there is no doubt about the primacy of academics. With the acquisition of land on the west shore of the Hudson River in 1992, facilities for outdoor sports, perhaps including football, may come into existence, and NYU become, once again, active in such sports. But, as with basketball, there will be no doubt as to the primacy of academics.

Reserve Officer Training Corps (ROTC)

For over half a century, from World War I to 1973, University Heights had an active ROTC unit with a significant number of Commerce students participating. But student opposition to the Vietnam War stimulated disagreement with the continuance of ROTC. At NYU such opposition did not succeed in killing the program until 1972, when the Heights campus was sold to the City University of New York and the facilities at Ohio Field were no longer available for drilling and related activities. Actually, NYU students can still participate in ROTC, but to do so they must join active units at John Jay College in Manhattan or Polytechnic University in Brooklyn. No doubt there continue to be students who find participation in ROTC attractive, for reasons both patriotic and practical. Among the latter is surely the tuition subsidization provided for ROTC participants. But they are few in number.

The Alumni

The most cursory reading of any university bulletin will quickly reveal those aspects of the institution cited as evidences of strength and attractiveness, reasons buttressing an applicant's desire to enroll. Prominent among the aspects put forward will be the quality of the faculty, the student body, the physical campus and plant (the academic and other facilities available), and the success and prominence of the alumni. The quality of the alumni will be a reason to boast.

Product and Promotion

This heading may seem odd for a discussion of alumni. But it has direct relevance, because alumni are a major output or product of the university. The other major output is research, through which knowledge is extended. Both alumni and research have a promotional aspect: the former through word-of-mouth and organized activities in behalf of the alma mater; and the latter through reputation and status for intellectual and scientific eminence associated with the institution.

From its beginnings, the School of Commerce took pride in its alumni. Thus, the earliest bulletins of the School listed the names and addresses of students, and presented survey data showing the earnings of graduates. The thrust of the survey data was clear; come to Commerce and enhance your future income. In later years the School's publications boasted of alumni accomplishments in broader terms, remarking on achievements in the professions (Law, Accountancy), in public offices (Congress, other legislative and elective offices), and in corporate leadership positions. A similar record marked GBA's experience.

Alumni are especially significant in promoting a school. One promotional aspect involves *recruitment* of new students. Of importance here is the personal word-of-mouth recommendation of a graduate who speaks glowingly of his or her alma mater. Such a recommendation is testimonial by a satisfied "customer," who affirms that the school added value to his or her knowledge base and understanding and thereby enhanced his or her ability to function successfully both in career and broader terms. A danger inherent in organized use of alumni in recruiting new students is that some alumni may misunderstand their role, and assume that it gives them a key to admitting students. That must not be the case, because it may entail a serious abuse (the admission of academically unqualified students). But, properly used, alumni can be powerful promoters of their alma mater.

A second promotional aspect of alumni involvement in school promotion has to do with *fund-raising*. Alumni are prime prospects as a source of external funds. They provide both *restricted* (endowed Institutes, Centers, Chairs, scholarships, fellowships, and named buildings and facilities) and *unrestricted* (general purpose) funds. They are also a vitally important source of volunteer fund-raisers. Alumni who have themselves donated are especially motivated and effective as solicitors of donations from others. The record of the Stern School certainly bears out the accuracy of this assertion.

A third promotional aspect of alumni involvement is *placement* of graduates. This facet of alumni involvement, like the other two, is not unique to any one school. All universities seek, in greater or lesser degree, to build alumni networks that will be effective in enhancing the employability of graduates, as well as in recruitment and fund-raising. Perhaps most successful have been America's Ivy League schools, but the sense of a bond between older graduates and new alumni exists in any school. To work, the older alumni need to feel well disposed to their alma mater, and need to regard it with pride and affection. In this respect, the Stern School, as one of the nation's prestigious business schools, is well positioned to employ actively its alumni in recruitment, placement, and fund-raising.

The Alumni Federation and the Alumni Council

NYU's alumni relationships were not formally structured and organized until October 1925, when the NYU Alumni Federation was chartered by the State of New York.[1] The Federation was set up as an autonomous body legally independent of the university, although its objectives were to organize the alumni for the benefit of the university. It worked to organize alumni associations related to each school and college at NYU, and these associations, in turn, were represented on the Federation's Board of Directors. The Federation's major activities were: (1) working with the individual school associations; (2) fund-raising; (3) developing and maintaining a list of alumni names and addresses; and (4) selecting or nominating alumni as recipients of alumni meritorious service awards and alumni trusteeships on the university's Board of Trustees.

For almost 60 years the foregoing activities constituted the Federation's operations. For 58 of those years, from 1925 to 1983, the Federation was served by two Commerce alumni as full-time paid executives; Ben Ross, Commerce '25, from 1925 to 1959, and George Carlock, Commerce '41, from 1959 to 1983. Whether a reflection of their relationship to the School of Commerce, or whether a result of the huge number, prominence, and affluence of the Commerce alumni body, undoubtedly a strong impression existed that Commerce alumni exerted a disproportionate influence in the affairs of the Federation. The Commerce alumni association was one of the most active of the School associations, and Commerce alumni were, over the years, strongly represented among the Alumni Trustees of the university, and among the recipients of the annual Alumni Meritorious Service Awards. The Alumni Trustees were voted by the university's Board of Trustees, but from three nominees put forward by the Federation (with a private indication by the Federation as to its preference). The Alumni Meritorious Service Awards were decided by the Alumni Meritorious Service Awards Committee of the Federation. Generally, these kudos reflected achievements in the recipient's career (trusteeships) or outstanding activity and performance in behalf of the university (meritorious service awards). Prominent among recipients, in addition to Commerce graduates, were alumni of other active groups, namely Law, University Heights, Dentistry, GBA, and Medicine. Not so prominent were Washington Square College of Arts and Sciences, Graduate Arts and Sciences, Public Administration, Social Work, and Education.

There were those who felt achievements and performance were not always the ruling criteria; that on occasion a kudo was gained through internal politics and the favor of an inner clique. As the years passed, gradually added to these critics were those who questioned the Federation's effectiveness in fund-raising, in building the alumni list and using it efficiently, and in bringing younger alumni into the individual school associations. Some deans became restive over the independence of the Federation and the tie it had to their school's alumni association. A number of NYU presidents, probably beginning with Henry Heald, were no less unhappy.

These dissatisfactions coalesced and erupted finally in the early eighties, not long after John Brademas became NYU's president. By 1982–1984 the university insisted that the Federation's fund-raising and other activities be embraced more clearly within the university's frame of control. Specifically, the university demanded that the executive vice president of the Federation report to the president as well as to its board. This demand was resisted by the Federation's board and some of the Alumni Trustees.

The university created an alternative alumni organization, the NYU Alumni Council, which worked closely with the university's external affairs offices in fund-raising. The council also became the body to which the individual school associations were allied. And the Council became the entity which nominated Alumni Trustees, recipients of Alumni Meritorious Service Awards, and Great Teachers Awards (this last award had earlier also been under the control of the Alumni Federation). The Council has an annual dinner at which these kudos are presented, along with the Eugene J. Keogh Award (for public service and in memory of the late Congressman and Commerce alumnus who fathered the famous Keogh Act that established the legal basis for so-called Keogh retirement plans). The NYU Alumni Council is a large body, of over 70 members, with five from each school of the university. Of those five, one is the president of the school's association, two are appointed by the school's dean, and two by the school's association. Each school's administration now has some meaningful input into its association's activities. I think that is desirable. I see only trouble and a lack of effectiveness when a school's administration and its alumni organization are at odds.

Note should be taken of the statesman-like role played by alumni trustees Boris Kostelanetz and Marvin Leffler, both Commerce alumni, in achieving an amicable, dignified resolution to the Federation-university dispute. Both men received warm expressions of appreciation from President John Brademas, along with university presidential citations.[2] President Brademas wrote:

We have now enjoyed a full year's benefit of a united alumni front made possible by the judicious, appropriate and business-like agreement negotiated.

As the result of your successful diplomacy, our alumni relations offices have moved to consolidated activities, improving efficiency and productivity and bringing to an end duplication of effort, dissipation of energies and confusion among alumni.

New York University once again speaks to its more than 200,000 graduates around the world with a single voice—stronger, more consistent and to better effect. Your work in forging the compact between the University and the Alumni Federation has meant:

—increased financial support for alumni donors;

—greater opportunities to serve alumni needs;

—more ways, in addition to fundraising, in which alumni can take an active role on behalf of their alma mater; and

—a heightened sense of loyalty and a firmer bond between the University and its graduates.

Perhaps a further point should be made, because note has been taken of the prominence of Commerce alumni in the Federation. Of special interest is the fact that no Commerce dean ever attempted to exert influence on the university's central administration through the Commerce Trustees. No indication of any such effort can be found in any of the records researched for this history. Yet, we have read sometimes bitter complaints by Commerce deans (Johnson and Madden) that the university was shamefully exploiting Commerce and using it as a "cash cow." Part of the explanation is undoubtedly the feeling by the deans that such politicking was simply not done, and would have been both dishonorable and a violation of their sense of loyalty as part of the university's overall administrative structure. Part of it may have been a concern that such an effort, once discovered, would have precipitated a collision between president and dean requiring the removal of one, or possibly both, by the Board.

The Stern School's Alumni Organization

Before the 1983–1984 dispute between the Alumni Federation and the university, Commerce (BPA) and GBA each had its own separate alumni association. The two associations had their own boards, officers, activities, awards, dinners, and dean's days (alumni homecoming). When the dispute developed between Federation and the university, the associations found it necessary ultimately to associate with the university's new Alumni Council. But an important new element in the situation was the development of an Alumni Office and organization in the Stern School itself.[3] The office (Office of Alumni Affairs) is part of a larger entity in the Stern School (the Department of External Affairs). The Office of Alumni Affairs concentrates its efforts in three broad areas: (1) the worldwide alumni network; (2) recent graduate cultivation and development; and (3) alumni benefits and services. The office believes that these efforts benefit the school in fund-raising, recruitment (admissions), and placement.

A "fly in the ointment" is that the Alumni Office perceives problems in the continued existence of separate graduate and undergraduate alumni associations. One significant problem seems to be difficulty in organizing and orienting the two associations' objectives and activities so that they are consistent and mesh with those seen as vital by the Office of Alumni Affairs. Reading between the lines, there may be a struggle over influence in organizing and directing the associations' activities. It appears that the preference of the Alumni Office is to create a single Stern School Alumni Association. But that is easier said than done. Deep loyalties and emotional ties exist among GBA and Commerce (BPA) alumni to their respective schools, even though many Commerce (BPA) alumni are also GBA alumni. But many others are not. The likelihood can be considered that an alumnus's tie to his or her undergraduate school is deeper than one to a graduate school. Consequently, this is an area where deans are likely to tread carefully. Meantime, the organizational pot appears to be simmering, although surface appearances are placid and cordial. A sunnier tomorrow may be dawning as various affairs are now merged and become Stern School rather than graduate or undergraduate. A prominent example is the joint Alumni Homecoming Day which has replaced the two separate affairs that preceded it.

In any case, in July 1992 the Alumni Office proposed a plan for achieving greater unity of purpose and direction in the activities of the two associations. The central feature of the plan was the creation of a "supranational" so-called Alumni Cabinet. The Stern School deans were to create the Cabinet by bringing together a prestigious group of representative alumni, consisting of one or two representatives each from the graduate and undergraduate associations. These representatives were to be the president and vice president of each association, plus representatives of the Dean's Executive Roundtable, the Board of Overseers, the Partners Steering Committee, the Haskins Steering Committee, the Commerce/BPA alumni body, a recent Stern School BS graduate, a recent graduate representative from the MBA Steering Committee, two international chapter presidents, two domestic chapter presidents, the chair of the Alumni Admission Council, and several others. The Cabinet would be charged with reviewing overall alumni activities and making recommendations for improved programming. More significantly, the cabinet would: (1) have jurisdiction over the two associations' activities and budgets; (2) make recommendations relative to alumni governance; and (3) communicate those recommendations to each association and its board. Beginning immediately, however, the Alumni Office would decrease its support for the boards of the two associations, and the deans would concurrently reduce their involvement with the boards.

A second major thrust to the July 1992 proposal involved the development of a "worldwide alumni network." The rationale was evidently twofold: first, it reflected the belief that the Stern School's alumni body had changed dramatically and is today an "internationally competitive alumni body"; and, second it reflected the presence of a significant number of foreign alumni, a presence that goes back many years and which has probably grown. But this thrust borders on being radical in terms of past practice and experience. One must ask how the resources required to make it work (to organize alumni chapters abroad and to provide necessary support for their activities) would square with the basic objectives of fund-raising, recruitment, and placement. One must ask further what the likely payback would be for dollars committed to such an international program, compared with the expenditure of the same dollars domestically. On the other side, as business grows increasingly global, an effort to develop and organize the Stern School's foreign alumni has merit. Perhaps the answer lies in readiness to respond positively to initiatives which arise among our alumni abroad, rather than exercising an expensive initiative of our own in anticipation of an enthusiastic response abroad.

One thing is certain. As of late 1993, neither thrust had been implemented, no doubt because the "political" and financial considerations need careful, deliberate thought. Equally certain is the fact that Dean George Daly will be confronted with the problem and will have to work his way through to decisions. I hope he will have strong support from influential alumni. Lacking such support, these initiatives are not likely to succeed. In any case, the disparate loyalties and interests of the graduate as compared with the undergraduate alumni will have to be dealt with. It is a very sensitive and subtle matter.

The John T. Madden Award and the GBA Alumni Achievement Award

Dean John T. Madden died in 1948. By 1950, a group of Commerce alumni, led prominently by Professor Jules Backman, created the *Dean John T. Madden Award* in his memory. The award was to be given each year to one-three Commerce alumni who had distinguished themselves through outstanding success and leadership in their careers. Between 1951, when the first awards were made, and 1992, when the last one was given, 115 were issued. In 1993 the Madden award was discontinued and succeeded by the Dean Abraham L. Gitlow Award, probably because so few alumni remained alive to treasure Madden's memory. The Gitlow award was similar in nature to its predecessor, with one major difference: recipients, in addition to outstanding success in their careers, had to have made an important contribution to society in a second area of activity. This feature came from recognition of Dean Gitlow's emphasis that education for business should avoid narrowness of vision and positively pursue intellectual breadth and broad interests.

The roster of Madden awardees is extraordinarily rich in remarkable people. While they were not all equally outstanding, an unusual proportion was truly exceptional. Based on my memory of the individuals on the list, at least 38 were chief executives. Included among them are Laurence Tisch, CEO of CBS and Loew's and chairman of NYU's Board of Trustees; Leonard N. Stern, CEO of Hartz, Inc.; Edward E. Barr, of Sun Chemical; Bruno Bich, of Bic; William Bernbach, of Doyle, Dane, Bernbach; William Catacosinos, of Long Island Lighting; John Creedon, of Metropolitan Life Insurance Company; Frank Dunnigan, of Prentice-Hall; Richard P. Ettinger, a co-founder of Prentice-Hall; John A. Ewald, of Avon Products; Arthur C. Fatt, a co-founder of Grey Advertising; Arthur B. Foye, a Managing Partner of Haskins and Sells; Harold S. Geneen, of International Telephone and Telegraph; Raymond C. Hagel, of Macmillan; Leo Jaffe, of Columbia Pictures; Abraham Krasnoff, of

Pall Manufacturing; Lawrence Lachman, of Bloomingdale's; Gustave L.
Levy, of Goldman Sachs; Allan Murray, of Mobil Oil; John E. Raasch,
of John Wanamaker; Richard L. Rosenthal, of Citizens Utilities; Lewis
Rudin, the real estate developer; Leon Shimkin, of Simon and Schuster;
Walter Shipley, of the Chemical Bank; John Ben Snow, of Woolworth's
and Speidel Newspapers; Asa T. Spaulding, America's first black actu-
ary and CEO of North Carolina Mutual; and, Henry Taub, a founder of
Automatic Data Processing (ADP). Others are omitted because of the
limitations of my memory, not because of a lesser order of significance.
While the CEOs are probably the largest single block, the other Madden
awardees included many prominent accountants (like the late Jack Seidman, a onetime N Y U trustee), attorneys (like Boris Kostelanetz), a chairman of the Board of Governors of the Federal Reserve System (Alan
Greenspan), a U.S. Senator (Rudolph E. Boschwitz), two U.S. Con-
gressmen (Eugene J. Keogh and Charles E. Rangel), a famous Holly-
wood designer (Orrie R. Kelly), several prominent academicians (Jules
Backman, Solomon Fabricant, Victor R. Fuchs—a president of the
American Economic Association, and Robert A. Kavesh), a great basketball player and coach (Thomas E. "Satch" Sanders); and, sadly, only
one woman (Carmen Webster Kelly). In the years ahead the representation of women will increase considerably, as it should, since their number among the alumni has increased greatly and their prominence is
becoming more evident.

But, other than the recognition of their success, what benefit has
accrued to alma mater from the creation of the Dean John T. Madden
Award, in terms of fund-raising, recruitment, and placement? Substantial benefit has resulted, especially in fund-raising, although one cannot
say that the contributions made to N Y U by this group would not have
been forthcoming, even if there had never been a Madden award. Relying again on my memory, the Madden awardees contributed at least $93
million to the university. Only 10 of them accounted for $88 million of
the total (those contributing at least $1 million), and two (Lawrence
Tisch, with his brother Bob Tisch, and Leonard Stern) represent some
$75 million. The other eight include Theodore Racoosin, Stephen Chan,
Abraham Krasnoff, Carmen Webster Kelly, Vincent Ross, Lewis Rudin,
Leon Shimkin, and John Ben Snow. The Madden award served to kindle
alumni interest in N Y U and the business school and to make that interest
active in its behalf. Another thing is clear and important in fund-raising.
A small percentage of donors contributes the lion's share. Hence, fund

campaigners do well to study and involve prospective major givers. From the promotional standpoint of recruitment and placement, the prominence of these alumni must have been attractive to some prospective students and had to open employment opportunities to some graduates.

One must conclude that the Madden awards, in addition to doing honor to the memory of the late dean, were a great success in other, more pragmatic respects.

GBA did not have a named award like the one honoring Madden. But it did have an Alumni Achievement Award similar in nature that honored outstanding graduates. In the years it was awarded, from 1956 to 1990, it had 58 recipients. Five of them were Commerce alumni, who also received the Madden award. The five double awardees are Jules Backman, William J. Catacosinos, Alan Greenspan, Leonard N. Stern, and John H. Vogel. Although the list is half as long as for Madden, it includes two women (Marion O. Sandler and Madeline McWhinney Dale). Otherwise, it was similar in its overall characteristics to the Madden awardee roster. It included a number of chief executives, prominent figures in the accounting and legal professions, some academicians, such prominent figures in the investment community as Henry Kaufman and George H. Heyman, Jr., the motion picture producer Ismail Merchant, and a posthumous award to Perry Ellis, the designer. The group had a positive but somewhat smaller impact on the school than the Madden awardees in terms of fund-raising, recruitment, and placement. The GBA Alumni Association discontinued the award in 1990.

The Charles Waldo Haskins Award

Initially presented in 1980, the Charles Waldo Haskins Award differs from the Madden, Gitlow, and Alumni Achievement Awards. Unlike them, it is a nonalumni award, given to distinguished Americans whose careers, like that of Charles Waldo Haskins, embrace multidimensional achievements in public service and/or education, as well as in business. By emphasizing the outstanding and multifaceted involvement of business leaders in our society, it sought to change the stereotype that typically characterized them as people of narrow minds and perceptions.

The Haskins award has become very prestigious, reflecting the quality of the awardees. It has thereby enhanced the luster of the Stern

School. The 14 awardees, beginning in 1980 and named chronologically, are: Arjay Miller, George P. Shultz, Robert S. McNamara, Arthur F. Burns, Juanita Kreps, Harold M. Williams, John C. Whitehead, W. Michael Blumenthal, Peter G. Peterson, John L. Weinberg, A. W. Clausen, Edgar M. Bronfman, William H. Donaldson, and Norman R. Augustine. Some started their careers in business, moving later to leading roles in public service and/or education. Others traveled a reverse route. But all spanned the broad sectors of societal activity, and accomplished remarkable results in all their endeavors.

Candor compels recognition of another aspect of the Haskins award: namely, enlarged alumni involvement with the School and, hopefully, enhanced fund-raising results. This aspect involved an elegant annual dinner at which the Haskins award was presented. Held originally at New York's St. Regis Hotel, the dinner has more recently been held at the Plaza. Alumni and other friends of the School, who contributed $1,000 or more per year, were designated as Charles Waldo Haskins Associates and received invitations. The Haskins Associates became a significant source of School support, generating funds beyond the minimum required to become a member of the group. An earlier attempt had been made to use the Madden award in a similar way, by creating Madden Associates of the School (at a minimum level of $500), but that program did not have substantial results. One reason may have been that the award was presented at the annual alumni dinner of the School, which may have diffused its impact because of the scope of the evening's program. Another reason may have been that for many years the award was presented to three awardees, which may have also lessened its impact. Yet, as noted above, the Madden awardees were themselves a rich source of support for the School.

Other Evidence of the Success of Stern School Alumni

Since 1975 Standard and Poor's[4] has been conducting a college/executive survey to discover which universities produce the largest number of the nation's top business executives. The survey results are culled from data provided by approximately 70,000 top business executives to Standard and Poor's *Registry of Corporations, Directors, and Executives*. The 1992 report included 973 institutions and provided data on 58,405 executives with undergraduate degrees and 28,571 with graduate degrees.

New York University is prominent among the top dozen schools. Among executives possessing graduate degrees, NYU ranked second with 1,316 graduate executives, outranked only by Harvard with 3,061. Columbia University ranked third with 1,125. If the ranking is based on the number of business leaders with combined degrees from the same institution, then Harvard and NYU still rank first and second, respectively. In 1992 Harvard counted 3,992 alumni in this category and NYU 2,115. These two universities have held these ratings since 1980. The University of Pennsylvania ranked third in 1990 and 1992, with 1,693 alumni in the latter year. The rankings change significantly if one restricts them to executives with undergraduate degrees only. From that perspective, the City College of New York (part of CUNY) ranked first in 1990 and 1992, having displaced Yale University (Yale led between 1980 and 1990). Continuing with the undergraduate alumni count, the University of Wisconsin ranked second in 1992, and Yale was third. New York University was in ninth place, followed by Princeton.

Note that the 1992 survey reflects alumni executives who graduated from college more than 20 years ago. In fact, the largest number graduated in 1950 (2,149). The second most popular year for graduation was 1969, followed by 1964, 1965, 1968, and 1959. To the degree the top institutions have undergone major changes in the academic characteristics of their student bodies, as well as in other respects, differences in the rankings may be anticipated in the years ahead. Thus, the survey observed that "Ivy League schools in the top 12, with the exception of Cornell University and the University of Pennsylvania, dropped down in the standings."[5] This result reflects the growing number and academic strength of non–Ivy League schools in the postwar period.

Interesting evidence of the prominence of Stern School alumni is probably the degree to which they are represented in the university's Board of Trustees.[6] Prior to 1950, only five trustees were Stern School alumni (all graduates of the School of Commerce). The first to appear was Percy S. Young, Commerce '08, who became a trustee in 1922. Since 1950 37 more have served. As of October 1993, 13 trustees were Stern School Alumni. Three of them held the graduate division's MBA degree, while the other 10 were holders of the undergraduate division's baccalaureate degree. Clearly, the presence of Stern School alumni among the trustees exploded in the last decade.

The Alumni's Role in the Academy

Our discussion has been one-sided to this point. Our entire emphasis has been on the support the alumni can give to the university, through fund-raising, recruitment, and placement. Is there no *quid pro quo,* no tangible and/or intangible return? That there might be none would seem odd in a society so often perceived as characterized by an attitude that everything can be bought. Think for a moment of the perception that advertisers control the media, that politicians are in the pockets of their largest contributors, that business is interested only in the pursuit of profits, legally or illegally, and that medicine is marked by large-scale fraud in billing and in widespread unnecessary procedures. Our cinema adds color to the picture with films like *Indecent Proposal,* where a newly married woman surrenders her virtue for $1 million as the outcome of a bet that she can be bought if only the price is sufficiently high. It is true that the picture shows unpleasant consequences, with the marriage destroyed and the love which marked its beginning torn asunder. But the basic point is that anything can be bought. In that context, why would anyone be surprised at the perception that unqualified students can buy admission to prestigious universities through generous contributions, or the influence of important alumni sponsors? More, why would one not believe that trusteeships or other significant honors cannot be obtained through similar means? Perhaps most important, why would one not believe that powerful alumni could influence university policy on a variety of issues that involve the intellectual integrity of the university?

Earlier in this chapter we hinted at the possibility that alumni used in recruitment might misunderstand their role, be led astray, and lead others astray. In the chapter on student life we discussed the Hatchett Affair, when a black militant on campus so outraged many alumni that fund-raising suffered seriously for a time. Is there a problem? If so, how serious is it?

Categorical denials that there is a problem would be specious. Too much evidence exists that university campuses, where sports involve big-time programs and money, are marked by scandals, ranging from buying athletes to ignoring or covering up their academic deficiencies. Too often in these situations alumni play a prominent role. The other side of the coin is that many universities, generally embracing the nation's most prestigious research institutions, have dropped big-time,

big-money sports. As we noted, NYU did so with football in the 1950s
and with basketball in the 1960s. Its present revival of activity in intramural and intermural sports grew out of the construction of the Coles
Sports Center and the acquisition of property on the west shore of
the Hudson.

It would be an outright lie to say I was never asked to admit an
unqualified student, or that the request was not sometimes accompanied
by broad hints or outright offers of generous contributions. Alternatively, there were occasional suggestions that support previously given
would be cut off. Adamantly and bluntly, I state that I never surrendered
to either blandishments or threats. But there are subtleties, involving
admissions cases on the margin. Thus, a dean may face an admission
decision between two students *equally qualified* in academic and other
respects, but one is sponsored by an alumnus and the other has no such
connection to the school. In such a situation, I see nothing wrong with
granting preference to the one over the other. To come down contrariwise is to say, in effect, that purity of purpose is always compromised if
one fails to "spit in the eye" of one's supporters. For those who find that
sort of behavior ennobling of the spirit, there can be no answer that is
both sensible and satisfying.

Perhaps a small item reported in the *Wall Street Journal* will prove
relevant and revealing.[7] Reporter Amy Gamerman writes about an interview with Janice H. Levin, a relatively unknown benefactor of the
Metropolitan Museum of Art. Mrs. Levin, who has become a significant
collector of French impressionist art, donated $3 million to help the Met
build its nineteenth-century galleries. The reporter points out that, in
gratitude, the museum named a room of Corots the Janice H. Levin
Gallery. But, included in the story, is this paragraph: "Mixed in with the
Pissarros, Vuillards, Morisots, et al, are Chinese snuff bottles, 19th
century gilded clocks and just plain kitsch such as the embroidered
throw pillow that urges, 'Go First Class . . . Your Heirs Will.' There are
also many tokens of the Levins' philanthropy: a framed photograph of
the community center the couple built in Beersheba, Israel; *an honorary
doctorate from Rutgers University. I gave a business school, Mrs. Levin explains. So I'm Dr. Levin*" (italics added).

No doubt the perception of Rutgers University is that the honorary
doctorate was awarded because of patronage of the arts and additional
substantial charitable activities that advanced social well-being. No
doubt Mrs. Levin's perception implies some *quid pro quo,* although no

one probably ever spoke in such terms. On such subtleties are conflicting perceptions constructed.

What about political correctness and campus fund-raising? Or, put the other way around, is a failure of alumni support, based on disenchantment over the efforts of some students and faculty to enforce political correctness, a wrong and inadmissible attempt to compromise academic freedom? No, for the one begets the other. Error lies on both sides. Academic freedom requires the right to think and to speak, to search and to report in the never-ending pursuit of understanding and truth. No one has a monopoly in this pursuit, and the integrity of the academy necessitates recognition of that basic fact by faculty, students, administrators, trustees, alumni, and others who come to the support of the institution. Any attempt to impose any form of political correctness on the academy is an anomaly; indeed, it is a travesty of academic freedom. Civility must be the hallmark of institutions of higher learning. Anything less compromises their integrity, and imperils their precious freedom.

The Outlook

As we turn our gaze to the future, what do we see? We see a transformed business school at New York University, a school which has contributed greatly to the transformation of the university itself. The sources of its strength are great and evident. They embrace: (1) an excellent faculty; (2) an excellent student body; (3) strong programs of study; (4) a beautiful state-of-the-art physical plant; (5) location in one of the world's leading cosmopolitan urban centers; (6) being part of a prestigious university; (7) the esteem of the university and important constituent communities (trustees, central administration, alumni, business, etc.); and (8) great élan, a pervasive spirit that past adversity has been overcome and that present strength is sufficient to future tests.

Of course there is exposure to adverse elements. The School continues to be heavily dependent on tuition revenue, while its current teaching load, curriculum, and compensation policies are those characteristic of schools with richer endowments and a significantly lesser reliance on tuition. The School's faculty and administration face issues involving priorities in the years ahead, even with major fund-raising advances. The variables which are sure to be visited and revisited will include degree programs, average class size, numbers of courses offered, staffing profiles, and teaching load policies. Among these variables are some that touch raw nerve endings of the faculty, such as a review of PhD programs which may subject them to a harsh cost-benefit analysis. Remember that the PhD is the cultural and psychological heart of the Academy. If some departments have doctoral programs and some do not, there is an inherent and implicit qualitative judgment. That it may also, and more immediately, be a market judgment will not easily overcome the qualitative inference in the perceptions of the faculty. A related priority issue that touches the faculty's value structure is the tension between research and teaching, and most importantly so when undergraduate teaching is involved. Still another issue bearing on value structure and mind-set is the tendency of faculty to be specialized along departmental and functional lines, when organizations are becoming increasingly global and needing to be seen and governed as complicated entities or systems, rather than as a collection of functional divisions or departments.

As we look ahead, let us look back also and compare the Stern School's culture and characteristics today with what they were at the beginning, a century ago. Recall that the School began as an undergraduate, two-year evening (part-time), nonresidential, practical program, staffed by businessmen, lawyers, and accountants who were practitioners, not academics. It was housed in part of a commercial building at Washington Square, along with the Law School, the School of Pedagogy, and the Washington Square Division of the University College of Arts and Sciences. The heart of the university had moved to the Bronx, where Chancellor MacCracken saw its future development. Enrollments mushroomed quickly, to gargantuan proportions, making the School the largest enterprise of its kind in the nation. Indeed, in the world! Considerable pride was taken in its size, which was seen as an extraordinary indication of its success. There could be no question that the School was meeting a market test, and satisfying an enormous demand for the educational service it provided. Unfortunately, the seeds of eventual disaster lay in that success, for the enormous cash surpluses generated were siphoned off to general university support, and very little was reinvested in the School of Commerce. The student body, originally mature, fully employed, and overwhelmingly male, was a cosmopolitan group, with a small, yet significant, sprinkling of Japanese and other foreign students. More importantly, it was substantially comprised of newly arrived immigrants and first-generation Americans. And, it soon included numbers of women. Despite its mass admission-mass attrition nature, the School was the vehicle that bore thousands of eager, ambitious people through the doors of opportunity, to the realization of the American dream of material success. But in the early and middle years of the century, the sad truth is that it did not command the academic respect of the older, more traditional divisions of the Academy.

This was the case, despite the development of the original, very limited two-year BCS degree program to a three-year, 96-credit hour one, and, in 1926, to a full, four-year, 128-credit hour BS degree program with a large general education component of Arts and Sciences courses.

The Graduate School of Business Administration, established in 1921 as a degree-granting entity separate from the School of Commerce, was in many ways culturally similar to its undergraduate progenitor. In other ways it quickly showed separate tendencies. GBA was similar in its origin as an entirely evening, part-time program. It continued to be so characterized for many years after Commerce developed a large, full-time, day program of studies. GBA moved into a day program only after Dean Joseph Taggart stimulated that development in the sixties. It shared also Commerce's mass admission-mass attrition character. But its growth was inhibited by the physical constraints imposed by its housing in the old Trinity Church building at 90 Trinity Place. Indeed, GBA's physical facilities were far worse than those available to Commerce, for the undergraduate school had moved into its own 11-story building at Washington Square in 1926. Nonetheless, the MBA program served successfully to advance the careers of thousands of graduate students. Most of those students came from the canyons created by New York City's downtown skyscrapers, buildings occupied by investment and banking firms constituting the financial center of the nation.

Professor Emeritus Michael Schiff recalls that, when he came to GBA in 1946, the student body was more homogeneously "American" than was the case at Commerce. The faculty consisted of many part-time practitioners, along with full-time Commerce professors. Professor Schiff recalls only six *full-time GBA faculty* at that time; Professors Marcus Nadler, Jules Bogen, Lewis Haney, W. Edwards Deming, Peter Drucker, and himself. The doctoral program, which was initiated shortly after the School's establishment, was not noted for its academic standards. Originally, it was authorized to award the DCS degree, although the faculty had aspired to the PhD. Only after some 20 years had passed was approval to award the PhD received, and the DCS discontinued. Although the curricular requirements for the doctorate looked reasonable on paper, it was loosely administered, and as many as an estimated 1,200 students were carried on the doctoral rolls as candidates. A very small proportion of that number ever succeeded in completing the program, but others were permitted to hang on for years.

That situation changed radically after Professor Ernest Kurnow became director of the doctoral program. He had a mandate to make the program academically of high quality, and he did.

GBA was different from Commerce in its academic aspirations, which were almost immediately made evident. In particular, the faculty working on the graduate programs of study pressed hard to establish a research orientation and thrust. Inherent in this direction was an emphasis on staffing with faculty possessing the doctorate, and having significantly smaller teaching loads. That was the ideal and aim, although its accomplishment came about only with the passage of many years. Also, it took many years before GBA was able to stand on its financial feet and get along without the supportive resources of the School of Commerce. The breaking away, begun toward the end of Dean George Collins's term in office, came to fulfillment under Dean Joseph Taggart in the sixties. That change was undoubtedly made easier for GBA by the sharp drop in enrollments and the financial collapse of Commerce.

The Things That Changed

The Stern School's centennial marks a profound transformation in this extraordinary and pioneering educational enterprise. That transformation is manifested mainly in its academic, financial, and physical characteristics, and in both its undergraduate and graduate divisions.

Academically, a highly practitioner-oriented school, employing a large adjunct faculty alongside a full-time faculty heavily engaged in outside consulting, changed into a research-oriented institution dominated by faculty with doctoral credentials. Its curricula, baccalaureate, master's, and doctoral degrees, became intellectually rigorous and sophisticated, and demanded advanced quantitative and analytical aptitudes and skills of its students. The undergraduate program, long an educational resource to evening, part-time students, became overwhelmingly a day, full-time program. The same trend appeared at the graduate level in the sixties, and has already gone far. It will go farther, and current plans are being implemented to that end. The doctoral program has been brought under control, and it is now prestigious.

Until the sixties, the baccalaureate program was characterized by a considerable degree of specialization and multiplicity of majors and minors. By the middle of that decade, the situation had changed dramatically. By the early seventies, a curricular revolution had been accomplished. The undergraduate degree comprised a genuine general education base of Arts and Sciences courses, surmounted by a business core covering the several basic functional areas and a major. A considerable range of electives was available, both in the Arts and Sciences and the professional areas, so that a student could arrange double majors. Half the program involved Arts and Sciences (general education) courses, and, if a student desired, up to 72 out of the 128 credits required could be taken in Arts and Sciences courses. The old stereotype of the business student as a narrowly focused, vocationally trained specialist was buried beneath the new reality. A development that bears particular emphasis is the degree to which the modern baccalaureate business curriculum requires extensive and intensive quantitative skills, including computer familiarity. What makes this point noteworthy is the conviction that quantitative and computer skills are of fundamental importance to effective operational functioning in modern society, and should therefore be a required part of *any and all* undergraduate curricula, including the humanities.

By the mid-nineties, there was some reversal in the degree of flexibility offered in the baccalaureate program. But it was offset by a major effort to develop a cross-disciplinary approach in the business core courses. This development is welcome. It is a belated move to recognize the reality that modern organizations must be seen, studied, and understood as total systems rather than as a collection of functional divisions or departments. Unfortunately, this is not a simple or easy change to implement. It encounters the specialized research orientation and interests of the faculty, whose doctoral education tends to produce narrowness rather than broad generalism. This source of tension will have to be resolved in the years ahead.

For much of the century, the nature of the MBA curriculum paralleled that of the business baccalaureate. Once one got past the half of the program comprising the Arts and Sciences general education component, one encountered the two years required for the business core, the major (and minor in earlier years), and electives. As in the case of the baccalaureate, until the sixties the program was more specialized than general, and offered a multiplicity of major and minor fields of study. In fact, until the post World War II years, undergraduate and graduate students were co-mingled in presumably graduate courses. Even after that practice was ended, a careful comparative analysis of texts and syllabi used in graduate and undergraduate courses would show more similarity than not. In reality, a student having an undergraduate business baccalaureate degree could easily get the MBA with one year of additional study. Recognizing that fact, a combined BS-MBA five-year program was developed. But there has been a certain lack of enthusiasm with that program at the graduate level, probably reflecting discomfort with the parallelism between the undergraduate and graduate programs. The widespread adoption, at N Y U and other prestigious graduate business schools, of a requirement that MBA matriculates have several years of full-time work experience is probably intended to emphasize the greater maturity, sophistication, and differentiation of the graduate from the undergraduate courses. It continues to perplex me that the work experience required of MBA students is not matched by a comparable requirement for the faculty.

In any case, the MBA program has wrestled over the years with the issue of generalism versus specialism. Of course the MBA degree is, by nature, supposed to be generalist. And with fits and starts, it has developed consistent with that concept. Of particular interest is the MBA curriculum implemented in 1993–1994, with its cross-disciplinary emphasis. As noted above in connection with the baccalaureate, this is a major move, and its success is a worthy, indeed a vital objective. Note should be taken of the eventual dropping of the thesis requirement by the eighties. Originally viewed as a significant exercise in research and analysis, it finally lost out to the AACSB-required capstone business policy course, or satisfactory alternatives to that course. These remarks do not put the quietus on the specialism issue, for specialized MS programs were created in Accounting and in Quantitative Analysis. Of them, the Accounting program has been a clear success, with synergistic effects on the MBA program and the School.

It is not enough to simply mention Accounting and pass on. The adoption by the AICPA of a 150-credit hour program, as a requirement to take the CPA exam, and its support by many states for implementation in 2000, will have a major impact on the business schools. The 150-credit hour program involves a five-year program of studies, including the two years of the undergraduate general education component. For holders of *nonbusiness baccalaureates,* it means three additional years of graduate work. Of course that makes the professional preparation of the accountant similar to that of the attorney. Will it encourage the establishment of free-standing graduate schools of accounting, separate from the business schools? The outcome is not unthinkable. Where universities have business schools embracing both baccalaureate and graduate programs, as at NYU and Wharton, the outcome could be otherwise, with the new Accounting program comfortably housed in the B-school as at present. I have no doubt about one thing: the B-schools will contest strongly the establishment of separate schools of accounting.

The doctoral program is by its nature specialized. What is remarkable at NYU is that this program matriculated and carried thousands of students in its earlier years. But then it was transformed and brought under control. Today, it is a rigorous program, and the Stern School PhD is a prestigious degree.

The Stern School is also light years away from its progenitors, the School of Commerce and the Graduate School of Business Administration, in the uniformly high quality of the students it matriculates. It is not the huge educational factory that it once was. In place of the 10,000 or so enrolled students at Commerce in post World War II years, there now appears a reasonably steady state enrollment of some 2,100. While that is not small, it is compared to the masses crowding the School's halls and classrooms prior to the enrollment collapse of the sixties. And today's students, as we have seen, are intellectually first rate, comparable to those admitted to the nation's most prestigious universities. The operation is no longer mass admission-mass attrition. Having suffered for decades as being academically inferior, the School now stands as a premier part of NYU, and is so recognized nationally and internationally. The story is similar at the graduate level, where GMAT scores average around the 600 level and undergraduate GPAs average 3.13. However, the requirement of full-time work experience for admission to the MBA program, which averages four years, is a nonacademic variable which conditions the application of the GMAT and GPA variables. The graduate program, like the undergraduate one, has been downsizing from past peaks. Today, enrollment stands at roughly 4,000, with about two-thirds part-time evening and one-third full-time day students. Those proportions are scheduled to change further in favor of full-time students.

Financially, the Stern School is also light years away from its forerunners. While it is still 90 percent dependent on tuition revenues, it is moving to build its endowment and the revenue thereby generated. With an endowment of some $50 million in 1994 and annual expected income of some $4 million from it, the trend is right. No less, and perhaps even more, significant is the agreement with the university that recognizes the correctness of returning surplus funds to the School from the revenues it generates. That agreement was set in Dean West's tenure. After indirect overhead allocated costs and an indexed annual surcharge for university support (at slightly over $2 million in 1994), remaining surplus revenues (about $4.5 million in 1993–1994) remain with the Stern School, being allocated to restricted accounts ($3.5 million) and a portion ($1.0 million) to the school's endowment. The School's long exploitation as a cash cow appears to be ended, and in that fact lies a major reason to hope that its strategic plan for the future will come to complete fruition. We should remember in this connection that the university no longer relies so heavily as it once did on surplus revenues produced by the Commerce-GBA tuition stream. The $88.4 million 1993–1994 revenue of the Stern School is only 5.5 percent of the university's entire budget of some $1.6 billion. Of interest is the satellite MBA program at Manhattanville. It seems a success, producing $2.7 million of revenue in 1993–1994 at a cost of $575,000. And the executive MBA program also seems a success, with indicated income of $5.3 million in 1993–1994, and estimated expenses of $4.0 million.

We must not lose sight, however, of the underlying fragility of a revenue stream which is 90 percent dependent on tuition. The essential fact, and the faculty and administration had better not lose sight of it, is that the Stern School is subject to the discipline of the academic marketplace. That has important implications for maintaining excellence in teaching as well as research, and in the curricula offered. This point cannot be overemphasized, especially when one realizes that the school is labor-intensive, as is all education. At the Stern School, compensation of full-time and adjunct faculty, along with nonfaculty personnel, amounted to $40.0 million in 1993–1994, or some 48 percent of total costs (including university overhead allocated charges and the indexed tax). If those charges are eliminated ($16.9 million), then the labor input becomes 60 percent of total expense. Viewed from another angle, these numbers indicate how vital it is for the School to continue to press ahead aggressively in its efforts to build its endowment.

Physically, the Stern School of today is in a quality constellation remote from that which characterized its beginning. The Washington Square location is the same, but the plant and facilities would not be recognizable to the founders. The School's three-building, L-shaped

Management Education Center faces Gould Plaza, constituting a handsome, spacious complex. The plant is state-of-the-art, providing comfortable private faculty offices of generous dimensions, classrooms and lecture halls of varied sizes, lounges for faculty, students, and staff, housing for Institutes and Centers, ample areas for administrative and support services, and personnel and conference facilities. The latest computer and other electronic equipment is available throughout the complex. Every office space is equipped with a PC and students have readily available equipment.

Contrast the present situation with the picture drawn in earlier sections of this history. The School of Commerce was characterized by overcrowding from its earliest days to the time in 1972 when it occupied Tisch Hall, the 11-story building that is one of the structures comprising the present complex. Between 1900 and 1926, Commerce shared space in the Main Building with the Schools of Law and Pedagogy. Its rapidly expanding student body, and extension to daytime from its original evening program outran the space available. The pressure forced the opening of satellite locations, in the Wall Street area at the old Trinity Church structure, and also in Brooklyn.

In 1926 Commerce moved into its own 11-story building (now Shimkin Hall), bordering the southeast corner of Washington Square. But that structure was quickly crowded. At its best, it did not provide the sort of physical space and amenities that would encourage faculty to spend much time at the school. After all there were no private faculty offices. The faculty were provided rather with desks which many shared with other faculty, in large, bull-pen offices. Department chairpeople and deans got private offices, but those were far from luxurious. It was truly more a factory in its atmosphere and ambience than a place for fostering study, research, and teaching. That those outcomes still occurred, and with frequency, was a testimonial to the spirit of many teachers and students. In 1972 Commerce occupied its present home, moving into a modern age of first-rate education in first-rate facilities.

The story at the graduate level was less pleasant than at the undergraduate. The old Trinity Church building at 90 Trinity Place has been described in some detail. It is not stretching things too far to say that those quarters bordered on being squalid. It was not that they were dirty and messy, but rather that they were decrepit, noisy, distracting, altogether inadequate and unprepossessing. That a great educational enterprise eventually emerged is a testimonial to the triumph of the human spirit, and an unquenchable desire to pursue an ideal no matter how great and how adverse the odds.

The turnabout came at GBA in 1960, shortly after Joseph Taggart became dean. It was his good fortune to carry out the construction of Nichols Hall, which enabled GBA to undertake its academic transformation. The addition of Merrill Hall in the early seventies advanced the School's progress. But, truth be told, both structures were inadequate to the objectives envisioned by administrators and faculty. While enormously improved, office and other spaces continued to be tight and inadequate. The School continued to need significant amounts of rented space for library and other purposes. And, the continued separation of the graduate and undergraduate operations interfered with optimizing the human and physical resources that were available. It was Dick West's good fortune to create the conditions for the next great advance.

Leonard N. Stern's $30 million gift in 1988 enabled the School to move finally toward the achievement of its greatest aspiration, to be truly recognized as one of America's top business schools. We move into the twenty-first century with reasonable confidence that we can do it, and the physical home of the School is the external manifestation that the aspiration is real, and not just a dream.

Ethnically and geographically, as well as by *gender,* the composition of the Stern School's student body has changed dramatically over the decades, with significant differences between the undergraduate and graduate populations. For several generations, Commerce reflected like a mirror the character of its metropolitan home. It was a commuter School, serving basically New York City and its surrounding counties in New Jersey, New York, and Connecticut. It had also a small contingent of foreign students, especially from Japan. But the overwhelming majority were first-generation Americans, born of immigrant parents from Central, Eastern, and Southern Europe. While the School accepted and educated them, there was an undercurrent of sentiment among some faculty and administrators that the School would be improved by a larger presence of more "American" students. Also, the School was overwhelmingly male, although a significant number of female students were enrolled by the mid-thirties.

The undergraduate picture today is quite different. Women have become a large presence in the student body, and in the early eighties they exceeded half of it. By the early nineties their proportion had dropped to a bit less than half, and there was a possibility that we were witnessing some reversal of interest in business careers among women. I am not ready to accept that as a conclusion, believing that a significant economic and social loss would result if that turned out to be the reality. Only time will tell. Of equal interest, the growth of dormitory facilities for resident students has enable the School to draw a larger proportion of its students from outside the metropolitan New York area. One-third of the freshman class entering in Fall 1993 came from outside New York City and the surrounding 17 metropolitan counties. Forty percent came from the city, and the rest from the 17 counties. The large immigrant stream served in the early years continues to be served, but its composition no longer originates in Europe. Instead, it comes from Asia, and in Fall 1993 47 percent of the newly matriculated freshmen were Asian.

At the graduate level, the situation does not altogether parallel the undergraduate. Women, while a large presence, are not as numerous proportionately as at the undergraduate school. Only 26 percent of the entering MBA class in Fall 1993 was female. The relatively smaller presence of women at the graduate level than at the undergraduate is not a new phenomenon, having been the case also in the School's earlier years. More significant differences appear in the ethnic and geographical composition of the student body. Professors Hotchkiss and Schiff commented that GBA's student body up to the post World War II years was more homogenous and "American" in character than was the undergraduate one. In geographic terms, 38 percent of the Fall 1993 new MBA students were from abroad. Interestingly, Japanese students continue to display a high level of interest in the Stern School. We have seen that this interest goes back to the earliest years of the school. Perhaps its continued strength reflects, at least in part, the existence of our Japan-U.S. Center on trade. In any case, the student body at the graduate level is today ethnically more diverse than it was in the past. Also, where 68 percent of the new undergraduates in Fall 1993 came from the metropolitan area, only 37.7 percent of the new MBAs originated there. Twenty-four percent came from states outside the metropolitan New York region.

The Stern School, while continuing to be cosmopolitan, is gradually becoming more national and less regional. That is a healthy development. It enhances the School's long-run stability by enlarging the population base that feeds its enrollments.

Having noted the long history of Japanese students at the Stern School, it seems appropriate to tell the story of Jo Sakai.[1] Jo was born in

Miyazu, Kyoto prefecture, Japan, in August 1874. He graduated from Kyoto's Doshisha University, and came to the United States at the dawn of the twentieth century to find employment with Thomas Edison, the great inventor. Unsuccessful, he matriculated in the new School of Commerce, Accounts, and Finance and graduated in 1903. At that time and through a coincidence of fate, James Ingraham, president of Florida's Model Land Company (a subsidiary of the Florida East Coast Railroad), contacted a former college friend who was on the faculty of New York University. Ingraham shared with his friend the idea of creating a colony of Japanese farmers in Florida, who would help build the state's agricultural industry. Similar efforts were under way in Texas, in the Houston area. In any case, Jo Sakai became aware of the Florida opportunity, and, armed with a letter of introduction to the state's governor William Jennings, he arrived in Tallahassee in the Fall of 1903. The governor was receptive as were other Floridians. Sakai examined land offered by the Model Land Company, but there was some question about land ownership by the Japanese. Generally, Floridian landowners were accustomed to a tenancy or sharecropper system. This was not the status envisioned by Sakai. Ingraham agreed, and the Model Land Company offered land for sale, so that the prospective Japanese colonists would be landowners, not tenant laborers.

Jo Sakai returned to Japan to recruit his colonists. Before leaving the United States, however, he visited with officials of the U.S. Department of Agriculture and Bureau of Immigration in Washington, D.C., where he received approval to bring a group of his countrymen to Florida. In Japan, he ran into difficulty with the Foreign Ministry, which raised barriers against providing the exit papers needed by the colonists, perhaps due to the Russo-Japanese War of 1904–1905. One can speculate that the opposition may have been no less due to sensitivity over the considerable opposition in the United States at that time, by labor and other groups, to Asian immigration as a source of cheap, un-American labor. But Jo Sakai was indefatigable, and found influential, cabinet-level ministers to help him in his efforts. This approach, as well as others orchestrated in the United States by Ingraham, were unavailing. Finally, Sakai hit on a clever device. He would have each of his prospective colonists apply for passports individually, on the pretext of going to the United States to study. This was an objective favored by the Japanese Foreign Ministry, and the passports were forthcoming. And so the first of the Japanese colonists began to arrive in Florida in August 1904.

Unfortunately, the land designated as the colony's site, along the Hillsboro River west of Boca Raton, was not yet drained, and so unsuitable for cultivation. As a short-term solution, the Model Land Company rented alternative acreage for an "experimental crop" to be cultivated by the Japanese with the advice of Captain Richards, an agent of the company (which provided equipment and supplies). Sakai had financial support also from Japanese backers, principally one Manzaburo Oki. The harvesting of the first crop, tomatoes, brought controversy between the colonists and the Model Land Co. The issue involved the insistence of Chase and Harney, the shipping company, that the packing operation was not in accordance with contract specifications. Ingraham sought to win Sakai and the settlers agreement to conform to Chase and Harney's demands. Instead, Sakai decided he would seek an alternative site for the colony. Some months of controversy and negotiations followed, with a solution and settlement being arrived at on July 12, 1905. At that time Sakai and the Model Land Company agreed on a new site for the colony. It consisted of an area some two miles by one mile in area, known as the Keystone Plantation, that was already under cultivation with pineapples, plus additional undeveloped adjacent acreage owned by the Florida East Coast Railway. With that, the Japanese colony was settled, becoming known as the Yamato Colony. It was successful, and flourished for some eight decades. Today, its location is the site of a lovely, small museum, built in Japanese architectural style, that tells the story.

The Thing That Is the Same

The tale of Jo Sakai and his Yamato Colony is included in this history of the Stern School because it illustrates the role the School played in bringing energetic immigrants into America's mainstream. Although Asians were only a small part of the stream that flowed through Commerce and GBA until the eighties, they are now a large presence. Today, however, they will not be farmers, but will move instead into every area of the nation's economy. And it is here that the Stern School remains as it was, in its core mission, the very mission that was set down for New York University by its founders over 160 years ago.

NYU's founders envisioned a school for the children of workers and small business people, rather than for the Brahmins of American society. The university, and its several schools and colleges, have been true to that mission, and none more so than the Stern School. If today it is selective in its admissions, even elite, its selectivity is still not based on class and culture, but on ability and ambition. It is, as always, the door that opens on opportunity, for everyone able and willing to do the work, embracing both sexes and every race and creed.

Problems That Persist

There are other things that, while changing in degree and proportion, remain as persistent problems. Perhaps most notable among them are: (1) the continuing tension between research and teaching; (2) the continuing tension between generalism and specialism; and (3) the continuing, heavy reliance on tuition as the major source of revenue.

The tension between research and teaching is profound, and involves the two essential purposes of the university and its schools. Those purposes are: (1) to do research, thereby seeking knowledge and extending the boundaries and depth of human understanding of the world about us and of our own natures; and (2) to instruct the younger generation in knowledge accumulated, plus inspiring them to extend further the boundaries and plumb the depths.

The foregoing duality of university purpose and mission was not accepted by Thorstein Veblen, the great institutional economist of the late nineteenth and early twentieth centuries. He expressed his opinion in his book *The Higher Learning in America*. Observing that the "conservation and advancement of the higher learning involves two lines of work, distinct but closely bound together," he identified them as: (1) scientific and scholarly inquiry, and (2) the instruction of students. He went on:

> The former of these is primary and indispensable. It is this work of intellectual enterprise that gives its character to the university and marks it off from the lower schools. The work of teaching properly belongs in the university only because and in so far as it incites and facilitates the university man's work of inquiry. . . .
>
> The student's relation to his teacher necessarily becomes that of an apprentice to his master, rather than that of a pupil to his schoolmaster. . . .
>
> *No man whose energies are not habitually bent on increasing and improving the domain of learning belongs legitimately on the university staff. The university man is properly, a student, not a schoolmaster. . . .*

The schoolmaster and his work may be equally, or more, valuable to the community—but in so far as his chief interest is of the pedagogical sort his place is not in the university. . . .

The difference between the modern university and the lower and professional schools is broad and simple; not so much a difference of degree as of kind. . . .

The lower schools (including professional schools) are, in the ideal scheme, designed to fit the incoming generation for civil life; they are therefore occupied with instilling such knowledge and habits as will make their pupils fit citizens of the world in whatever position in the fabric of workday life they may fall. The university on the other hand is specialized to fit men for a life of science and scholarship; and it is accordingly concerned with such discipline only as will give efficiency in the pursuit of knowledge and fit its students for the increase and diffusion of learning. . . .

Doubtless the larger and more serious responsibility in the educational system belongs not to the university but to the lower and professional schools. Citizenship is a larger and more substantial category than scholarship; and the furtherance of civilized life is a larger and more serious interest than the pursuit of knowledge for its own idle sake. But the proportions which the quest of knowledge is latterly assuming in the scheme of civilized life require that the establishments to which this interest is committed should not be charged with extraneous duties; particularly not with extraneous matters that are themselves of such grave consequence as this training for citizenship and practical affairs. These are too serious a range of duties to be taken care of as a side-issue, by a seminary of learning, the members of whose faculty, if they are fit for their own special work, are not men of affairs or adepts in worldly wisdom. (Italics added)[2]

Contrary to Veblen's categorical view, an opposing opinion sees scholarship and research as imperatives for schoolmasters who seek success in their task. In the latter view, the schoolmaster is not seen as a pedant, a doctrinaire individual who simply regurgitates the pap of established academic fare. He is seen rather as a teacher consumed with curiosity, a person ever seeking to expand his or her knowledge and understanding, and to pass it on to the next generation. This combination of curiosity and the search for knowledge is essentially the hallmark of the scholar-researcher. Consequently, while Veblen's views can sharpen our insight into the tension between research and teaching which has bedeviled our universities over the years, they do not make his solution correct, that is, separation between the work of the scholar-researcher and the schoolmaster. The two functions are married in our universities, and will continue to be wedded there. Philosophical neatness and organizational simplicity will not rule. Consequently, pragmatism dictates candor and openness about the problem, and a coupling of integrity and honesty in finding and implementing a solution. That solution, in my mind, involves a clear demarcation between the work of doctoral programs, which conform in purpose and plan with Veblen's view of the university, and the work of master's and baccalaureate programs, which conform in purpose and plan with Veblen's view of the schoolmaster's task. They do coexist, but they could do so to better effect if their nature and respective needs were better understood and respected.

The doctoral program and degree is by its nature specialized. But the business baccalaureate and MBA degree programs require a mix of the general and the specific. The Stern School is well positioned to press forward in its search for the best balance. Apart from the general education component at the undergraduate level, which is the critical ingredient at the baccalaureate level that provides a necessary broad base for cultural and scientific understanding, the upper two undergraduate years and the MBA programs are essentially parallel. Parallel but not identical, for the greater maturity and experience required for admission to the graduate program must be reflected in greater sophistication and rigor in the curriculum and the conduct of its implementation. However, in both cases there is a business core, a major, and electives. The core is a key element, inherently and necessarily required to be general. Unfortunately, the core has until recently been a collection of courses that are specialized by functional area. What needs to happen here is a truly cross-disciplinary approach that focuses on organizations as total entities and systems, as organic wholes rather than as a group of separate functions and disciplines. This insight is difficult to implement, for the faculty who are the key are specialists, not generalists. It is their mindset, which is a product of the specialized training they receive as doctoral candidates, that must be altered. They must think and communicate across functional lines, a pattern of thought and action that seems strange and uncongenial. But it *must* happen. Fortunately, the present thrust of curricular reform at both baccalaureate and MBA levels in the Stern School is consistent with that direction. Added to this cross-disciplinary approach there also needs to be a *weltanschauung*, a worldview. It is no longer a brilliant insight to observe that technology is driving us truly to a world economy, or, at the least, huge regional economies (Asian, European, and American). I hope the former will emerge and prevail, so that regional rivalries are contained and the promise of peace enhanced. In any case, the business organizations of the future are likely to be even more multinational and global than they are today.

The major is the specialized component in the business degree, and it is there that specialized skills are to be developed and honed. The trick will be to keep it from growing and overwhelming the generalist character of the core. Then there is the component of elective courses, which may be used to strengthen the student's overall (that is, general) grasp, or to buttress the specialized skills acquired in the major. I prefer that some balance be achieved here, although the student's interests must be recognized, otherwise he or she will no longer be provided with electives and free choice.

At the graduate level, the desire for a greater degree of specialization than is afforded by the MBA can be made available through MS programs. But they should be limited, because the primary purpose and mission of the graduate business school should continue to be the preparation of managers, although the program should encourage the development among them of entrepreneurs and leaders.

We are left with the preparation of accountants, which should continue to be housed in the business school. That belief is based on the profound importance of accounting and business to each other, as well as on history and the educational infrastructure already in place. The new 150-credit hour requirement for the CPA exam, which is to be implemented by 2000, involves a three-year program of studies above the undergraduate general education component. It will be most easily accommodated in universities having both undergraduate and graduate business programs, although an extra year at the graduate level in a non-MBA master's program could also do the job. Of course the latter arrangement involves a curriculum probably not in synchronization with the MBA, and may implicitly take on the aura of an autonomous School of Accounting within the B-school.

The continued importance of tuition as a primary source of revenue is also a source of persistent tension, for fluctuations, especially downward, create serious pressures on faculty and administration to review curricula, number of course offerings and sections, class size, teaching loads, and staffing profiles (use of adjuncts and assistants). This tension is not all bad, for it keeps the faculty facing the market. Insulation from market pressure, provided by huge endowments and unrestricted contributions, are comforting to the faculty and permit it to pursue its own narrow interests in research. But complete insulation is undesirable. While excellent research must continue to be a hallmark of the Stern School, excellent teaching must be seen as having equal importance. And the market test, through the medium of tuition revenue, compels the faculty to keep that purpose high on their list of priorities.

If it is not yet evident, then it must be said explicitly. The key to future success is the faculty, for they are the normal governors in America's research universities today.

A Vision for the Future

The Stern School has established itself as one of America's premier business schools, with powerful undergraduate and graduate programs of study. Its many sources of strength were noted at the beginning of this chapter, including quality of faculty, students, plant, university, curricula, alumni, and location in one of the world's great cosmopolitan centers. But that is not sufficient to insure future greatness. To that end, the school's dynamic thrust to achieve an overarching view of society and its organizations, both nationally and internationally, must be continued, extended, and deepened. It must also be infused with an ethical sense, a bedrock of moral values that go beyond and transcend the pure pursuit of profit, especially in short-term time frames. A longer view has to be explicated, even preached. And central to that view must be an emphasis on quality and consumer satisfaction, as well as a humane concern for the well-being of labor and other suppliers of the resources going into production. In so doing the school will be true to such great former members of the faculty as W. Edwards Deming and Peter Drucker, as well as to the many others whose names have appeared in this chronicle.

If faculty and administrators are dedicated to these values and hold them dear, then the School will meet any market test. It will also attract additional support for endowment, to strengthen further the excellence and range of its research output. After all, endowment and other nontuition revenue sources make possible more generous staffing arrangements, with benefits on both the research and teaching sides of the enterprise. Withal, the School must remain true to its heritage as a school of opportunity. That is at the core of what it has been, is, and should aspire to be.

The School should seek an enlarged and more focused emphasis on entrepreneurship and leadership. Dean Dill penned a poignant appeal on this point, saying: "An unfulfilled opportunity for leadership . . . exists at NYU. What other school boasts as many graduates who have gone from stark and simple beginnings to huge successes—not just pioneers in building businesses, but in growing them into major players in the economy and community? What other school has an opportunity to look at 'business' entrepreneurship, not only in business per se, but in the arts, medicine, and other parts of the not-for-profit world as well?"[3] The Stern School should be first in bringing to its students an understanding of the elements of entrepreneurship and leadership. While it may not make entrepreneurs and leaders of those lacking the necessary innate characteristics, it can stimulate and make more successful those who do.

If the School does these things, it cannot fail.

Notes

NOTES TO CHAPTER ONE

1. Professor Emeritus Michael Schiff notes that the *essential nature* of the CPA exam, set down in 1896, remained unchanged for 98 years, to May 1994. Also, while candidates for the CPA were allowed to use an abacus or slide rule in earlier years, they were not permitted to use a pocket (electronic) calculator until 1994. Professor Schiff is a former chairman of the Stern School's Department of Accounting and was dean of the Sy Syms School of Business at Yeshiva University.

2. *The American Association of Collegiate Schools of Business, 1916–1966* (Homewood, Ill.: Richard D. Irwin, 1966), 1–2.

3. New York University, Annual Reports, 1912, 89.

4. New York University, School of Commerce, Accounts, and Finance (hereafter SCAF), *Announcement for 1900–1901*, 6.

5. Thatcher F. Jones, editor, *History of New York University* (New York: New York University Press, 1932), 357–58.

6. George Burton Hotchkiss, Unpublished autobiographical excerpts from a manuscript discovered in files, Dean's Office, Commerce-BPA, July 2, 1993, 3–5.

7. NYU Bulletin, SCAF, 1910–1911, Vol. X, No. 9, May 11, 1910, 11.

8. *Ibid.,* 9–10.

9. NYU Bulletins, SCAF, annually, 1900–1901 through 1914–1915.

10. New York University School of Commerce, Accounts, and Finance, *Glimpses of the Faculty,* 1936, 40.

11. New York University, *The Commerce Book, 1942–1943,* A student handbook, Vol. V, 15.

12. NYU Bulletin, SCAF, Vol. VIII, No. 10, May 16, 1908, 44–63.

13. NYU Bulletin, SCAF, Vol. IX, No. 15, June 19, 1909, 32–33.

14. *The Commerce Handbook, 1942–1943,* 15.

15. NYU Bulletin, SCAF, Vol. III, 1902–1903, 7, 10.

16. NYU Bulletin, SCAF, 1912–1913, Vol. XII, No. 18, June 28, 1912, 17.

17. *Ibid.*

18. NYU, *Report of Officers to the Chancellor of the University, for the Academic Year 1936–1937,* 171–74.

19. *Ibid.,* 171–72.

20. *Ibid.,* 172.

21. *Ibid.,* 166–67.

22. Jones, *History,* 225–26.

23. *Ibid.,* 233–35.

24. NYU, *Report of Officers, 1919–1929,* 200.

25. Hotchkiss, Unpublished excerpts, 32–34.

26. NYU Bulletins, SCAF, annually, 1900–1901 through 1916–1917.

27. Hotchkiss, Unpublished excerpts, 13.

28. NYU, SCAF, *Glimpses of the Faculty,* 1–2.

29. NYU Bulletin, SCAF, Wall Street Division, 1920–1921, Vol. XX, No. 14, May 29, 1920, 8–10.

30. NYU Bulletin, SCAF, Wall Street Division, 1921–1922, Vol. XXI, No. 13, May 14, 1921, 9–13.

31. NYU Bulletin, SCAF, Wall Street Division, 1930–1931, Vol. XXX, No. 18, 8–13.

32. Hotchkiss, Unpublished excerpts, 24–25.

NOTES TO CHAPTER TWO

1. A university official who represents the institution and transacts its business. Perhaps equivalent now to a provost, chancellor, or executive vice-president. The Syndic was Dr. John MacCracken, son of Chancellor MacCracken.

2. NYU, *Annual Reports of New York University,* "Report of the Syndic," New York, N.Y., 1912, 57.

3. NYU Bulletin, SCAF, Wall Street Division, Vol. XXIII, No. 11, 1923–1924, April 21, 1923, 14–15; and NYU Bulletin, SCAF, Wall Street Division, 1924–1925, Vol. XXIV, No. 10, April 23, 1924, 14.

4. NYU Bulletin, SCAF, Wall Street Division, 1928–1929, Vol. XXVIII, No. 14, April 2, 1928, 18.

5. NYU Bulletin, SCAF, 1947–1948, Vol. XLVII, No. 9, February 21, 1947, 24.

6. NYU Bulletin, SCAF, Wall Street Division, 1924–1925, Vol. XXIV, No. 10, April 12, 1924, 15–19.

7. NYU Bulletin, SCAF, 1901–1902, Vol. I, No. 9, July 1, 1901, 13.

8. NYU Bulletin, SCAF, 1902–1903, Vol. II, No. 10, June 30, 1902, 6–7.

9. NYU Bulletin, SCAF, 1904–1905, Vol. IV, No. 9, May 16, 1904, 10.

10. *Ibid.*

11. NYU Bulletin, SCAF, 1907–1908, Vol. VII, No. 9, May 11, 1907, 11.

12. NYU Bulletin, SCAF, 1908–1909, Vol. VIII, No. 10, May 16, 1908, 11.

13. NYU Bulletin, SCAF, 1912–1913, Vol. XII, No. 18, June 28, 1912, 16–17.

14. NYU Bulletin, SCAF, 1913–1914, Vol. XIII, No. 16, June 13, 1913, 21.

15. NYU Bulletin, SCAF, 1914–1915, Vol. XIV, No. 17, June 26, 1914, 25.

16. NYU Bulletin, SCAF, Wall Street Division, 1920–1921, Vol. XX, No. 14, May 29, 1920. 15.

17. NYU Bulletin, SCAF, Wall Street Division, 1924–1925, Vol. XXIV, No. 10, April 12, 1924, 22.

18. NYU Bulletin, SCAF, Wall Street Division, 1923–1924, Vol. XXIII, No. 11, April 21, 1923, 16–17.

19. NYU Bulletin, SCAF, Wall Street Division, 1924–1925, Vol. XXIV, No. 10, April 12, 1924, 22.

20. NYU Bulletin, SCAF, Wall Street Division, 1925–1926, Vol. XXV, No. 12, May 2, 1925, 22–23.

21. NYU Bulletin, SCAF, Wall Street Division, 1926–1927, Vol. XXVI, No. 15, April 10, 1926, 22–29.

22. *Ibid.*, 21–22.

23. NYU Bulletin, SCAF, Wall Street Division, 1929–1930, Vol. XXIX, No. 14, April 6, 1929, 26–27.

24. NYU Bulletin, SCAF, Wall Street Division, 1926–1927, 24.

25. NYU, *Reports of Officers to the Chancellor of the University for the Academic Year 1936–1937*, 165. Sixty-Four credit certificate programs continued to be offered.

26. NYU, SCAF, *Glimpses of the Faculty*, 34–35.

27. NYU, SCAF, *Programs of Study Leading to BS Degree*, 1948–1949, 24.

28. NYU Bulletin, SCAF, Wall Street Division, 1926–1927, 87–90.

29. NYU, SCAF, *Programs of Study Leading to BS Degree*, 1948–1949, 2.

30. NYU Bulletin, SCAF, 1908–1909, 12.

31. NYU Bulletin, SCAF, Wall Street Division, 1921–1922, 9.

32. *Ibid.*, 17.

33. Personal records kept by Professor Emeritus Ernest Kurnow, onetime chairman of the doctoral program at GBA.

34. U.S. Bureau of the Census, *Historical Statistics of the United States, Colonial Times to 1970*, Part 1, Washington, D.C., 1975, 379.

35. U.S. Bureau of the Census, *Statistical Abstract of the United States: 1992* (112th edition), Washington, D.C., 1992, 144.

36. *Ibid.*, 145.

37. A. L. Gitlow, *Being the Boss: The Importance of Leadership and Power* (Homewood, Ill.: Business One Irwin, 1992), 195–96.

NOTES TO CHAPTER THREE

1. New York University, *School of Commerce Dean's Annual Report, 1970–1971*, 31.
2. New York University, *Self-Study Final Report*, New York: New York University Press, 1956, 1.
3. *Ibid.*, 23–24.
4. NYU Bulletin, *Reports of Officers to the Chancellor of the University*, Vol. XXXI, No. 2, December 8, 1930, 105.
5. NYU, *Self-Study Report*, 182–83.
6. *Ibid.*, 191–92.
7. Robert A. Gordon and James E. Howell, *Higher Education for Business*, New York: Columbia University Press, 1959; and Frank C. Pierson, *The Education of American Businessmen*, New York: McGraw-Hill, 1959.
8. Thomas L. Norton, *The Undergraduate Business Curriculum*, The Ford and Carnegie Reports, 1.
9. *Ibid.*
10. *Ibid.*, 2.
11. *Ibid.*
12. *Ibid.*, 3.
13. J. Victor Baldridge, *Power and Conflict in the University*, New York: Wiley, 1971, 47.
14. NYU, *A Presentation from New York University to the Ford Foundation Special Program in Education*, Part II, November 1963.
15. *Ibid.*, 16.
16. *Ibid.*, 32–41.
17. NYU, School of Commerce, *A New Vista for Collegiate Business Education*, Report of the "Think" Subcommittee of the Curriculum Committee, September 29, 1964, 3.
18. *Ibid.*, 1–2.
19. NYU, *Faculty Committee to Study the Schools of Business*, minutes of Committee meetings commencing April 5, 1965 and ending June 2, 1965.
20. Baldridge, *Power and Conflict*, 53–55.
21. *Ibid.*, 53.
22. *Ibid.*, 54.
23. *Ibid.*, 53.
24. *Ibid.*, 55.
25. NYU, School of Commerce, *1968–1969 Dean's Annual Report*, 14–15.

26. Gitlow, *Being the Boss*, 116–17.

27. N Y U, *Reports of Officers, Registrar's Report, 1947–1948*, Tables I, IIIA, IV, and VI.

28. These figures are from the bulletins of N Y U, SCAF, for the years noted. Professors Emeriti are not included in the figures.

29. N Y U *Annual Report of the Dean*, SCAF, 1946–1947, 2.

30. The U.S. Consumer price index, with 1982–1984 equal to 100.0, was 22.3 in 1947 and 144.5 in 1993, so that a 1947 dollar was equal to $6.48 in 1993. *Handbook of Labor Statistics*, U.S. Department of Labor, Bulletin 2340, August 1989, 475, and *Economic Indicators*, Washington, D.C.: U.S. Government Printing Office, March 1994, 23.

31. The N Y U *Self-Study Report*, 266, came to conclusions on this point consistent with those of Dean Madden. But the Self-Study observed that Chancellor Heald announced a limit of one day per week on outside activity for remuneration, effective in the academic year 1955–1956. However, individual exceptions were allowed. Heald himself made such an exception for Professor Darrell Lucas, chairman of the Marketing Department.

32. Letter, Professor Emeritus Darrell B. Lucas to Dean Emeritus A. L. Gitlow, June, 1993.

33. N Y U *Self-Study Report*, 266.

34. N Y U, School of Commerce, *Dean's Annual Report, 1965–1966*, 19.

35. N Y U, *School of Commerce Bulletin, 1956–1957*, 34–35.

36. Table 3.1 and course data are from: N Y U, School of Commerce, *Dean's Annual Report, 1965–1966*, 11–12.

37. N Y U, School of Commerce, *Dean's Annual Report, 1967–1968*, 30–38.

NOTES TO CHAPTER FOUR

1. Change in name of School explained on 91–92.

2. N Y U, School of Commerce, *Dean's Annual Report, 1965–1966*, 38–39.

3. N Y U, School of Commerce, *Dean's Annual Report, 1965–1966* (38–39) and *1966–1967* (18–19).

4. Another development, the growth in enrollment of Asian students, is noted on page 103.

5. At her death in 1993, Edlyn Racoosin bequeathed some $2 million more to the Racoosin Scholarships endowment, thereby bringing its aggregate corpus to some $3½ million.

6. N Y U, School of Commerce, *Dean's Annual Report, 1966–1967*, 20.

7. Data provided by dean's office, undergraduate college, Stern School of Business.

8. U.S. Bureau of the Census, *Statistical Abstract of the United States: 1993* (113th edition), Washington, D.C., 1993, 481.

9. At Harvard, Northwestern, and Pennsylvania's Wharton School, the percentages of *tenured* faculty who were women in 1993 were respectively 5 percent, 12 percent, and 9 percent. *BusinessWeek*, July 19, 1993, 60.

10. NYU Bulletin, College of Business and Public Administration, 1976–1977, 53.

11. NYU Bulletin, College of Business and Public Administration, 1982–1984, 20–21.

NOTES TO CHAPTER FIVE

1. NYU, *Reports of Officers for the Year 1919–1920*, 25.

2. *Ibid.*, 204.

3. *Ibid.*, 25–33.

4. *Ibid.*

5. NYU, *Reports of Officers to the Chancellor of the University for the Academic Year, 1936–1937*, 217.

6. From an unpublished statement prepared by Dean Madden in February 1937, discovered in the files of the dean's office, 2.

7. *Ibid.* and NYU, *Reports of Officers to the Chancellor, 1936–1937*, 221.

8. Robert E. Gleeson, Steven Schlossman, and David Grayson Allen, "Uncertain Ventures: The Origins of Graduate Management Education at Harvard and Stanford, 1908–1939," *Selections* The Magazine of the Graduate Management Admission Council, Spring 1993, Vol. IX, No. 3, 10.

9. *Ibid.*, 15.

10. NYU Bulletin, Graduate School of Business Administration (hereafter GBA), 1921–1922, Vol. XXI, No. 5, March 19, 1921, 10–11.

11. NYU Bulletin, GBA, 1923–1924, Vol. XXIII, No. 7, March 24, 1923, 18–19.

12. NYU, GBA, Faculty Meeting Minutes, February 21, 1923.

13. NYU Bulletin, GBA, 1922–1923, Vol. XXII, No. 10, April 22, 1922, 15.

14. NYU Bulletin, GBA, 1923–1924, Vol. XXIII, No. 7, March 24, 1923, 19.

15. Records of Professor Emeritus Ernest Kurnow, former Chairman of the GBA doctoral program.

16. *BusinessWeek*, July 19, 1993, 58–65.

17. NYU Bulletin, GBA, 1937–1938, Vol. XXXVII, No. 24, May 11, 1937, 13–16.

18. NYU Bulletin, GBA 1921–1922, Vol. XXI, No. 5, March 19, 1921, 9–10.

19. NYU Bulletin, SCAF, 1930–1931, 110–111; and NYU Bulletin, GBA, 1929–1930, Vol. XXIX, No. 21, May 25, 1929, 12–13.

20. Letter, Dean William Dill to Dean Emeritus Abraham Gitlow, Dec. 24, 1993, 2.

NOTES TO CHAPTER SIX

1. Unpublished statement by Dean John T. Madden discovered in the files of the dean's office, 3.

2. NYU Bulletin, GBA, 1965–1966, 68–71.

3. Rough draft of *Report of Study of Former Students*, Memorandum, W. Edwards Deming to Dean William R. Dill, March 30, 1976, 9.

4. Letter, Professor Emeritus Michael Schiff to Dean Emeritus Abraham L. Gitlow, January 15, 1994.

5. Letter, Dean William Dill to Dean Emeritus Abraham L. Gitlow, December 24, 1993, 3–4.

6. NYU Bulletin, GBA, 1960–1961, 19–21.

7. NYU Bulletin, GBA, 1972–1973, 55.

8. Peter F. Drucker, ed., *Preparing Tomorrow's Business Leaders Today*, Englewood Cliffs, N.J.: Prentice-Hall, 1969, 262–63.

9. W. Edwards Deming and William R. Dill, "How Can a School of Business Better Serve Its Students?" unpublished manuscript, February 3, 1977, 3–4.

10. Memo, Professor Emeritus Ernest Kurnow to Dean Emeritus Abraham L. Gitlow, December 27, 1993, 1–2.

11. George Sorter is Vincent Ross Professor of Accounting in the Stern School, a past chairman of the Accounting department, and a past director of the Ross Institute for Accounting Research.

12. Letter, Dean William Dill to Dean Emeritus Abraham L. Gitlow, December 24, 1993, 10.

13. Letter, Dean William Dill to Dean Emeritus Abraham L. Gitlow, December 24, 1993, 7.

14. Ernest Kurnow, "The New York University Careers in Business Program," in *Teaching and Beyond: Nonacademic Career Programs for Ph.D.s*, The Regents of the University of the State of New York, Teaching and Beyond Project, Albany, New York, October 1984, 8–20.

15. Letter, Dean William Dill to Dean Emeritus Abraham L. Gitlow, Dec. 24, 1993, 8.

NOTES TO CHAPTER SEVEN

1. NYU, *Building For the Future*, Formal dedication, Management Education Center, April 23, 1993, 5.

2. *Ibid.*, 2.

3. *Ibid.*, 6.

4. Economics involves two courses, for a total of 6 credits. Accounting involves two courses, for a total of 4.5 credits.

5. *Establishment of PPRCIII to Review Other Degree Programs,* memo of Dean George Daly to Faculty Council, August 30, 1993.

NOTES TO CHAPTER EIGHT

1. NYU Bulletin, *School of Retailing,* April 15, 1944, Vol. XLIV, No. 20, 11.
2. NYU Bulletin, *School of Retailing,* April 26, 1948, Vol. XLVIII, No. 17, 20.
3. Memo to File, Vice-Dean Hawkins, November 25, 1980.
4. Minutes, Faculty Council, School of Business, November 25, 1980.
5. Memo, Professor Ingo Walter to Faculty Council, June 3, 1981.

NOTES TO CHAPTER NINE

1. Richard T. Wines, Associate Director of Accreditation and Eunice K. Lange, Assistant Director of Accreditation, AACSB, were very helpful in preparing this chapter. They provided relevant publications and records, e.g., minutes of annual meetings.

2. *New York Times,* January 28, 1994, A19.

3. *Ibid.,* January 30, 1994, 16.

4. *The American Association of Collegiate Schools of Business, 1916–1966, Fiftieth Year,* Homewood, Ill.: Richard D. Irwin, 1966, 183.

5. *Ibid.,* 184.

6. *Ibid.,* 188–89.

7. *Ibid.,* 197.

8. *Ibid.,* 199–200.

9. *Ibid.,* 201.

10. *Ibid.,* 206–7.

11. *Ibid.,* 210–11.

12. *Ibid.,* 200–201.

13. *Ibid.,* 214–15

14. *Ibid.,* 234.

15. *Ibid.,* 222–24.

16. *Ibid.,* 229.

17. *Ibid.*

18. *Ibid.,* 239, 243.

19. *Ibid.,* 243–44.

20. *Ibid.,* 247–48.

21. AACSB, *Accreditation Council Policies Procedures and Standards, 1990–92,* St. Louis, Mo., 24.

22. AACSB, *Achieving Quality and Continuous Improvement Through Self-Evaluation and Peer Review,* St. Louis, Mo., 1.

23. *Ibid.,* 17.

24. *Ibid.,* 13–14.

25. *Ibid.,* 15.

26. AACSB, Minutes, Board of Directors Meeting, April 30, 1976, Appendix A, 9.

27. AACSB Memorandum, Final Report of Executive Vice President, April 21, 1976, 4.

28. AACSB, Minutes, Board of Directors Meeting, October 20–21, 1976, 6.

29. AACSB, Minutes, Board of Directors Meeting, November 8–9, 1979, Appendix 1.

30. AACSB, Minutes, Board of Directors Meeting, June 9–10, 1980, 5.

31. AACSB, *Achieving Quality,* 41.

32. AACSB, Minutes, Accreditation Council and Assembly Business Meetings, April 20, 1993, 2.

33. American Assembly of Collegiate Schools of Business, *Newsline,* Fall 1993, Vol. 24, No. 1, 11.

34. *The American Association of Collegiate Schools of Business, 1916–1966,* 192–93.

35. *Ibid.,* 193.

36. *Ibid.,* 211.

37. *Ibid.,* 219.

38. *Ibid.,* 221.

39. *Ibid.,* 202.

40. An incident of external influence was reported in the press, but it was not political. It involved the University of Rochester, which turned away some Japanese students from a program being attended by Kodak managers. The Rochester action was apparently in response to Kodak fears that the Japanese would learn their trade secrets. Those fears allegedly led Kodak to convey its concern to the university, which then took the action noted. Subsequently, the university stated its resolve not to act in response to external pressure.

41. Wade Lambert, "Suit Says ABA Accreditation Is Out of Date," *Wall Street Journal,* November 24, 1993, B1 and B3.

NOTES TO CHAPTER TEN

1. N Y U, SCAF, *Commerce Violet,* May 1910, 14.

2. *Ibid.*

3. Theodore G. Ehrsam, ed., *The History/Handbook of Alpha Kappa Psi, Seventh Edition,* Indianapolis, Ind.: Alpha Kappa Psi Foundation, 1993, 38–45.

4. NYU, *Commerce Violet*, Vol. I, 1908, Editorial (pages not numbered).

5. *New York Times*, September 19, 1993, 1.

6. Abigail Thernstrom, "Affirmative Action Backfires at Harvard Law Review," *Wall Street Journal*, November 18, 1992, A17.

7. NYU Bulletin, SCAF, 1940–1941, 43.

8. NYU, *The Student's Guide to NYU*, 1993–1994, 43–52.

9. NYU, SCAF, Faculty Meeting Minutes, No. 6, December 10, 1947, 104. Of the 44 cases, 32 involved suspensions, 4 probation, 1 reprimand, 3 dismissals, 2 withdrawals, 1 no jurisdiction, and 1 denial of a certificate.

10. *Ibid.*, October 8, 1947, 81–92.

11. *New York Times*, May 31, 1994, A7; June 4, 1994, 6.

12. *Ibid.*, June 6, 1994, 16.

13. Memorandum, Associate Dean John Guilfoil to Stern Faculty Teaching Undergraduate Sections, "Grading Guide Lines," September 25, 1992.

14. Telephone interview, Dean Emeritus Abraham L. Gitlow and Dan Quilty, December 2, 1993.

NOTES TO CHAPTER ELEVEN

1. George Carlock, telephone interview, October 11, 1993 and Bea Jones, telephone interview, October 11, 1993.

2. Letter, President John Brademas to Boris Kostelanetz, May 9, 1990.

3. NYU, Stern School of Business, *Departmental Plan for the 1992–1993 Academic Year*, July 8, 1992.

4. Standard and Poor's, *1992 College/Executive Survey*, June 25, 1992, 25 Broadway, New York, NY 10004.

5. *Ibid.*, 2.

6. Fred Knauth, former Acting Secretary, NYU, October 26, 1993.

7. *Wall Street Journal*, October 19, 1993, A18.

NOTES TO CHAPTER TWELVE

1. *Morikami Newsletter*, The Friends of the Morikami, December 1983, July 1984, August 1985, Boca Raton, Florida.

2. Thorstein Veblen, *The Higher Learning in America*, Reprints of Economic Classics, New York: Augustus M. Kelley, 1965, 16–21.

3. Letter, Dean William Dill to Dean Emeritus Abraham L. Gitlow, December 24, 1993, 10.

Subject Index

in 1965–66, 66
in 1970–1990, 105–6
in 1994–1996, 169–73

Day program, 9–10
Delta Sigma Pi, 223
Discipline, student, 237–42
Doctor of Commercial Science, 35, 115–16
Doctor of Philosophy, 35, 122–27, 136–40
Dormitories, 225

Ecole des Hautes Etudes Commerciales, 155
Endowments, 177–79
Enrollments
    admission standards, 40
    community college transfers, 40
    flat fee tuition, 40
    forces affecting, 39–41
    Gordon-Howell Report, 40
    numbers, graduate, 119–22
    numbers, undergraduate, 7–8, 53, 56, 92–95
    NYU Self-Study Report, 40
    Pierson report, 40
    population shifts, 40
    veterans, 39
Evening studies
    beginnings, 6
    Professional Program in Business, 88–89
Executive MBA Program, 151–52
External evaluation. *See* Accreditation
External influence, 297 n.40

Faculty
    Committee to Study the Schools of Business, 50–51
    compensation, 16, 18, 60, 77–78, 80–81, 175–77, 214–15
    consulting, 59, 293 n.31
    dominance of PhD, 100–103
    full-time, 22–24, 58–59
    number, 54
    part-time, 16
    PhDs, 22–24
    research, 17
    retirement "buy-outs," 55, 66
    staffing profiles, 79
    teaching, 15–16
    teaching loads, 60–61, 116, 172–75
    women, 103, 294 n.9
Federation, Alumni, 256–59
Fencing, 252
Financial Aid
    funded, 99–100
    merit based, 97–98
    need based, 98
    unfunded, 98–99
Football, 252–54
Ford Foundation
    general, 206
    Gordon-Howell report, 44–45
    NYU proposal, 46–48
    $25 million grant, 45–46
Founders, 1
Fund raising
    impact, 164–65, 256, 263
    and political correctness, 269
Future, outlook for, 287–88

General Course department, 32–33, 64
Generalism-specialism tension, 141–43, 285–86
Gitlow Award, Abraham L., 262
Glucksman, L., Institute for Research in Securities Markets, 197
Gordon-Howell report, 44–45
Grade inflation, 242–48
Grades, 28–29, 53
Graduate School of Business Administration
    Alumni Achievement Award, 264
    Alumni Association, 259
    certificate programs, 128, 157–58
    culture, 111–18
    debate over location, 133–34
    early dependence on Commerce, 108
    enrollments, 119–22
    external support, 109–10
    Masters' programs, 32–33, 128, 140–52, 156–57
    NYU's concept of the Business School, 108
    origin as a division of Commerce, 34–36, 107
    PhD program, 122–27, 136–40, 156–57

Name Index

McNamara, Robert S., 265
McWhinney Dale, Madeline, 264
Merrill, Charles E., 132
Miller, Arjay, 265
Moskowitz, Charles C., 85, 106
Murray, Allan, 104, 263

Nadler, Marcus, 131, 272
Narodick, Kit, 104
Netzer, Dick, 74
Newcomer, Mabel, 38
Newman, Benjamin, 48, 50
Newsom, Carroll, 64
Nichols, C. Walter, 131–32
Norton, Thomas L., 44–45, 56, 66

Peterson, Peter G., 265
Pierson, Frank C., 44
Price, Harold, 197
Prime, John, 48, 52, 56, 66

Quilty, Dan, 253

Raasch, John E., 263
Racoosin, Edlyn, 97, 293 n.5
Racoosin, Theodore, 96–97, 263
Rangel, Charles E., 263
Reidenbach, Richard C., 219
Reutiman, Gladys H., 10
Robinson, Daniel, 132
Robinson, James M. A., 219
Ronen, Joshua, 194
Rosenkampff, Arthur Henry, 17
Rosenthal, Richard, 105, 263
Ross, Ben, 257
Ross, Vincent C., 182–83, 194, 263
Rudin, Lewis, 263

Sakai, Jo, 280–82
Salomon, Arthur K., 132
Salomon Brothers, 192
Sametz, Arnold, 194
Samuelson, Paul A, 195
Sanders, Thomas E., 263
Sandler, Marion O., 264
Sawhill, John, 152
Sato, Ryuzo, 196
Schaller, Elmer, 190

Schaub, Lincoln, 111
Schiff, John M., 131
Schiff, Michael, xiii, 61, 130–31, 141–42, 156, 182, 194, 272, 280
Schlossman, Steven, 110
Schulman, Emily, 237
Seidman, Jack, 263
Sells, Elijah, 1
Shapiro, Moses, 104
Shapiro, Samuel, xiii
Shimkin, Leon, 263
Shipley, Walter, 104, 263
Shultz, George P., 265
Silber, William, 194
Simon, Charles, 193
Snow, John Ben, 96–97, 132, 263
Sorter, George, 151, 194, 295 n.11
Spaulding, Asa T., 263
Sprague, Charles Ezra, 1, 3, 16, 21
Stern, Leonard N., 164–65, 251, 262, 264, 279
Swanson, A. E., 200

Taggart, Joseph, 50, 52, 73, 119, 129, 134–35, 162, 272–73
Taub, Henry, 104, 263
Taylor, Archibald Wellington, 35, 107, 109, 110, 112, 129
Thomas, Allen, 162
Tisch, Lawrence, 104, 262
Tisch, Preston Robert, 263
Truman, Harry S, 133
Turner, Jon A., 198

Veblen, Thorstein, 283–84
Viola, Sylvia, xiii
Vogel, John H., 264
VonMises, Ludwig, 131

Walter, Ingo, 123, 194
Weeks, Richard R., 219
Weinberg, John L., 265
West, Richard, xiii, 74, 164, 166, 192
Whitehead, John C., 104, 265
Williams, Harold M., 265
Winder, Bayley, 74
Wines, Richard, xiii

Young, Percy S., 266

Printed in the United States
By Bookmasters